Robotics Sourcebook and Dictionary

Robotics Sourcebook And Dictionary

David F. Tver
and
Roger W. Bolz

INDUSTRIAL PRESS INC.
200 Madison Avenue
New York, New York, 10157

Library of Congress Cataloging in Publication Data

Tver, David F.
  Robotics sourcebook and dictionary.

  1. Robot industry — Directories.   2. Robots, Industrial
— Dictionaries.   I. Bolz, Roger William.   II. Title.
HD9696.R622T83   1983   629.8'92   83-135
ISBN 0-8311-1152-6

First Printing
ROBOTICS SOURCEBOOK AND DICTIONARY

Preface

Industrial robots are basically programmed manipulators designed to perform useful work automatically without human assistance. In a different definition, a robot is a commercially available, mechanical, programmable device that independently performs manipulative job functions. In this sense, robots fill the gap between special-purpose automation and human endeavor. The term robot derives from the Czech word "robota" meaning servitude or drudgery, and its old Slavic equivalent "robota" or work. Unlike science fiction concepts, however, today's robots are practical devices that offer flexibility in handling and processing functions, reliability, and control programmability.

Industrial robots are available in a wide range of capabilities and configurations. Basically, however, they consist of several major components: the manipulator or "mechanical unit," which actually performs the manipulative functions; the controller or "brain," which stores data and directs movements of the manipulator; and the power supply, which provides energy to the manipulator. A complete turnkey robotic system is said to consist of five elements: the robot or robots; computers for control; suitable sensors for feedback; computer software for intelligence; fixtures and material-handling units adapted for the work to be performed.

Robotics Sourcebook and Dictionary is a reference book covering most of the key aspects of current industrial robotics. An introduction provides an understanding of the basic types of robots that have been put into use. The second section contains a dictionary of general applications describing how robots have been put to use in today's industrial environment. Modern robotics is a combination of engineering and of computer science and software applications, hence, the third section is a glossary of robotics, control, and computer terminology that should be useful in understanding and developing robotic programs. Since there are more than 70 companies manufacturing robotics equipment today, the fourth section contains a list of the more-recognized companies in the field, along with a selection of typical products they manufacture and their capabilities. The authors are indebted to the companies in the listing of manufacturers for their courtesy in supplying basic information on their products.

Contents

Section 1

Introduction and Dictionary of Types

A robot is a mechanical device that can be programmed to perform some task of manipulation or locomotion under automatic control. Today robots are still on the threshold of research and development. However, industrial robots are available in a wide range of configurations and capabilities, from simple "pick-and-place" devices to computer-directed, servo-controlled, point-to-point, and continuous-path units. Programmable controls, memory systems, and up to seven articulations give a high degree of flexibility and adaptability to many tasks involving manipulation of objects and tools.

When the actual tasks that a robot can perform are studied in a real factory world, they boil down to moving parts in simple combinations of straight lines and rotations. Each task requires a different combination of motions, and each task requires different travel distances and imposes different weight loads on the robot. Generating such motions with jointed arms requires large numbers of joints.

While robots vary widely in shape, size, and capabilities, they generally consist of three basic components: the manipulator, the control, and the power supply that drives the manipulator. Manipulators are the mechanical devices that do the work and provide the dexterity by pneumatically, hydraulically, or electrically driven jointed mechanisms that can perform as many as seven independent coordinate motions.

The following Dictionary of Types defines the various characteristics of the basic robot styles available today.

assembly robot. A robot designed, programmed, or dedicated to putting together parts into subassemblies or complete products.

bang-bang robot. A robot in which motions are controlled by driving each axis or degree of freedom against a mechanical stop. (See also *fixed-stop robot, pick-and-place robot.*)

bilateral manipulator. A master–slave manipulator with symmetric force reflection where both master and slave arms have sensors and actuators such that in any degree of freedom a positional error between the master and slave results in equal and opposing forces applied to the master and the slave arms. A two-armed manipulator (can refer to two arms performing a task in cooperative movements, or can refer to two arms in the sense of a master–slave manipulator).

continuous-path robot. This robot operates, in theory, through an infinite number of points in space that, when joined, describe a smooth compound curve. This curve is usually developed during the programming or "teaching" phase, which is carried out by an operator. Load capacities of point-to-point continuous-path robots are essentially a function of width, motion, inertia, and other factors. Although the load capacities differ by individual manufacturers, as do sizes, a present-day capacity range of between 300–500 lb (136–227 kg) on a fully extended medium technology robot arm with ±0.008 in. (0.2 mm) accuracy on repeated positioning has been reported. Continuous-path control is used where the path of the end effector is of primary importance to the application, such as when used for spray painting. The unit is generally not required to come to rest at unique positions and perform functions as is common in applications employing a point-to-point control. Typically, a robot using this type of control is taught by the operator physically grasping the unit and leading it through the desired path in the exact manner and at the exact speed that the operator wishes the robot to repeat. While the device is moved through the desired path, the position of each axis is recorded on a constant time base, thus generating a continuous time history of each axis position. Every motion that the operator makes, whether intentional or not, will be recorded and played back in the same manner. Since the operator must physically grasp the robot, it must be designed to be essentially counterbalanced and free under no power so that the operator can perform the task; therefore, this control is generally limited to light duty robots. Since the operator is manually leading the robot through the desired sequence, the teaching is very instinctive, and there is no concern for the position of each axis. The programming is direct. Another characteristic of this type of control is that considerable memory capability is required to store all the axis positions needed to record the desired path smoothly. For this reason, magnetic-tape-storage means are generally used.

controlled-path robot. The controlled-path type of robot is less common and utilizes a computer control system with the computational ability to describe a desired path between any preprogrammed points. Each axis or degree of freedom can be controlled and actuated simultaneously to move to those points. The computer calculates both the desired path and the acceleration, deceleration, and velocity of the robot arm along the path.

cylindrical-coordinate robots. This robot type is represented by such models as the Pacer, Versatran, and Auto-Place. Its configuration consists of a horizontal arm mounted on a vertical column that, in turn, is mounted on a rotating base. The horizontal arm moves in and out, its carriage moves up and down on a vertical column, and these two members rotate as a unit on the base. Thus, the working area or envelope is a portion of a cylinder.

fixed-stop robot. A robot with stop-point control but no trajectory control; that is, each of its axes has a fixed limit at each end of its stroke and cannot stop except at one or the other of these limits. Such a robot can therefore stop at no more than two locations (where location includes position and orientation). Often very good repeatability can be obtained.

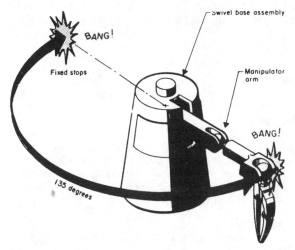

The range of motion for nonservo robots is limited by two fixed, but adjustable, stops for each axis. The robot arm moves from one to the other to perform its operation.

generation 1 robot. This is the robot in use today. It is characterized as being a programmable, memory-controlled machine with several degrees of freedom. It can be equipped with grippers of special handling attachments, which can hold and operate hand tools, welding guns, and power tools, as well as perform workpiece and material-handling, -manipulation, and -transfer functions.

generation 1.5 robot. This is the robot that will be sensory controlled and have capabilities to perform ''make'' and ''test'' functions. It will work on principles of electrooptics, pressure, torque, force-sensitive touch, and proximity. It will be capable of recognizing and manipulating workpieces, parts, and tools. The motion paths of the robot will be memory controlled with overrides of preprogrammed control depending on sensor inputs.

generation 2 robot. This is the future robot that will have hand-and-eye coordination control through machine-vision concepts. The robot will see objects and will be able with hand interactions to perform manipulative functions.

generation 3 robot. A ''factory-intelligence-controlled'' robot that will provide artificial intelligence to help solve ''factory'' problems.

hydraulic robot. This robot type normally includes a hydraulic power supply as either an integral part of the manipulator or as a separate unit. The hydraulic system generally follows straightforward industrial practices and consists of an electric-motor-driven pump, filter, reservoir, and, usually, a heat exchanger (either air or water). These robots normally operate on petroleum-based hydraulic fluid; however, most are available with special seals for operation on fire-retardant fluid.

industrial robot, degree of freedom. This type of robot is designed to emulate a human's physical capabilities. To accomplish this, it is necessary that the required degrees of freedom be such that they simulate human movements and activities, which is done by an articulated mechanical arm and hand having freedom of movement similar to a human's waist, shoulder, elbow, wrist, and fingers. Movement in five degrees of freedom is adequate in most material-handling functions, and, as a result, the more popular and most widely used programmable robots in industrial application are of this type. Robots with six degrees of freedom are also available. These have the ability to move in a longitudinal direction, which is required for tracking continuously moving operations such as automobile bodies on assembly lines.

industrial robot, design variations. Design variations existing in various industrial robots can be classified broadly into three different types. These are the rectilinear type, polar configuration type, and the anthropomorphic type. The rectilinear-type design has basic movements that are linear in nature, excluding the wrist and rotating movements. A robot designed with the polar configuration has prime movements with polar coordinates, except the arm-extend and -retract movement. The main difference between the rectilinear- and polar-type configurations is limited to the method of achieving the vertical up-and-down movement. A robot designed to be anthropomorphic in nature more closely simulates human movements; it has additional movements in the arm that simulate the human elbow.

jointed-spherical (jointed-arm) robot. This robot type has rotary joints in several places along the arm that roughly correspond to the human shoulder, elbow, and wrist. It is usually mounted on a rotary base.

manipulator-type robot. A method of classifying a robot by the manipulative function that it is capable of performing: (1) the pick-and-place type, where only three degrees of freedom are generally required, with a very simple gripper design for part clamping–unclamping; (2) the special-purpose type, which is designed to perform a specific function such as paint spraying, press load–unloading, or die-casting-machine load–unload and which usually employs unique features that make it suitable for its intended function; (3) the universal type, in that it can be used to perform any manipulative type of function and which is usually designed with five degrees of freedom, excluding special gripper designs or tools that can be attached to the robot's arm.

material-handling robot. A robot designed, programmed, or dedicated to grasping, transporting, and positioning materials in the process of manufacture.

material-processing robot. A robot designed, programmed, or dedicated to cutting, forming, heat treating, finishing, or otherwise processing materials as part of manufacture.

medium-technology robot. A medium-technology robot consists of a basic mechanical and electrical control package. Most units are self-contained and can be moved easily from one jobsite to another. Programming is fast and uncomplicated. This robot type is adaptable to most jobs since it can carry payloads of up to 100 lb (46 kg) and operate within a reach of up to 10 ft (3.1 m) across its sphere of influence.

mobile robot. A robot mounted on a movable platform.

nonservo robot, common characteristics. With this robot type a relatively high speed is possible, owing to the generally smaller size of the manipulator and the full flow of air or oil through the control valves. Repeatability to within 0.010 in. (0.25 mm) is attainable on the smaller units. These robots are relatively low in cost; are simple to operate, program, and maintain; and are highly reliable. However, they have limited flexibility in terms of program capacity and positioning capability.

nonservo robot, significant features. The manipulator's various members move until the limits of travel (end stops) are reached. Thus there are usually only two positions for each axis to assume. The sequencer provides the capability for many motions in a program, but only to the end points of each axis. Deceleration as the stops are approached may be provided by valving or shock absorbers. It is feasible to activate intermediate stops on some axes to provide more than two positions; however, there is a practical limit to the number of such stops that can be installed. Although this mode of operation is commonly used on the smaller robots, it is applicable to larger units also. The programmed sequence can be conditionally modified through appropriate external sensors; however, this class of robot usually is restricted to the performance of single programs. Programming is done by setting up the desired sequence of moves and by adjusting the end stops for each axis.

nonservo robot, typical operating sequence. Upon starting of program execution, the sequencer/controller initiates signals to control valves on the manipulator's actuators. The valves open, admitting air or oil to the actuators, and the members begin to move. The valves remain open and the members continue to move until physically restrained by contact with end stops. Limit switches signal the end of travel to the controller, which then commands the control valve to close. The sequencer again outputs signals. These may again be to the control valves on the actuators or to an external device such as a gripper. The process is repeated until the entire sequence of steps has been executed.

pick-and-place robot. A simple robot, often with only two or three degrees of freedom, that transfers items from place to place by means of point-to-point moves. Little or no trajectory control is available. Often referred to as a bang-bang robot.

point-to-point robot. This control method is perhaps the simplest and most frequently used. Teaching is done by moving each axis of the robot individually until the combination of axis positions yields the desired position of the robot end effector. When this desired position or point is reached, it is programmed into memory, thereby storing the individual position of each robot axis. In replaying these stored points, each axis runs at its maximum or limited rate until it reaches its final position. Consequently, some axes will reach their final value before others. Furthermore, because there is no coordination of motion between axes, the path and velocity of the end effector between points is not easily predictable. For this reason point-to-point control is used for applications where only the final position is of interest and the path and velocity between the points are not prime considerations.

programmable manipulator. A device that is capable of manipulating objects by executing a stored program resident in its memory.

record–playback robot. A robot for which the critical points along desired trajectories are stored in sequence by recording the actual values of the joint-position encoders of the robot as it is moved under operator control. To perform the task, these points are played back to the robot servo system.

rectilinear-Cartesian robot. A continuous-path extended-reach robot that offers the versatility of multiple robots through the use of a bridge and trolley construction that enables it to have a large rectangular work envelope. Being ceiling mounted, such devices can service many stations with many functions, leaving the floor clear. X and Y motions are performed by bridge and trolley, the vertical motions are performed by telescoping tubes, and additional axes can be used.

rectilinear-coordinate robot. This robot is mounted on a fixed base. All arm motions of the manipulator are in a straight line, either in–out, up–down, or side-to-side. Even though a pivoting wrist joint may be provided, the work envelope of this robot type conforms to either a cube or a rectangular solid.

sensory-controlled robot. A robot whose control is a function of information sensed from its environment.

sequence robot. A robot whose motion trajectory follows a preset sequence of positional changes.

servo-controlled robot. The typical operating sequence of a servo-controlled robot is as follows: Upon start of program execution the controller addresses the memory location of the first command position and also reads the actual position of the various axes as measured by the position feedback. These two sets of data are compared and their differences, commonly called "error signals," are amplified and transmitted as "command signals" to servo valves for the actuator of each axis. The servo valves, operating at constant pressure, control flow to the manipulator's actuators, the flow being proportional to the electrical current level of the command signals. As the actuators move the manipulator axes, feedback devices such as encoders, potentiometers, resolvers, and tachometers send position (and in some cases, velocity) data back to the controller. These "feedback signals" are compared with the desired position data, and new error signals are generated, amplified, and sent as command signals to the servo valves. This process continues until the error signals are effectively reduced to zero, whereupon the servo valves reach null, flow to the actuators is blocked, and the axes come to rest at the desired position. The controller then addresses the next memory location and responds appropriately to the data stored there. This may be another positioning sequence for the manipulator or a signal to an external device. The process is repeated sequentially until the entire set of data, or "program," has been executed.

servo-controlled robot, common characteristics. Smooth motions are executed with control of speed, and, in some cases, acceleration and deceleration. This permits the controlled movement of heavy loads. Maximum flexibility is provided by the ability to program the axes of the manipulator to any position within the limits of their travel. Most controllers and memory systems permit the storage and execution of more than one program, with random selection of programs from memory via externally generated signals. With microprocessors or minicomputer-based controllers, subrouting and branching capabilities may be available. These capabilities permit the robot to take alternative actions within a program, when commanded. End-of-arm positioning accuracy of 0.060 in. (1.5 mm) and repeatability of ± 0.060 in. (± 1.5 mm) are generally achieved. Accuracy and repeatability are functions not only of the mechanisms but also of the resolution of the feedback devices, servovalve characteristics, control accuracy, etc. Owing to their complexity, servo-control robots are more expensive and more involved to maintain than nonservo robots and tend to be somewhat less reliable.

servo-controlled robot, continuous path. Typically the positioning and feedback principles are the same as in a servo-controlled robot. There are, however, some major differences in control systems and some unique physical features. During programming and playback data are sampled on a time base, rather than as discretely determined points in space. The sampling frequency is typically in the range of 60 – 80 Hz. Owing to the high rate of sampling of position data, many spatial positions must be stored in memory. A mass-storage system, such as magnetic tape or magnetic disc, is generally employed. During playback, owing to the hysteresis of the servovalves and inertia of the manipulator, there is no detectable change in speed from point to point. The result is a smooth continuous motion over a controlled path. Depending on the controller and data-storage system used, more than one program may be stored in memory and randomly accessed. The usual programming method involves physically moving the end of the manipulator's arm through the desired path, with position data automatically sampled and recorded. The speed of the manipulator during program execution can be varied from the speed at which it was moved during programming by playing back the data at a different rate than that used when recording. Continuous-path servo-controlled robots share the following characteristics: These robots generally are of smaller size and lighter weight than point-to-point robots. Higher end-of-arm speeds are possible than with point-to-point robots; however, load capacities are usually less than 22 lb (10 kg). Their common applications are to spray painting and similar spraying operations, polishing, grinding, and arc welding.

servo-controlled robot, point-to-point. A typical servo-controlled robot is used in a wide variety of industrial applications for both part-handling and tool-handling tasks. Significant features are for those robots using the "record–playback" method of teaching and operation, initial programming is relatively fast and easy; however, modification of programmed positions cannot be accomplished readily during program execution. Those robots using sequence/potentiometer controls tend to be more tedious to program; however, programmed positions can be modified easily during program execution by adjusting the potentiometers. The path through which the various members of the manipulator move when traveling from point to point is not programmed or directly controlled in some cases and may be different from the path followed during teaching. Common characteristics include high-capability control systems with random access to multiple programs, subroutines, branches, etc., and great flexibility provided to the user. These robots tend to lie at the upper end of the scale in terms of load capacity and working range. Hydraulic drives are most common, although some robots are available with electric drives.

servo-controlled robot, significant features. The manipulator's various members can be commanded to move and stop anywhere within their limits of travel, rather than only at the extremes. Since the servovalves modulate flow, it is feasible to control the velocity, acceleration, and deceleration of the various axes as they move between programmed points. Generally, the memory capacity is large enough to store many more positions than a nonservo-controlled robot. For some sophisticated units this means access capability at as many as 4000 points in space. Given programs select and sequence activity points for a particular operating scheme. Programs can be varied to maintain the scheme while changing the activity points. Both continuous-path and point-to-point capabilities are possible. Accuracy can be varied, if desired, by changing the magnitude of the error signal, which is considered zero. This can be useful in "rounding the corners" of high-speed contiguous motions. Drives are usually hydraulic or electric and use state-of-the-art servo-control technology. Programming is accomplished by manually initiating signals to the servovalves to move the various axes into a desired position and then recording the output of the feedback devices into the memory of the controller. This process is repeated for the entire sequence of desired positions in space.

special-purpose robot. Offering more versatility in accommodating frequent changeovers and ease of installation and maintenance, a special-purpose robot, designed specifically for parts extraction and orientation, fills the gap between integrated custom machine equipment and a general-purpose industrial robot.

spherical-coordinate robot. Mounted on a rotary base and resembling the turret of a tank, the arm of a spherical-coordinate robot can not only extend and retract, but is pivoted so that it can swing vertically, allowing rotary motion about a horizontal plane. The end effector moves in a volume of space that is a portion of a sphere.

supervisory-controlled robot. A robot incorporating a hierarchical control scheme, whereby a device having sensors, actuators, and a computer, and capable of autonomous decision-making and control over short periods and restricted conditions, is remotely monitored and intermittently operated directly or reprogrammed by a person.

teleoperator. Although not classified as a robot in strict terms, the teleoperator unit covers industrial manipulators that are human-operated, with the operator in the control loop on a real-time basis. Teleoperator manipulators use master–slave operator control with force feedback. Balanced use of human and machine, which permits the operator to transmit his or her inherent intelligence and dexterity through the machine to the task, is based on cybernetic anthropomorphous machine systems (CAMS) technology. Teleoperator manipulators are cybernetic in that a human is retained in the system; they are controlled by a human operator with his or her responsive, decision-making capability. They are anthropomorphous in that they resemble a human in form and duplicate the human's manipulative powers. Essentially, the machine system serves as a physical extension of human's strength, endurance, and task-performing functions. For this reason, such machines are said to have "instinctive" control, which has proved of interest in satisfying the relatively unstructured applications of the foundry. The first application of a teleoperator manipulator in the foundry industry was for a shakeout application in an automotive foundry. Other applications have included furnace slagging, shotblasting, ladle skimming, palletizing, and metal-pouring installations. A load capacity range of 125–7000 lb (56–3150 kg) is presently available for manipulators of this type. Six degrees of movement include horizontal extension, hoist, azimuth rotation, yaw, pitch, and roll. A servo-control system transmits a small proportion of the load force to the operator's hand, thus giving him or her "instinctive control" of the job.

transfer devices. Transfer devices can be grouped into two main categories: bulk transfer devices, which transfer randomly placed parts, and orientation transfer devices, which hold the workpiece in transfer devices. Conveyor belts, sheet metal chutes or guides, and simple part slide mechanisms are all orientation transfer devices. The familiar tote bin, often assuming different names, is the most basic form of bulk transfer device. The overhead conveyor, which is a simple type of orientation device, can be configured in one of three ways: indexing from position to position, continuously moving, or powered and free. In a powered and free conveyor system, handling hooks or racks move continuously around a closed loop. When a work station needs a hook at a given point, it can divert the hook from the main conveyor system and rigidly lock it into position. After the hook is loaded with a product, it returns to the main loop, from which it can move to a different work station. Another type of orientation transfer device is the pallet conveyor. This device is simply a normal conveyor equipped with pallets for individual parts. Parts are placed into the fixture of a part pallet and then transferred to another work station, either by continuous motion or by indexing in controlled steps. By using shot pins and other mechanical devices, a robot can locate a palletized part within 0.005 in. (0.127 mm). A lift and carry device, which uses a mechanical linkage system to index parts from one work station to the next, is similar to a pallet conveyor. Other types of orientation transfer devices include the bulk hopper feeder with orienter and iron-man-type devices. The bulk hopper automatically feeds loose, randomly oriented parts from a bowllike vessel by elevating individual parts to a drop-off position.

Robotics Dictionary of Applications

assembly line (Harrison Radiator Division). A robot is used to remove 30-lb (14-kg) air conditioners from the end of an assembly line and place them in shipping containers every 19 seconds. At Harrison Radiator Division, General Motors Corp., the assembly lines run continuously, requiring the robots to pick up the assembled air conditioner units on the fly. Each shipping container holds 12 units, with a defined position for each unit. The distance through which the robot arm has to travel from conveyor to loading position and back again varies from one loading cycle to the next. Each robot is required to locate an air conditioner on the moving conveyor, pick it up, and determine the path to the loading position, then place the unit where it is intended, within a 0.25-in. (6.35-mm) tolerance. The robot has no "eyes" to see where the air conditioners are located on the moving conveyor. Instead, there is an encoder attached to the drive shaft of each conveyor; the encoder is actuated when a fixture carrying an air conditioner breaks the light beam of a photoelectric control mounted alongside the conveyor. The encoder sends signals to the robot's microprocessor control, enabling it to track the exact position of each fixture, within 0.050 in. (1.27 mm). A robot is mounted at the end of each assembly line, with its arm aligned with the centerline of the conveyor. This means the robot has only to extend or retract its arm to achieve precise alignment with the moving fixtures. The assembly line is a slat conveyor, over–under carousel design, with a series of fixtures mounted on 42-in. (1.1-m) centers. The air conditioner units are assembled directly on the fixtures. Loaded fixtures advance to the end of the line, the robot removes the units, and the empty fixtures return on the lower flight to the head of the assembly line. Each air conditioner is picked up by a mechanical grab at the end of the robot arm. The grab engages a flange on the top of the air conditioner and lifts it from the fixture. Then the arm quickly moves through a horizontal arc to the shipping container. Workers assist in the loading process. Empty shipping containers and steel racks are brought from storage by fork trucks and placed on a powered roller conveyor, which parallels the assembly conveyor. In each container there is reusable dunnage with molded inserts that the workers arrange for loading. A container with a bottom sheet of molded dunnage is advanced to the first loading position, where it is automatically lifted off the conveyor bed and clamped into place. The robot automatically transfers air conditioner units to the container, placing them according to a preprogrammed pattern. When six units have been put in place, the container advances to a second loading position. There a worker adds spacers between the units and a sheet of dunnage for the second layer of six units.

axle production (Saab-Scania). An ESAB A30A arc welding robot installed at the Kristinehamm works of Saab-Scania in Sweden reduced by 40% the time required to produce rear axles for the Saab 900 car. The robot freed skilled welders for other tasks and averted an anticipated shortage of workers; it also improved working conditions for the welders, who had previously been exposed to fumes and spatter of the arc. The robot welding station is programmed to execute a sequence of 31 separate welds with an aggregate length of 21.7 in. (550 mm). Using a single torch, it welds mounting points for rear suspension, brake pipes, and stabilizers onto a 2.1-in (54-mm) diameter axle tube in a cycle lasting less than 2 minutes. The completed assembly is 50 in. (1500 mm) long and weighs 22 lb (10 kg). The robot maintains a repetitive positional accuracy of ± 0.008 in. (± 0.20 mm), and, unlike special-purpose, multitorch stations, it can easily be reprogrammed to incorporate changes in axle design or to undertake different work altogether. The A30A equipment consists of the robot itself — an IRb6 industrial unit from ASEA; two specially designed manipulators for holding and positioning the work; a dc welding set based on ESAB's LAH 500 rectifier; and a computerized control unit with a removable programming keyboard connected by cable. The two main manipulators, which hold the axle tube between a head and tailstock, are set 90° apart around the robot, which alternately swings from one to the other. While one assembly is being welded, the operator sets up the next one. To direct the welding torch precisely where required, the robot has five independent movements powered by dc servomotors. The programmer moves the torch manually to successive key positions, using a sample workpiece as template. Parameters such as torch positions, required speed of movement between positions, and whether the motion should be point-to-point or continuous path are then entered into the computer memory with the portable keyboard. Movements of the manipulator can also be programmed in. The memory can store up to four selectable programs with a total of 500 positions.

bottle handling (chemicals). Through the use of a standard 2000B, five-axis Unimate industrial robot, the hazardous task of handling bottles of photographic chemicals was solved. The highly toxic photographic chemicals are contained in 4 or 5 quart capacity (3.8 or 4.8 liter) plastic bottles. The bottles are filled, capped, and marshalled to a transfer station via conveyor at the rate of 20 per minute. The Unimate robot picks up two bottles at a time and transfers them to boxes of various sizes accepting one, two, four, or six bottles. When the transfer of product is to a box accepting only one bottle, two boxes are presented back to back on the load conveyor and the robot fills both at the same time. If no boxes are present, the Unimate robot loads the bottles onto an auxiliary pallet until boxes are provided. The pallet pattern is 6 × 7 bottles requiring 24 transfers per pallet.

brick loading. A system for loading refractory bricks into oven cars using a 4000 Series Unimate industrial robot with special tooling, conveyors, and an oven car indexer–positioner. Formed bricks are ejected out of a press and pushed onto a metal pallet on a conveyor. A single pallet and brick can weigh up to 75 pounds (34 kg). Loaded pallets are accumulated in groups of three and picked up by the Unimate with its special tooling for loading into an oven car. The oven cars are divided in half, each of which has 12 shelves for holding six pallets at each level. Since the Unimate robot handles three pallets at a time, it goes to each level twice. In the first operation, one-half of the oven car is empty while the other half contains empty pallets. The Unimate picks up three full pallets from the output conveyor and loads them into the proper position in the empty half of the oven car. It then goes to the other half of the oven car, picks up three empty pallets and deposits them onto the input conveyor. Picking up three more full pallets, the Unimate loads them behind the first three in the oven car. The next set of full pallets will be loaded at the next lower level. This sequence continues until one-half of the car is loaded with full pallets while the other half is completely empty. The Unimate robot then proceeds to perform the second operation. The oven car indexing system shuttles the half-full, half-empty car and an oven car filled with only empty pallets into the proper position. The second half of the first car is loaded while the empty pallets from the first half of the second car are removed. When the second operation is completed, the Unimate robot programs back to the first operation, while the fully loaded car is indexed into position for removal by a fork lift truck.

casting, investment (Outboard Marine Corp.). Evinrude Motors Division of Outboard Marine Corp. utilizes Unimate industrial robots to make ceramic shell molds used in a variety of leisure-time products ranging from outboard motors to snowmobiles. The robots quickly adapt to changeovers from one type of casting to another. The investment castings range in weight from ¼ to 8½ pounds (0.11 to 3.87 kg). The ceramic shell molds usually require six coats. Coats one and two are flourfine slurries of colloidal silica followed by fine-grain stucco sand refractory. Coats three, four, and five employ coarser-grained slurries and stucco sand. The sixth coat is a slurry only and serves as a sealer to bind the previous stucco coats. After a drying period the wax pattern is melted out in a steam autoclave, leaving an empty shell. The shell molds are fired and metal is poured into the hot shell. In the first phase of automation robots make the molds. Workers supply trees to be coated and remove the coated trees. During processing, racks containing as many as 30 trees are wheeled to the robot's working area. Trees are hand-loaded individually onto a pick-up stand to which the robot reaches when ready to coat the next tree. The newly coated trees are put on a similar set-down stand to a positioning accuracy of ± 0.05 in. (1.27 mm). The stand is unloaded manually at this time. Following the last coat, the trees are dewaxed in a pressurized steam autoclave and fired at 1700°F (927°C) to fuse the grains of silica. In the second phase that is being planned, the degree of automation will be increased. A conveyor will carry the trees automatically to the pick-up point. Another conveyor will carry coated trees away from the coating area. Operation of both conveyors will be controlled and monitored by each individual robot served by the conveyors. The robot now controls the entire first phase of the operation, including slurry mixer motor, air valves for fluidizing the bed of stucco, and gate valves in the fluidized-bed dust control system.

ceramic mold making. This mold-making system is composed of a robot surrounded by five rotary slurry mixers, one fluidized bed, one rainfall sander, and three conveyors. All of the equipment is placed within easy reach of the robot. The 42-in. (1067-mm) diameter rotary slurry mixers contain 300 gallons (1136 liters) each of various slurries that are applied at different times during the mold-making operation. The mixers are controlled by variable-frequency drives and are stopped and started by the robot as the program dictates. Stopping and restarting is necessary because of the high forces generated against a wax airfoil pattern when it is dipped into a slurry moving with peripheral speeds in excess of 300 sfpm (91 m/min). The fluidized bed and rainfall sanders are also turned on and off by the robot as the program dictates. The separately driven, close-loop conveyors index mold envelopes to specific locations on command from the robot. The overall length of each conveyor was carefully calculated so that a group of mold envelopes enter, are processed, and leave the system as a batch. The wax clusters are mounted on dipping plates that are hung from old carriers mounted at 42 in. (1067 mm) intervals on the conveyors. The conveyors are indexed toward the load or unload stations, bringing the carriers to a point within the robot's reach. Each carrier is then clamped in place with a cylinder-operated clamping mechanism. This positions the carrier (and the dipping plate) optimally for repeatable load and unload operations. Programs stored in a memory are automatically accessed under normal operating conditions. (See also *investment casting.)*

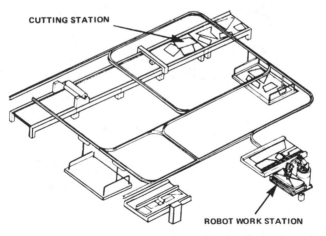

CUTTING STATION

ROBOT WORK STATION

This schematic of the ceramic mold-making system shows the robot and ancillary equipment it controls, including conveyors, sanders, and dip tanks.

composite structure robotization (U.S. Air Force). Through the use of a robot, equipment from the apparel industry, a material-handling system, and some ingenuity, the U.S. Air Force has developed a computer-controlled robotic work cell that completely automates the lamination process. Called the Integrated Flexible Automatic Center (IFAC), the robot picks up, orients, and transfers materials, and has reduced transfer time 65%. A broadgoods spreader developed by Cutting Room Appliances positions the prepreg on a cutting surface. A reciprocating knife cutter manufactured by Gerber Garment Technology, Inc., is mounted on a gantry across the cutting surface. The spreader and cutter work in tandem. After cutting, the curing surface is transported to the robot work station by a material-handling system nicknamed the "flying carpet." A carrier frame lifts the entire cutting table top and carries it along 230 ft (70 m) of electrified monorails mounted in the ceiling. Computers signals control queuing. The robot employed is a standard Cincinnati Milacron T³, modified with a foam-faced vacuum head. An electrooptical vision system mounted in the ceiling permits the robot to search and locate the ply required by a preprogrammed sequence. Once located, the robot lifts the ply. Once the precut piece is in place on the head, the robot rotates the ply to the proper orientation. The robot in the system lays the plies into a stool bed that has the contour of the finished part, and the foam head helps ensure compaction during the step. The robot can transfer various types of composites. The cutting table, before returning to the cutting station, moves to an area where any leftover scrap material is automatically raked off. A video camera mounted overhead checks the operation. In all, five image processing stations in the IFAC feed into the automated inspection and evaluation system to provide the required on-line quality assurance.

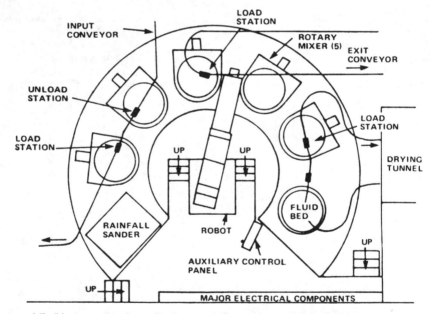

Integrated Flexible Automation Center (IFAC) automatically manufactures high-quality composite parts for use in aircraft construction.

conveyor line tracking (automotive). Line tracking is one solution to feeding a continuously moving conveyor accurately. The system was designed using a Series 2000 Unimate robot and associated equipment to transfer 72-pound (32.4-kg) engine heads from an assembly conveyor to a continuously moving monorail conveyor at a major automotive manufacturing facility. The system consists of a powered roller accumulating conveyor equipped with a positioning shuttle to locate the cylinder head for Unimate transfer. Monorail carrier guides were designed to ensure true position of the carrier during transfer. Unimation also designed and supplied a monorail pulley and mounting together with an encoder mounting and coupling arrangement. An encoder (position feedback device) is coupled to the continuously moving line. This encoder is automatically set to a zero position in reference to each individual carrier as the carrier arrives at the load station. The in/out motion of the Unimate is slaved to the line encoder, when the Unimate robot is in the tracking mode.

deburring (ASEA). The following description illustrates an example of a station for deburring forged steel blanks after drilling, tapping, reaming, and milling in a machining center. Two types of components are deburred in the station. A conveyor, with a buffer cartridge for 1 hour's production, feeds the parts to the robot. One item is moved forward to the pick-up position. A sensor issues a signal to the robot indicating what type of part it is to pick up. The robot can then select the appropriate deburring program. The items are deburred against a rotating tungsten-carbide file, the motor of which is mounted in a resilient toolholder in order to enable the file to cope with various working margins. When the deburring task is completed, the item is moved to a honing machine, which, at the same time, issues a signal to the robot to fetch the next item. In a station for deburring plastic items the robot selects the deburring program according to the type of part then in the fetch position. The robot also selects grip fingers. The robot then moves the part against a number of different deburring tools. A deburring station that includes ASFA's robot is arranged as shown in the figure: (1) a machining center attended by a pick-and-place robot, (2) a conveyor with a turret-shaped cartridge for 1 hour's production, (3) the pick-up position where the pallet is secured, (4) a vertical conveyor and the return route for empty pallets, (5) ASEA's IRb-6 robot for deburring against a rotary file, (6) the off-loading position on the input conveyor to the honing machine (8).

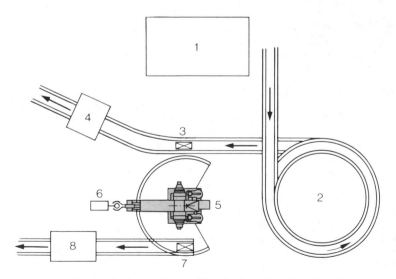

An example of station layout when an ASEA robot is used for deburring tasks.

deburring metal parts (ASEA). A significant number of installations composed of robots have been of the type where the robot holding a hand tool performs some operation other than material handling. Such installations include grinding, polishing, deburring, measuring and many others. Deburring after a mechanical operation is a common and expensive operation. One of the first generally usable and economical methods for automation of deburring uses industrial robots. By closely resembling the manual method the industrial robot can solve most deburring problems. The task is to remove the burrs generated from machining of a cast iron detail. The detail is part of a brake regulator used in trucks and other heavy vehicles. The burrs are generated inside the detail at the intersections between holes drilled from different directions. The sizes of the burrs vary between approximately 0.04 and 0.4 in. (1 and 10 mm). Two contours are to be deburred, one rectangular and one with continuous curves. In the installation, which uses an ASEA robot of type IRb-6, the robot works together with a parts magazine for the parts that are to be deburred, two deburring tools, and a conveyor for the finished parts. The robot handles the part itself, since the part is relatively lightweight. The part is picked from the magazine. It is then moved by the robot between the two tools and manipulated in such a way that those tools vary accurately with controlled speed and follow the contours that are to be deburred. At the end of the cycle, the part is placed on the conveyor belt and the robot continues the operation. The cycle time is approximately 40 seconds. The magazine is arranged as a rotating index table and holds approximately 1 hour's production. This allows the robot to work continuously even with very limited supervision. The two deburring tools used in this application are a rotating hard metal tool and a rectangular reciprocating file, which is used especially to reach the sharp corners at parts of the contour.

die casting (Doehler–Jarvis). The parts handled by the Unimates are aluminum automatic transmission cases ranging in weight from 25 to 75 pounds (11.25 to 33.75 kg). The robot's function begins with it in a "ready" position waiting for the die casting machine to open. If the machine does not open, the robot does not move, but an alarm is sounded. When the machine opens, the robot enters the die and signals the machine to eject the casting. It then grips the casting and places it on a chute to an inspection table. As safety precautions, the part must touch an electrical limit switch in the chute before it is released by the robot. After removal of the casting, the Unimate activates the timer-controlled water sprays used to cool the casting die. In its next operation the robot grasps a spray gun, enters the die, activates the gun, and lubricates all die surfaces. It sprays in a precise, programmed pattern, reaching all areas of the die, withdraws, and signals the machine controls to close for the next cycle. At the end of the cycle it puts down the gun, returns to the start position, and waits for the machine to open again.

die casting (Du-Well Products, Inc.). Du-Well Products produces parts for the automotive and appliance industries and for communication equipment, calculators, office machines, photocopiers, office furniture, architectural accessories, farm machinery, and garden tractors. Parts being cast include one for an automatic washing machine for Westinghouse and a shift lever housing for GMC's Saginaw Division. The robot unloads two 800-ton machines, cycles and puts both parts into a quench tank, and readies them for the trim press. The operation starts with the closing of the die casting machine to the robot's left, which is casting four parts for a washing machine. When the die casting machine opens, the robot extracts the part from the die. Next, the die is sprayed with a lubricant and the part is moved past a sensor into the quench tank. The die casting machine is then recycled, as the robot moves to the die casting machine on its right, removes a transmission housing, and readies for recycling. Should both units open simultaneously, the robot automatically services the faster die casting machine. Although, normally, the robot serves one and then the other, it can run either separately.

fastner application (automotive). In the assembly of formed-wire springs for automotive seats, industrial robots apply crimp-on fasteners that clamp two parallel wires together to permanently assemble the spring sections. Special fixtures are needed to pre-position the components and shuttle them past the robot. A tubular feed arrangement, suspended overhead, supplies clamps without restricting the movement of the application tool.

flexible assembly system (compressor subassembly). D.E.A. of Torino, Italy designed and developed a Pragma A 3000 robot for assembly operations for precise and intelligent parts handling. The Pragma robot system has a single or multiple element configuration, which is determined by incrementing the number of robot arms. The single arm is composed of modular parts. It is not constrained by fixed structures, except for the slideway of one rectangular axis, which has to be mounted alongside of a workbench to accommodate from one to six aligned robot arms. The arm axes are Cartesian linear; the wrist actions are rotary. The control unit supervises both the whole assembly cycle of different arms and arm interfacing with dedicated tooling through control of the position loop of each axis. In this way it can make logical decisions with reference to the feedback signal received from the sensors that are located in the wrist and gripper. A high-level programming language simplifies the cycle programming. Its editing feature permits direct program modification. During programming or reprogramming, it is possible to input significant cycle, part, or station data through a manual self-teach phase. Specific applications of Pragma robots are the assembling of two compressor subassemblies. Two separate automatic systems, each including the robots, are employed. One of the subassemblies is a cylinder head assembly, which is composed of 12 parts. There are four elements in the other assembly, which is a mating of a crankshaft and an external bearing. Since both are parts of the same product, the same production rate is required from both systems: 300 groups per hour. The valve assembly machine is composed of two arms aligned on a workbench that also carries the automatic tooling. The bench is less than 67 in. (1700 mm) long and 59 in. (1500 mm) wide. The control supervises the cycle by controlling arm operations, interfacing the tools, and activating the electrovalves employed. Gripper sensors are used at each station to detect the presence of and to correct the position of parts, thus ensuring precise handling and proper assembly. The valve parts are exhaust valve leaf, leaf lock, two rivets, valve plate, valve body, gasket, suction valve leaf, and four screws.

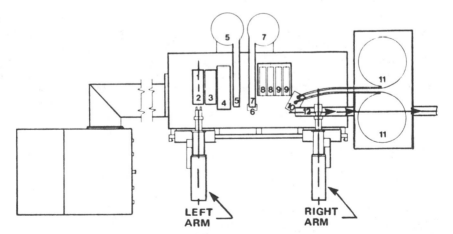

Schematic of the system used for cylinder valve assembly. It consists of two robot arms, automatic tooling, and a workbench.

flowline manufacturing system (ASEA). A flowline system has the machine tools grouped according to some well-defined combination of processes and capacity required. Material handling within the system is reduced, while the manufacturing control is increased. The ultimate goal of such a system is the manufacture of a complete family of parts. There are many flowline systems on the market, especially in Europe. A typical European flowline system, schematic, is located at the ASEA Electric Motor Plant in Vastarras, Sweden. The system consists of a turning center, a rotary table surface grinder, two turret drills, a flip-over station, a parts conveyor, and a robot. The cell manufactures three different parts, each made in six sizes. Parts of one size are machined at each setup, minimizing production and delivery problems as well as the cost of flexible tooling. Some retooling is required between batch runs. The cell is manned for one shift and runs unmanned for the remaining two shifts. During the manned shift the raw stock conveyor is loaded, the finished parts conveyor is unloaded, and any required tooling changes are made. In order to justify a system of this type, batch sizes must equal the production of three or more shifts. This requires lot sizes of 200 or more parts for this particular operation.

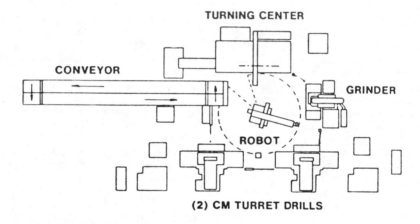

TURNING CENTER

CONVEYOR

GRINDER

ROBOT

(2) CM TURRET DRILLS

forging steel cylinders (Taylor–Wharton Co.). This company forges high-pressure steel cylinders for compressed gases on a high-production basis. An industrial robot (Unimate Series 4000) was installed to handle hot, heavy chrome–molybdenum steel alloy billets. The operating cycle of the robot begins when the forge press cycle is complete and a piston has pushed the cup-shaped preform up in the forge pot to a position that is accessible to the Unimate. The robot grasps the forged preform, lifts it from the pot, swivels approximately 180° to a tilt-table at the draw bench, deposits the preform on its side on the tilt-table, withdraws, swivels back, immerses its "hand" in a tank of cooling water, then stops poised at the forge press ready to grasp the next preform. The cylinder preform weighs 143 pounds (65 kg). This particular run of preforms is drawn into compressed gas cylinders with 0.222-in.-thick (5.6-mm-thick) walls. Forge press cycle time is approximately 45 seconds and robot cycle time is approximately 35 seconds, resulting in a 10 second wait. The point-to-point industrial robot has an electronic memory with a capacity of from 128 to 1024 steps, depending on the job requirements. A "teach" control on an umbilical cord permits an operator to teach the robot a new job by leading its hand through the steps needed to perform the job. Once taught, the robot will repeat the cycle endlessly.

forging systems (hammer equipment). A manufacturer of hammer forging equipment has been selling automated forging systems, consisting of a die forger controlled by an industrial robot. The robot removes a hot piece of stock from an electrically heated magazine, transfers the stock to the first of two die stations, triggers the forging hammer, which delivers a series of blows, while the robot holds the workpiece steady in the first impression. It then moves the workpiece to the second impression, triggers the hammer again, may transfer the workpiece to other impressions, and then deposits the forged "platter" of parts on a conveyor. Noise levels can be well in excess of 90 dBA, with blows equivalent to a ton of force being delivered at rates up to 100 per minute. One person monitors the operation from a remote, quieter area where he or she is not exposed to heat and fumes customary in forging. For the production of crankshafts at another plant, a large version of a Unimate takes 2200°F (1200°C) forgings from a nest, loads each into a twisting machine that does the preliminary forming of the crankshaft, then unloads the forgings onto pallets. The weight of each forging is in excess of 200 pounds (90 kg), some types weigh more than 300 pounds (135 kg).

forging, three-pass upsetting (auto tie rods). The robot grasps the bar located at the pick-up point outside an induction heater, transfers it to the first horizontal die, and signals the upsetter to cycle. At the completion of this first pass, the robot turns the bar 90° and positions it in the second horizontal die. After the second pass, the robot places the bar into a vertical die, signals the upsetter to cycle, and finally places the formed part in a floor tote. The robot's gripper is offset to permit it to maneuver around the pick-up point end stop and the upsetter backstops. A wrist-swivel action by the robot allows the part to be twisted out of the upsetter dies. A slide mechanism feeds bars to the induction heater. Heated bars emerge and are accurately positioned for pick up by the end stop. An infrared detector focused on the bar at the pick-up point provides a go/no go signal that establishes whether the bar has been heated properly and may be formed. The robot is programmed to reject improperly heated bars. Production rate is 140 parts per hour.

foundry mold preparation (Caterpillar Tractor Co.). At the Caterpillar Mapleton, Illinois iron foundry Unimate series 2105B industrial robots have been installed on several mold cope and drag lines. Some of the lines are indexing, others are continuously moving. Some robots wield spray heads to spray refractory wash into the copes and drags. Following this, additional robots play gas torch flames onto the mold to dry them. Each robot has up to 16 programs in its local memory. Identification of the molds as they come down the line triggers proper selection of the program developed for that mold configuration. The flexibility of the robot provides a cost effective means for performing these operations in a batch-processing environment. Using the robots to spray ensures coverage of all critical surfaces without overspraying.

functional manufacturing system (Fujitsu Fanuc). A functional layout uses machines in specific groups, where the criterion for grouping is essentially the type of machining being done. This is the traditional organization of a batch-type manufacturing plant. When the part family concept is applied, either partially or wholly, machines are occasionally regrouped into cells, each of which handles all operations required on parts of certain size and configuration. The part family thus created comprises a large number of more closely defined part families, sufficient to permit the use of two or more like machines of each functional type required. Such a cell arrangement retains advantages of function organization, which facilitates application of group technology principles. Work travel distances are relatively short, and automation of the type offered by modern robots can be applied with still further improvements in work flow and productivity. One of the best known functional robot automated manufacturing systems is a subset of a DNC system at Fujitsu Fanuc in Japan. Among the 18 NC machine tools are eight lathes with relatively short part machining times. Because of the frequency of loading and unloading, a robot was installed to handle the parts. The robot is mounted on rails above the machines and is allowed to move between the machines to perform its designated duties.

furnace tending (valve bodies). Manual loading and unloading of a furnace with tongs is a task in which heat-induced fatigue can lead to carelessness and increased risk, regardless of the protective clothing worn. At one plant, an industrial robot loads and unloads a rotary-hearth furnace for firing ceramic coatings on interiors of valve bodies. Formerly, a worker was stationed in front of the 1800°F (980°C) furnace. Valves and fittings of various sizes and shapes must be processed in this application; therefore, a library of programs has been established. A tape containing the appropriate program is withdrawn from the library and electronically transferred to the robot's memory before each different lot of parts is processed. Program transfer takes a maximum of 3 minutes. When the parts are completely new, the robot is taught the new program in the conventional manner. An operator plugs a hand-held teach control into the industrial robot and uses it to lead the arm and hand of the robot through the required steps. Later, the new program can be put on tape and filed for future reference.

glass manufacturing (automotive). The automation of an edge grinding operation on flat window glass for an automotive manufacturer utilizes robots. Each 2000B Unimate used, loads and unloads two automatic glass edge grinding machines alternately in less than 17 seconds. Maximum glass size is 28 in. × 68 in. (71 cm × 173 cm), weighing up to 35 pounds (16 kg). An auxiliary unload assist device on the glass grinder raises the finished part to allow the Unimate hand to move under the finished part into a nest on the grinder. A special double hand allows handling two pieces of glass so that a finished part is deposited on an output conveyor as a new piece is picked up from the input conveyor. The hand consists of two sets of dual vacuum cups mounted back to back so that an unfinished glass is supported by the lower cups and a finished piece supported by the upper cups. Three clamp operators combined with special valves and timer allow independent programming of vacuum and/or blow-off on either side of vacuum cups. The hand is supported from a hand gear train housing and the angular position of the vacuum cups can be varied ±20% by swivel motion. The position of the cups relative to the wrist is adjustable. The programmable swivel and adjustable cup position allows handling a large variety of part shapes.

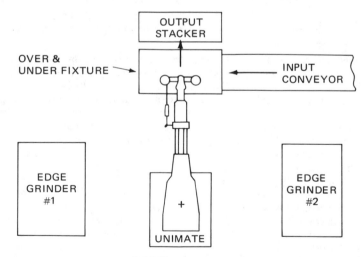

Installation arrangement.

glueing (automotive). The following is an example of a glueing process utilizing ASEA robots. In this glueing plant for car body components two ASEA robots (type IRb-6) work in parallel. The car body items are fed forward to the glueing section by a conveyor and are then secured under each robot. Each robot then receives a signal to start its work cycle. The glue strings are then laid out according to a pattern programmed into the robots. In this case, a thin string is applied along the outer edge of the plate and short thick strings are applied to the center of the plate. The thickness of the glue string can be varied by changing the speed of application or by a flow regulator in the glue extrusion head. The components are then moved away automatically and in the next stage are joined to stiffening plates. A robot-served station for glueing of sheet-metal items can be arranged as shown in the diagram. Here two robots cooperate with each other. The items are moved via a conveyor to the robots where they are secured in position. Since the process is fully automatic, no personnel need be exposed to volatile constituents in the glue or to any residual detergents.

Sheet-metal items

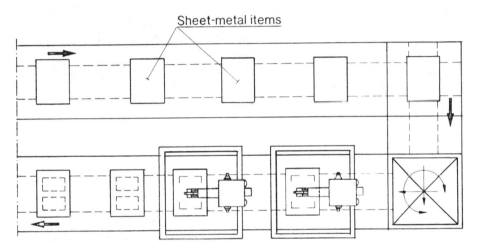

An example of a station where car body components are glued together with the aid of two ASEA robots.

grinding and cleaning (iron castings). In a number of applications in the grinding field where robotic precision, contouring capability, and force sensing are important attributes, the ASEA industrial robot model IRb-60 has been used successfully. When grinding is performed by a robot, a certain pressure must be exerted against the casting. Any variation of fin contour must be removed without damaging the surface of the casting. Normally a robot is programmed around a finished casting. As the robot follows the contour of the casting, with fins of various sizes along the parting line, there is a variation in pressure from the robot as it attempts to maintain the original programmed path. The larger or higher the fin on the parting line, the greater the pressure exerted by the robot. In addition, the force depends on the robot's rigidity and the distance of the programmed path from the casting. It is preferable that the robot handle the casting from magazines rather than being fed by a worker. There may be several operations necessary on the casting requiring several grinding machines. It is possible to install a number of grinding machines within the working range of the robot for more than one application. In some cases the casting is too heavy to handle. The grinding unit is then attached to the robot and the casting placed in a fixture. It is necessary to have the following equipment for cleaning of castings in an automatic grinding installation: (1) Grinding equipment with sufficient horsepower. (2) An industrial robot with good positional accuracy to perform the movements required and apply the grinding pressure needed for the application. The robot must be rigid but have the capability of adjusting to the application and must have force sensing, which can determine when the grinding is completed for a variety of fin sizes. It must also be able to compensate for grinding wheel wear. It should be possible to read out the contact force digitally if required. (3) The gripper should be attached to a well-defined surface and removable fins located in accessible positions. Inside fins should be avoided unless they are on radius. The automatic grinding installation is thereby simple and more effective.

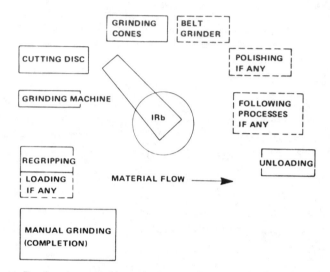

Drawing of a practical layout for automatic grinding with the ASEA IRb.

grinding of milling segments (ingots). The grinding of milling segments that have passed an ingot cutting station. The milling segments are made of stainless, acid-resistant steel, which has good dimensional characteristics. The gripper is hydraulically actuated and is equipped with a pressure switch controlling the gripping force to approximately 2 tons (17.8 kN). The station layout is illustrated. The overall robot station is housed in a large enclosure for environmental reasons. Grinding operations are accomplished by two electrical stand grinders. The machine has a power of 7½ hp (5.6 kW) with a disk diameter of approximately 20 in. (500 mm). The robot can compensate automatically for disk wear of up to 0.2–0.4 in. (5–10 mm). the machine grinds the narrow areas in the rear side of the milling segments. The work sequence is as follows: The robot operator loads magazine one once per hour. The robot picks up the casting in a fixed position and moves it to fixture two for regripping to obtain an exact gripping position. The robot then moves to machine three, where the inner radius and one side are ground. The search program, which has a built-in torque detector to compensate for disk wear, is used as the operation proceeds. Small grinding operations are done on machine four. The casting is placed in fixture two, where it is regripped and the outer radii on the other side are ground in machine three. After the grinding operation is completed the casting is put on the pallet in a programmed pattern. The total time cycle, including some manual grinding, is approximately 6 minutes per detail.

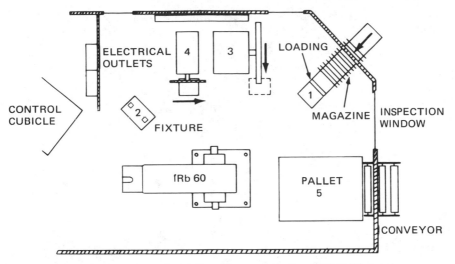

Equipment layout for grinding milling segments with an ASEA IRb-60.

grinding (cutting ingots). The industrial robot is used with a hydraulic cutting machine of 75 hp (55 kW). The disk has a diameter of approximately 12 in. (300 mm), and the cutting speed is 3.25 sec/in.² (0.5 sec/cm²) cutting area. The casting is manually placed on a turntable with two fixtures. While the cutting takes place the operator removes the cut workpiece and loads the fixture with a new workpiece. When the cutting is completed, the robot signals the operator to index the table 180°. The robot is placed in a large cage for effective protection from noise, dust, and possible disk breakup. To compensate for cutting disk wear, it is equipped with a torque detector connected to the search function. By using a robot for cutting operations the company achieves faster cutting, more accurate cutting, and better working conditions. In addition, the ASEA robot automatically slows down to cutting speed when the disk comes into contact with the workpiece; it maintains the same cycle time independent of the disk diameters.

handling (harrow disks). The automation of grinding harrow disks uses a Series 2000 Unimate industrial robot with three degrees of freedom and equipped with a special vacuum-air double hand. In operation, the Unimate robot's hand blows off excess dust from the blade and vacuum lifts it to a registration table where it is oriented, allowing the Unimate robot to regrip in a centered position. This is necessary because incoming stacks of blades can lean as much as 1 in. (2.54 cm) from a centered position. Having oriented the blade, the robot loads grinder 1 with its left hand, and removes a finished blade with the right hand. The robot then deposits the finished blade at the nearest output station, where it picks up another from the incoming lift table. After orienting this blade and loading grinder 2, the finished blade is removed and the cycle is repeated. The hand consists of a group of suction cups attached to spring-steel fingers set on an angle compatible with the concavity range involved. Each hand has its own pneumatic system enabling it to be independently programmed. All pneumatic lines are fitted with quick disconnect couplings allowing rapid changeover from one size to another. The hands are pivoted above a self-aligning bearing allowing them to properly seat themselves on the leaning stacks of blades. Lift tables are provided, and through an electric eye indexing system, keep incoming blades at a fixed height. This eliminates the need for a wrist on the Unimate robot, allowing the 2000 model to lift the 90-pound (41-kg) disks (two at a time), normally requiring the heavier 4000 unit.

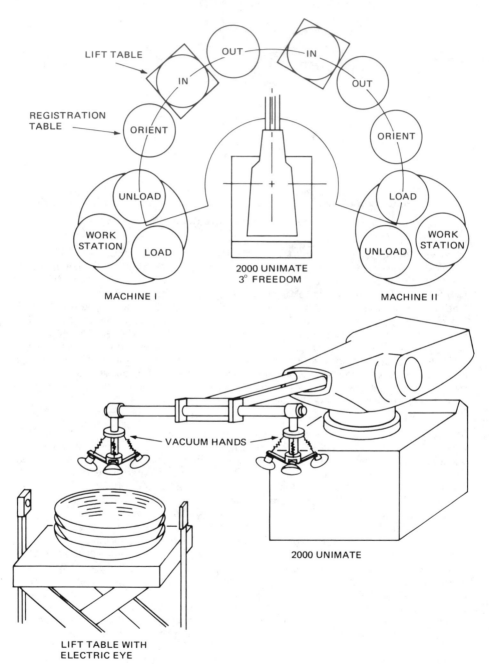

LIFT TABLE

OUT

IN

IN

OUT

REGISTRATION TABLE

ORIENT

ORIENT

UNLOAD

LOAD

WORK STATION

LOAD

UNLOAD

WORK STATION

2000 UNIMATE
3° FREEDOM

MACHINE I

MACHINE II

VACUUM HANDS

2000 UNIMATE

LIFT TABLE WITH
ELECTRIC EYE

heat treating and forming line (International Harvester). Heat treating and forming line for hollow disks using austempering process. Blanked disks of AISI 1085 steel with edge-turned bevels are loaded one at a time onto the entry conveyor of a 1650°F (900°C) surface combustion furnace by a Unimate industrial robot. At the exit end of the furnace the disks pass through a stamping station where they receive an ID number. Disks then enter a 550°F (290°C) salt bath quench. Upon emerging from the quench, each disk is presented to a second Unimate by a pop-up station. The robot transfers the hot disk into heated dies of a 400-ton (3.6 MN) Warco press. The press dishes the disk, and the disk is removed from the die area by a third Unimate robot. The formed disks are then transferred to the entry conveyor of an Ajax washer and dryer by the same robot. Dry disks then proceed by conveyor to the next operation – priming and painting. Unimate No. 1 at the entry conveyor for the tempering furnace has a vacuum-cup pick-up hand, which comes down vertically from the end of the robot arm. The hand then lifts the top disk from the palletized stack of about 50–60 disks. The robot transfers the disk and deposits it on the entry conveyor for the 1650°F (900°C) furnace. When no disks remain in the stack, the three vacuum cups come to rest on the open framework of the pallet, and a pneumatic pressure sensor detects absence of the usual negative pressure buildup. The sensor signal terminates the program and initiates advance of a new stack of disks into position. When a new stack is in position, a signal restarts the program. The second and third robots on the line each have one two-fingered hand to grip the disk on the OD. The basic hand tooling remains the same for all disks and only fingers are changed for gripping different diameters. The robots at International Harvester Canada each have an electronic memory and control system to direct the actions of the hydraulically powered arm. The memory also sends electrical signals to control the equipment that the robot automates, and receives signals, typically from limit switches or other sensors, from the other equipment to synchronize operations.

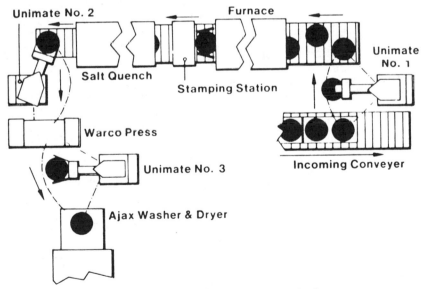

Floor plan of International Harvester's austempering line.

investment casting (automated shelling). Howmet Turbine Components Corp. produces precision investment castings primarily for turbine engines using the lost wax process. In the general layout of the automated shelling system, the 4000 Unimate is located in the center to permit access to all auxiliary equipment. To provide the required versatility to do the complete shelling operation, the Unimate is mounted on a shuttle mechanism so that it operates in two positions, as shown in the diagram. Around the Unimate in the front area, the ceramic slurry pots, the stucco sanders, and a loading station are arranged in a circular pattern. Also, in this area is the logic control center, the Unimate control console, and the program control console. In the rear area are three conveyors: (1) a two-tier conveyor for first and second dip coats, (2) a conveyor for back-up dip coats, and (3) an output conveyor for final drying. In the rear to the left of the conveyor is the environmental control equipment for the conveyor rooms. The Unimate on this automated line has 16 programs of 64 steps in each program. Fourteen of the programs are consumed by the various shelling cycles with two programs remaining open for any special programs and for troubleshooting. They are equipped with a heavy duty wrist gear train to allow greater load capacity, and, owing to the very abrasive atmosphere in the area, wear becomes a problem and the heavy duty gear train gives longer life. The Unimates have five programmed articulations with the fifth axis of movement, which is the wrist yaw, converted to constant spin. This permits constant rotation of the clusters during any mode of the robot. The Unimate console has been modified to include extra time delays and a random program selector (RPS). The Unimate is electrically interfaced with the other equipment so that it controls the operation at the proper time in the programs.

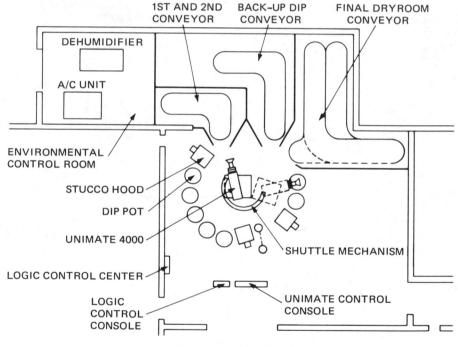

Dover automated shell line.

investment casting, mold making (TRW Metals Division). The robot-controlled mold-making system was designed to produce ceramic molds as required in an investment casting foundry, which utilizes the lost wax casting technique. The product mixture consists of blades, vanes, and some structural components as used in airborne and land-based gas turbine engines. The system is composed of a robot surrounded by five rotary slurry mixers, one fluidized bed, one rainfall sander, and three conveyors, all of which have been placed within the reach of the robot in order to operate well under the maximum physical limitations imposed by the robot manufacturer. The 42-in. (107-cm) slurry rotary mixers contain 300 gallons (1137 liters) each of various slurries that are applied at different times during the mold-making operations. These mixers are controlled by variable frequency drives and are stopped and started by the robot as the program dictates. The fluidized bed and rainfall sanders are also turned on and off by the robot as the program dictates. The conveyors are separately driven closed-loop conveyors that index mold envelopes to specific locations on command from the robot. The wax clusters are mounted on dipping plates, which in turn are hung from mold carriers affixed to the conveyors on 48-in. (122-cm) center-to-center distances. As the conveyors index toward the load or unload station, the conveyors take a path that brings the carrier to a tangent point within the robots rotary and vertical reach and normal to the arm of the robot when rotated to that point. The carrier is then clamped in place with a cylinder-operated clamping mechanism. This positions the carrier (and the dipping plate) in the optimum position for repeatable load and unload operations. The robot stores programs in its memory and these programs are automatically accessed under normal operating conditions.

loading and unloading, machine tool. Used in this operation to load and unload two double chucking Bullards, the Unimate is a Series 2000A with a special random program selector. This allows the robot to service each Bullard sequentially or individually should one of the Bullards by inoperative for any reason. The robot loads and unloads both chucks on machines 1 and 2 in approximately 30 seconds per machine. Parts are manually loaded and unloaded from the conveyor system by one operator for the two machines.

loading and unloading, parts. In this application the robot was mechanically modified to handle a greater load. Part weights range up to 300 pounds (136 kg), and the gripper weighs 200 pounds (91 kg) for a total weight of 500 pounds (227 kg). The robot is required to take a workpiece from the end of a roller conveyor to one lathe, then to a second lathe, next to a drilling station, and then to an output station. The parts running through this machining system are similar in geometry but vary in size. The robot services these machines on a demand basis and in the proper sequence. The conditional branch feature is used to enable the robot to function on this demand basis. High position repeatability is required since special fixturing to center the part in the machine is not used. Cycle time is critical, and the use of controlled acceleration and deceleration allows the use of high velocities. The large reach volume of the jointed arm is also required in this application. The programming for the intricate moves required to place the large workpiece between centers in the lathe is made easier by using the coordinate axes control.

loading and unloading, presses (truck wheels). This system incorporates two separate Versatran Model FB robots, both operating under the command of a single control and both powered by a single hydraulic power supply. The movements of the two robots are coordinated so that they function essentially as one robot with two arms. In the manufacturing plant they are positioned adjacent to a forging press for loading and unloading heavy-duty 400-pound (180-kg) aluminum truck wheels. Wheel blanks delivered on a conveyor to an input station next to the press are picked up by the first robot and placed in the forging die. Following the forging operations, the second robot picks up the wheel and deposits it on an outgoing conveyor. Placement of the robots on either side of the press leaves the front area clear, permitting easy access for press and die maintenance or repair. A single microcomputer control system monitors the operation of both robots, avoiding any chance for interference, and eliminates the need for special interfacing and programming between multiple robots. Movements of the two robots are coordinated in such a way that neither of the robots must wait while the other completes its programmed moves. The programmed moves of the loading robot start from a position 5 ft (1.5 m) out from the center of the press. From there the Versatran arm swings over to acquire a wheel from the input station, swings back, and advances to a "home" position 3½ ft (1.1 m) from the press. As the preceding part is removed by the second robot, the arm advances into the press, lowers the next part 6 in. (15 cm) into the forging pocket, releases the part, raises 6 in. (15 cm), and retracts 5 ft (1.5 m) to clear the press. The robot travel from the "home" position, into the press, and back out to the fully retracted position takes only 3 seconds.

loading and unloading, pinion line. An automated machining line for planetary pinion gears that utilizes three robots, nine machine tools, and a transfer system to produce gears from forged blanks is used by Massey-Ferguson. Massey-Ferguson's line was designed to handle five sizes of pinion gears, ranging from a 29-lb (13-kg), 6.8 in. (17.3 cm) OD, 3.2 in (8 cm) width, 25 tooth, 4.0 pitch gear, down to a 6-lb (2.7-kg), 3.6 in. (9 cm) OD, 2.5 in. (6.4 cm) face width, 16 tooth, 5.0 pitch gear. The process consists of broaching the ID of a normalized rough forged blank, turning the faces and OD, shaping the teeth, tooth deburring, and gear shaving to produce a pinion gear ready for heat treating. The three robots are Unimate 2105 G, 5° models. They differ primarily in hand-tooling configuration and programmable controller systems. The modifications necessary to adapt the machine tools for robot loading were primarily in the areas of control circuitry to enable the machines to send and receive signals from the robots, chucking systems to facilitate loading, chip removal, and part in-position sensors. The Fab-Tec transfer system transformed the manufacturing process from a group of machining centers to an integrated machine line, retaining most of the flexibility of the independent machining centers. The key elements in the flexibility of the system are the storage units positioned between machining centers. Maintaining these storage units in a half-filled status during normal operation permits the machines ahead of the unit or below the unit to be down for approximately half a shift without affecting the overall line production. The balance of the transfer system is conventional in that it is composed of gravity conveyors, pump up lifts, elevators, and various metering devices. The unconventional feature of this transfer system is the way it is integrated into a transfer line that automatically transfers parts as needed. Much of this flexibility is due to the programmable controller system.

machining (Iveco). A system designed and produced by Comau for Iveco, a European manufacturer in the motor vehicle industry. It is a flexible manufacturing system (FMS) fully controlled by a central process computer; with appropriate software, it controls the entire production cycle from optimized pallet management to the control of individual NC machines. The system primarily manufactures different types of engine covers for trucks, tractors, and construction machinery, but is capable of machining front and rear gearbox assemblies and complete gearboxes. This flexible machining system consists of the following elements: several machining centers (for metal-cutting operations) equipped with NC; a pallet handling system, including positioning, clamping, and storing equipment; a centralized computer to control and monitor all operations; ancillary systems for the loading and unloading of workpieces; chip removal and workpiece cleaning; inspection and test stations. The entire system is capable of processing a random part mix as efficiently as batch-type systems. The central control system of a flexible machining line normally consists of two computers operating in parallel. The TR95 consists of 12 special NC machining modules linked by a modular conveyor system for pallet transfer and recirculation. The machining units are designed to perform specific machining operations such as milling, drilling, tapping, turning, boring, and various other operations. Work may be performed on parts up to 24 in. × 24 in. (600 mm × 600 mm) in size. Loading and unloading takes place at a special station on the pallet transport system, where the parts, after identification, are loaded and transported to the appropriate machining modules. At each station the pallet is reidentified, and the central computer, on the basis of the various part programming and process optimization data, decides whether the pallet is to continue on the main conveyor line or be shunted off to the machining station. All the NC modules in this system are single spindle units with automatic tool-change capability, except for the multihead unit with automatic head change. On either side of the work position is a head storage carrying six interchangeable multispindle heads. The average daily output of the line is 220 parts in two shifts.

materials handling (gearboxes). Items can be forwarded to a robot in several ways. In some cases, they arrive on conveyor fixed trays or pallets on which they are arranged in some sort of pattern. In other cases, they arrive one at a time on a conveyor belt. Pallets are advantageous in that the items can easily be further conveyed by manually or automatically operated trucks. Before reaching the robot, a roller conveyor must be terminated with a stop or sorting facility incorporating an orientation device. To further increase the degree of utilization and the economic yield, the materials-handling operation can often be combined with tasks involving serving machine tools, cleaning, or mechanical processing. A materials-handling station can be arranged as shown in the diagram. A robot with limited travel movement picks gearbox items from a conveyor after they have passed through a sandblast booth. The robot places the items patternwise on pallets, which are fed forward and positioned in front of the robot. Approximately 35 different types of items pass through this station. When the robot is to begin picking a new type of item, a completed program in an article-numbered cassette is entered into the control system of the robot. At the same time, the gripper is adjusted to suit the new item.

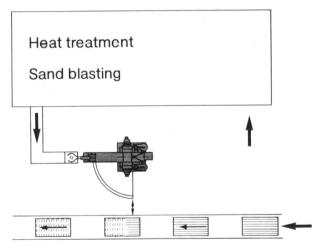

Example of a materials-handling station built around an ASEA robot.

measuring car bodies. Robots measure car bodies by checking 120 points on the body at the end of a spot welding line to a repeatability within 0.02 in. (0.5 mm). Two 13.2-pound (6-kg) robots are mounted on tracks up to 16 ft (5 m) on either side of the body line; these robots can traverse 10–16 ft (3–5 m), and reach the whole length of the car when it is in the measuring station on the line. Cars come down the line at a rate of 40 per hour, and to keep pace with the line, the robots check one-quarter of the points on each car.

Therefore, after every four cars all of the 120 points have been checked. Each robot checks about 15 points in the front section of one car, then another 15 points in the next car, and so on. The system, calibrated against a master body, measures X, Y, and Z departures from the nominal size at each point. Deflections are measured by a three-dimensional probe on the robot arm, the robot itself moving to present position. This solution was preferred to putting a sensor on the robot's arm to make contact with each point and to measure the displacement directly from the robot's resolvers. A special computer is programmed to receive and interpret the data from the probe. Dimensional data can be analyzed statistically to identify trends and correct errors promptly. Points important in the check include shock absorber and engine mountings, window and door openings, and hood and truck frames.

nut-running and tightening, drilling (arsenal). General purpose industrial robots are especially well suited for performing nut-running and similar operations in hazardous environments. Drilling and countersinking with the aid of a positioning guide is another application. Mechanical guides will increase the locating accuracy of the robot and will also help to shorten positioning time. Without such guides, both accuracy and positioning time suffer, and a human worker is often faster. In the application shown the positioning guide surrounds the impact wrench that unscrews a lifting lug from the nose of a projectile in a munitions plant.

operator override (arc welding). Manufacturing processes upstream from a welding operation or distortion during welding at times create a seam that deviates from the programmed straight-line path. In order to prevent reteaching the robot for each part, a feature called Operator Override has been developed. This feature uses the human as the feedback mechanism for adjusting for deviations in the weld seam. The operator, through a set of switches, can cause the robot to deviate from or shift its straight-line paths. The deviations are made in a direction normal to the line of the weld in the X-Y plane, and also vertically in the absolute Z direction of the robot. The maximum deviation is limited by software to 0.5 in. (12.7 mm) in all directions. At the end of the move, the robot will automatically return to the programmed end point, cancelling out the path deviations input by the operator.

palletizing (arsenal). A two-projectile depalletizing system uses a 4000 Series Unimate. Empty projectiles come to the arsenal from special manufacturing facilities that forge and machine the projectiles. They arrive on standard wooden pallets and are transported to the depalletizing area for loading into tank cars. The system must remove and dispose of banding and remove plastic protective grommets and pallet tops. These operations are accomplished as part of a power and free palletized conveyor system, which then presents the projectiles to the Unimate. Four 4000A, five-axis Unimates, two working the 6.1-in. (155-mm) and 6.9-in. (175-mm) line, and two working on the 8-in. (203-mm) line, remove the projectiles from the wooden pallets and put them into tank cars. The projectiles weigh up to 200 pounds (91 kg). The first Unimate engages a lift lug, which is screwed into the nose of the projectile from the six or eight position pallets to an intermediate nest. The Unimate unscrews the lift lug and deposits it onto a conveyor as it returns for the next projectile. The second Unimate in the team picks up the projectile by engaging the internal threads in the nose and transfers the parts to one of fifteen positions in the tank car. Two types of hands are employed in this application. The first hand incorporates two features. One is a contoured cup driven by a pneumatic impact wrench to seek, find, and unscrew the projectile lift lug. The second feature is a pneumatically operated lift pin to engage the lift lug eye for transport of the projectile. The second hand contains a threaded, pneumatically operated internal expanding mandrel for transporting the projectile with the lug removed by engaging the internal nose threads. Both hands include long cylindrical fingers to prevent projectile sway and are inherently fail-safe on loss of air or electrical power.

palletizing (converters). A 2100B Series, five-axis industrial robot with hand tooling is used to stack 58 catalytic converters into wire cage-type transports in proper preprogrammed sequence. These converters are placed accurately and in the proper position in every tote cage. The converters are fed from a transport onto a small conveyor, which has the capability of tilting the converter at a 72° angle for Unimate pick-up. It then delivers the converter to the Unimate to pick the converter up and place it into its proper location. Accuracy of placement must be maintained as converter surfaces are critical to the final finished product. The only difficulty experienced in programming was the odd shape of the converter, having left and right plumbing on its ends. The solution was a programming technique combined with alternate end feeding from the input conveyor.

palletizing, glass tubes (lamps). Open-end uncoated glass tubes measuring 92 in. (2337 mm) in length, produced for fluorescent lamps, are palletized, with a typical load being made up of 25 layers of tubes, each layer having 31 tubes. After the last production operation, the fluorescent tubes are conveyed to the work station of the robot. The robot's task is to build up a pallet load of tubes and, once a pallet is full, to trigger another conveyor that moves the filled pallet away while bringing an empty pallet into position for loading. At one plant installation hot glass tubes with necked ends are carried away on a conveyor with the tubes located in parallel positions for air cooling and delivery to the robot's pick-up point. The parallel tubes are automatically moved closer together into a queue at the end of the conveyor. The head of the queue advances into the pick-up area as another tube joins the rear of the queue. When the queue contains 31 tubes, the capacity of the pick-up area, the head tube has moved to a point where it trips a limit switch. The switch performs two functions. It signals the robot that it can pick up a load and it operates a gate that halts tube number 32. The following tubes form a buffer storage until the robot has palletized the other tubes (they will subsequently form the next group of 31). The robot picks up all 31 tubes in the pick-up area, turns 90° to its left, and deposits the layer of tubes on a staked-sided pallet that can accommodate 26 layers. Conical plugs on the robot's gripper fit into each end of every tube to retain them during transfer. The tubes are released by the gripper a fraction of an inch above the last pallet layer. This short drop aids the nesting of tubes in each layer and ensures that accumulated stacking height deviations do not cause the robot to press a new layer against those below it. A complete transfer of 31 tubes takes approximately 10 seconds.

plastic molding. A number of plastic product manufacturing plants use general-purpose industrial robots that tend compression molding and injection molding machines. In one plant, each of two industrial robots alternately unload parts from a pair of eight-cavity compression molding machines. Employee turnover was high because of the heat and vapors. Now, two robots are working in a hazardous dump area of the machine, rather than the nine employees formerly. Besides unloading the machines, the 120 step programs in the robots' memories also control a magazine holding preheated parts fed one at a time to the molding machines. Elsewhere, elastomeric parts 5 ft (1.5 m) long are being unloaded alternately from two injection molding machines. The robot performing the job reaches into the press and strips the part from 395°F (202°C) dies, relieving two operators per shift from exposure to vapors as well as the heat. Previously, operators relieved each other at intervals to keep their exposure to the vapors within allowable time limits. Each elastomeric part consists of two usable pieces joined by a runner and sprue. After stripping the part from the die, the unit draws the part over two parallel blades on a cutting table, severing the pieces from the central sprue. Finally, the robot drops the usable pieces on a conveyor and turns to the second injection molding machine as it opens. On the way, the robot drops the sprue in a box.

pressloading/unloading (R. E. Chapin Manufacturing Works). Chapin manufactures an extensive line of compressed air sprayers for the application of weed killers, pesticides, and general spraying solutions. Major elements in the stamping line at Chapin include three presses and five robots. The robots are standard Series 50 models built by Auto-Place. In the operation, sheet metal blanks for forming into funnels are delivered to the press line on a chute. The first robot picks up a part off the chute and places it into the first die, where it is drawn and formed. The second robot removes the part and places it in the die on the second press for trimming and piercing. The third robot removes the part, turns it over, and places it on a pedestal between the second and third presses. Robot No. 4 removes the part from the pedestal and places it in a cam die in the third press where it is reformed and curled. The last stamping operation presented a critical and time-consuming unloading problem. The curled edges of the part form a vacuum, and the operator had to use a tool to pry the part out of the die. The fifth Auto-Place robot in the line easily overcomes the vacuum, removes the part, and drops it into a chute leading into a bin of finished parts.

press loading (body panels). A Unimate 2200A is used to load a body panel into a cam pierce die. The panel is delivered to the load position on a double-width conveyor. The robot picks the panel up and loads it into a die, then moves back to receive the next panel. The die is automatically cycled by a standard press autocircuit, followed by panel rejection to the exit portion of the conveyor belt.

rubber bale handling (Firestone). At this rubber plant a 2000B Unimate is being employed to palletize automatically 75-pound (34-kg) rubber bales into shipping containers. A series of conveyors transport the bales from the manufacturing area to the packaging and shipping area. Here, automatic machines wrap the rubber bales in plastic film bags for placement into shipping containers. Each conveyor delivers a specific grade of rubber to be

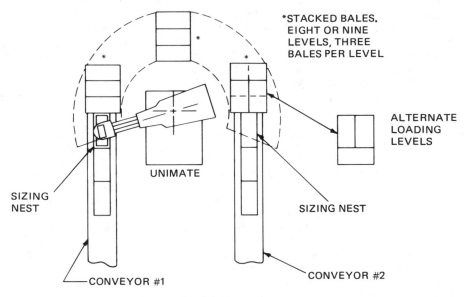

Installation arrangement.

palletized into a selected shipping container and configuration. The Unimate is adapted with a special hand mechanism to transfer the bales from the conveyors into the appropriate containers. The conveyors accumulate the bales in groups of three (one layer) before calling for the Unimate program to transfer that layer of parts to the container. Just prior to transfer, each bale is resized to ensure that cold flow of the material has not distorted its shape. Two types of containers are used; a cardboard container with vertical dividers holding three bales per layer, eight layers high in three vertical rows, and a wooden box with no dividers. The bales are palletized in alternate hand patterns for each layer to key them together nine rows high. The same Unimate program is used for each common pattern layer for a given container position. A special control console allows selection of a separate program for each conveyor so that either conveyor output can be palletized in either type container at any of the three loading stations. Upon completion of a container, a material handler removes the full container and replaces it with an empty one. Since there are three container locations for the two conveyors, the operator can select an alternate program to load a second container while replacing the full container.

shaft cutting. A machine group for production of shafts for gear boxes includes a Boehring lathe, a Hurth milling machine, a Nyberg and Westerberg grinding machine, measuring fixtures and removal conveyance. The machine is provided with a bar magazine. The bar is automatically fed forward, the material is cut to length and centered, and the first shoulder is turned. The finished component is fed onto a conveyor belt with the shoulder toward the feeding direction. The robot changes components in the lathe and starts rough machining. The robot turns to the control equipment and puts the finished shaft into a measuring fixture. Two diameters and one linear dimension are measured. The measurement results are stored by measuring equipment and transferred to the lathe when the rough machining is finished and fine machining is started. Should the shaft be outside the tolerance zone, no starting signal is given for fine cutting; neither does the robot receive a signal to retrieve the shaft and to proceed to milling and grinding. The component is clamped with the turned end in the chuck (soft jaws) and with a pivot at the other end. Tools are provided to produce rough cutting, fine cut, parting-off chuck. A new (reserve) cut is changed after a preset number of shafts are turned. In measuring fixtures the fine cut is finally made. The fixture is axially and radially self-orienting by means of V-blocks and axial limit stops, which are easily adjustable for different shaft sizes by means of modules (not adjusting screws). The adjustment for the respective shaft is to remain repeatedly the same at rerigging. The measuring equipment is manually operable. In relation to the grinding machine the robot positions the shaft in the fixed pivot and provides a signal for the tail pivot to move forward. When the tail pivot is in position, a signal is given to the robot to release the shaft, withdraw, and start the grinding cycle. After the grinding cycle is completed, the robot removes the shaft in the reverse sequential order of the insertion cycle.

spot welding (automobile body on a moving line). In this application, an automobile body is already fixtured on a "body truck," which is moved by a floor conveyor. A rail system is used to guide the body truck and maintain proper alignment to the robot. The welding operation is done around the "wheel well" while the body is moving. The body truck position is measured relative to the robot base. The ability to program the body when it is stationary and to execute the program when the body is in motion and the need for only a minimum amount of modifications to the line have made this application economical.

spot welding, resistance (General Motors). The application of industrial robots for resistance spot welding has successfully been used by General Motors assembly plants in Lordstown, Ohio, and Norwood, Ohio. The robots were successsfully used on-line for various body welding operations. At each plant 22 robots were stationed alongside a synchronous indexing line, which has the capability of producing 100 body assemblies per hour. Each robot produced from 12 to 24 welds on each body. The accuracy required for this operation was to locate the spot welding gun and electrodes within a circle of 0.093 in. (2.4 mm) in diameter. In addition, it was essential that positive body, panel, and flange locations be achieved. More consistent panels were produced and used in conjunction with more positive means of panel location. As a result, a more consistent, higher-quality body was produced. Another factor that requires consideration when spot welding is the weight and configuration of the welding guns used. Heavy and deep throated guns with large throat areas limit the speed and accuracy attainable by robots. Lightweight and low-inertia guns are more desirable in order to minimize these problems. Model mix problems normally encountered in body assembly spot welding applications are easily resolved by the use of robots with multiple program capabilities. This allows selection of the proper robot movement and location when different models of a product are produced on the same line or machine. Variations are easily handled by interconnection with sensing devices such as limit switches, which detect model variation and select the appropriate robot program.

spot welding, resistance (General Motors). General Motors Assembly Division in Lordstown, Ohio, uses Unimate 2000 series on the main line shuttle to perform spot welding operations on "H" body exposed mating flanges. They also use four Unimates on the side frame shuttle to weld the quarter inner and wheelhouse panels. Four additional Unimates are used in a continuous maintenance and repair program. All robots are mounted in a fixed position, which allows for any one of them to be moved out for repair and an operating robot moved in to take its place.

spray painting (General Motors). Primer and finish color spray painting operations on urethane plastic bumpers have been automated with 16 servo-controlled robots at the General Motors Guide Division. The installation consists of four painting lines, with four robots in each line. The DeVilbiss Co. supplied the Trallfa robots, which provided the continuous-path motion necessary for precise duplication of the human sprayer's motions and techniques. Each of the four painting lines includes one robot for priming and three robots for applying color paint. The robot incorporates arm and wrist actions that provide six axes of motion. Its hydraulically powered manipulator features a unique patented Flexi-arm device, which essentially duplicates the pitch, yaw, and rotation motions of the human wrist. The horizontal sweep of the arm spans 135°, an optional feature selected over the standard 93° arm swing. The counterbalanced arm is also hydraulically depressurized while the robot is being programmed, making the arm easy to move manually. The microprocessor-based control for each robot consists basically of a microprocessor, a dual floppy disc memory system, and an LED display. Up to 64 spray programs can be stored in memory. Recall time for any one program is just 0.5 second. Other control features include random program selection, extended memory times, copy and edit capability, and synchronization with monorail movement. Solid-state circuits mounted on plug-in boards facilitate maintenance and troubleshooting. Synchronizing robot movements with the two monorails is an important requirement. In programming the robots, the operator attaches a teaching handle to the manipulator arm, and plugs it in electrically to a receptacle on the robot base. He then leads the arm through the desired program sequence to define the path and relative velocity of the arm and spray gun. When programming is complete, the operator removes the control from "programming" to "repeat" and puts the robot into the automatic mode.

testing and inspection, parts (Chevrolet Motor Division). Chevrolet uses four solid-state image cameras to determine visually if valve covers for V-6 engines are properly assembled and generates data that tell a robot when to accept parts or reject them according to the nature of the defect. The Auto-Place system installed and operating at Chevrolet consists of a dial index machine with six dual fixture stations on a 12-ft-diameter (3.7-m-diameter)

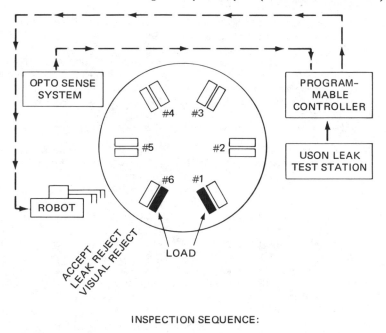

INSPECTION SEQUENCE:

St. No. 1: (left-hand fixture) load   St. No. 4: Opto Sense System
St. No. 2: Uson Leak Tester   St. No. 5: Auto-Place Robot sorts
St. No. 3: Idle position   and unloads valve covers
                         St. No. 6: (right-hand fixture) load

The "accept" or "reject" signals made by the Uson Tester and the Opto Sense System are replayed to the programmable controller where they are held in memory until the inspected parts reach station No. 5. At this point, the "accept–reject" decision signal is transmitted to the robot, which sorts and unloads the parts according to the nature of the defect.

aluminum table. To initiate the automatic testing and inspection routine an operator manually loads valve covers on fixtures at the right side of station No. 6 and the left side of station No. 1. Two styles of valve covers are inspected. The parts are placed on cast aluminum fixtures, which fill the valve cover to within 0.125-in. (3.175-mm) of the wall. Parts are seated on a urethane gasket to support and position them. At this point the operator pushes palm buttons to advance the parts to station No. 2 for 100% leak testing for weld soundness. Station No. 2 consists of a pair of Uson Corp. electronic memory pressure decay units interfaced with a Texas Instruments programmable controller (PC). Each fixture at station No. 2 has magnetic sensors to indicate the presence of a part. If a part has not been loaded on one of the fixtures, the Uson tester is instructed to test only the loaded fixture. When the presence of a part on a fixture is sensed, a vertically descending ram seals the holes in the top of the valve cover and clamps the bottom flange of the part to the urethane gasket to form a seal. The test cavity is then charged with approximately 5 psi air pressure through a solenoid valve controlled by the tester. Next, the solenoid valve is closed, and an electronic pressure transducer continuously measures pressure trapped in the part. After leak testing, the valve covers index to station No. 4, the visual inspection station. The visual inspection station is served by four General Electric Co. solid-state imagers with matrix arrays positioned to view the parts. They are mounted overhead in protective enclosures with Lexan windows. The cameras' lenses are focused on the valve covers, not the windows. The GE cameras are tied to the Auto-Place Opto Sense camera control and comprise what Auto-Place calls its Opto Sense System. The cameras have a solid-state matrix array with approximately 60,000 picture elements (pixels). Each element is sensitive to black, white, and shades of gray. The pairs of cameras work as a team with each viewing one-half of a part with a slight overlap in their fields of vision. If one pair of cameras is down, the line can still inspect at 50% of capacity because everything is programmed parallel. The final step in the testing and inspection sequence is indexing the parts to station No. 5, where they are sorted and unloaded by an Auto-Place Series 50 pneumatically operated robot.

thermometer processing (Chesebrough-Pond). One of the products produced by Chesebrough-Pond is mercury-in-glass, clinical (fever) thermometers. The process involves some 160 manufacturing steps, which include shrinking, expanding, and moving the mercury about in the thermometer in a process similar to that of kneading dough, so as to drive entrained gases out of the mercury. The process utilizes hot- and cold-water baths, vibrations, and centrifuging. In the automated system utilizing a Unimate 2100 the Unimate is located in the center, with its entire working envelope occupied by various auxiliary equipment of company design. Equipment includes warm- and cold-water baths, a vibrating table, holding and turning tables, several centrifuges, and both incoming and outgoing conveyors. The centrifuges, vibrator, and both conveyors are interlocked with the robot so that, for example, the centrifuges will signal that they have stopped and their lids have opened before the robot will attempt to reach into the machine. In like fashion, the incoming boxes of thermometers must trip a switch which indicates to the robot that the box is ready for pickup. On the outgoing conveyor, a photoelectric eye must be cleared before the Unimate will place another box on the conveyor. The boxes are made of perforated stainless steel, and hold 1100 thermometers each. All loading stations are equipped with beveled openings so as to accommodate any inaccuracies in box position, robot gripper, or box placement. The robot gripper is designed to handle either one or two boxes at a time and does both. The turning table is used for setting the boxes down while the hand is reconfigured as needed before the next equipment loading step. At certain steps in the cycle, time delays are programmed into the robot to allow warm water to drain from the boxes before they are placed in the cold-water baths. This lessens the heat load on a recirculating chiller which supplies the cold water. The centrifuges are equipped with speed switches and hardened steel cams and plungers. When the speed switches sense that the centrifuges have slowed to about 2 rpm, the plunger is actuated and engages itself in a detent in the cam. The cam is locked to the centrifuge drive shaft; hence, the centrifuges are stopped in the same position every time so that the boxes can be found by the robot. One operator runs the entire system.

tracking, stationary base line (automobile body side transfer). In this application automobile body sides are picked up from a continuously moving floor-mounted conveyor on which they are built, to an overhead continuously moving monorail conveyor. This application requires that the robot system has the ability to track two continuously moving lines, independently of one another. This application not only illustrates the concept of tracking but also the use of a heavy-duty robot with a large working range. The body side and the robot grippers together weigh approximately 250 pounds (113.5 kg), and the robot must reach to the floor-level conveyor to pick the body side up and raise it to a height of approximately 10 ft (3.1 m) to deposit it on the overhead conveyor.

tracking, stationary base line (automobile bumper transfer). In this application two automobile bumpers are transferred from a stop–go conveyor on which they are built to an overhead monorail conveyor system. The overhead conveyor stops approximately in sequence with the build conveyor, but its stationary position can vary widely from one cycle to the next. It is therefore necessary to utilize the tracking ability of the robot system to monitor the position of the monorail conveyor so that the bumpers may be placed correctly on the conveyor's cradle.

tracking, stationary base line (spot welding). Spot welding with robots is being carried out in automobile body assembly operations. In one operation the robot was taught to weld flanges parallel to the direction of the motion of the line, and also perpendicular to the line direction in both the horizontal and vertical planes. Abort and utility branches were fully utilized in these spot welding applications on moving car bodies. Different abort branches were taught for different weld areas of the body and, in a similar manner, different utility branches were also taught. Both the abort and utility branch concepts were fully proven, the abort branches being initiated by internal signals from the control and the utility branches by signals indicating stuck spot weld gun tips.

transfer molding (GTE Sylvania, Inc.). A Series 2100 Unimate industrial robot operates two 50-ton (0.5 MN) transfer molding presses. The robot has an articulated arm, with a gripper that is controlled by electronic memory, to unload the two presses alternately. The Unimate also performs secondary operations during the cycle times of the presses. There are three phases to the automatic transfer molding program: (1) The pill (molding compound) must be preheated and placed. (2) The part removed from the mold. (3) Secondary operations performed when practicable. Extruders that prepare the molding compound, preheat it, and supply a molding pill were selected because of their convenience in changing pill weight during production runs and the consistent pill temperature throughout. Although an extruder represents approximately three times the investment needed for a customary preheater, one extruder can serve two transfer molding presses even though different parts are run in each press. A special pill feeder was devised to supply pills from one extruder to the two presses alternately. The feeder consists of a pair of hydraulic-cylinder-operated arms, one arm for each press. Each arm has two cylinders: one to sweep the arm in an arc and the other to lengthen the radius of the sweep arc. Each arm transfers a pill in a cup from an extruder to the press and loads the pill in through the rear. To satisfy their objectives the industrial robot was included in the system to unload automatically the parts from the molds, synchronize the operation of the presses and feeder, and transfer parts to secondary operations, which could be performed automatically. The left-hand transfer press molds printed circuit card connector parts, while the right-hand press molds ``split block'' connector parts. Both parts are molded from glass-filled black phenolic with a left-hand pill weight of 2.6 ounces (72 g) and a right-hand pill weight of 2.1 ounces (60 g). The cycle time of each press is approximately 80 seconds. While the right-hand press is closed, the Unimate robot reaches into the two-cavity mold of the left-hand press, extracts the parts, moves them past a feeler-operated limit switch to sense whether the parts have been extracted, and deposits the parts in a box. The extruder and pill feeder load the left-hand press, which closes as the industrial robot turns to the right-hand press. As soon as the right-hand press opens, the robot extracts those parts from the two-cavity mold, presents the parts to the limit-switch sensor on that press, and loads the parts into special secondary operation equipment. Following this, the robot initiates the cycle of the secondary operation equipment, and resets the equipment upon completion of the right-hand secondaries as the transfer molding press closes. Next, the Unimate swings back to the left-hand press, poised to extract the next part and to repeat the entire cycle again.

transferring, components (appliances). Various appliance components require transfer from one moving conveyor to another. In this case, the parts are transferred from an unpalletized part conveyor to a conveyor that transports the parts to a dipping tank. After the parts have been dipped, they must go back to the original conveyor. The parts are appliance components, weighing from 10 to 15 pounds (4.5 to 6.8 kg) and coming in assorted sizes. A Cincinnati T³ robot, with a tracking option performs the transfer. It is equipped with special tooling that allows it to pick up a wide variety of parts. Both conveyors are continuously moving at different rates. Steel hooks carry the parts on the conveyor. The robot has a cycle time of from 4 to 7 seconds to transfer parts from conveyor to conveyor, depending on the part.

transferring, engine heads (automotive). Broached engine heads of four-cylinder engines need to be loaded onto pallets then transferred to another plant for machining. The parts must be unloaded from the pallets onto a conveyor that feeds a transfer machine. The engine head weighs 42 pounds (19 kg), and has the dimensions of 18 in. (457.2 mm) high by 4 in. (101.6 mm) wide by 0.75 in. (19.1 mm) thick. In this operation a 2000 Series Unimate robot works in conjunction with three pallet locators. The locators are fixed to the floor adjacent to the robot. Pallets loaded with 96 parts (six layers with 16 parts per layer) are placed into the locators for accurate positioning. The robot automatically selects the proper program for depalletizing a given pallet. When the robot finishes a layer of parts, it removes the dunnage (a device, often a plastic mold placed on top of a pallet to locate precisely the palletized object for a robot), separates and deposits them in another pallet location. The tooling is designed to indicate whether a part has been loaded properly into the dunnage. If the part has been loaded incorrectly, the robot hand tooling will signal the robot to select a different program in order to orient the part properly. After the robot has finished unloading one pallet, it will automatically select a program to unload the second pallet while giving a signal to an outside operator who placed a full pallet of parts in the empty parts locator. The entire engine manufacturing cycle time is 18 seconds, of which the robot takes 6 seconds.

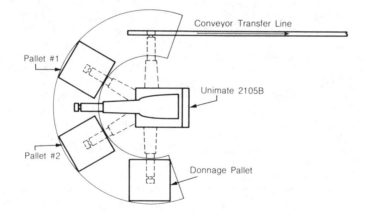

A Unimate 2000 Series robot unloads engine heads from parts pallets.

transferring, glass (automotive). The task is to transfer glass windshield and window panels from a washing conveyor to a glass de-edging station. The panels weigh from 6 to 48 pounds (2.7 to 21.8 kg) and range in size from 6 in. (15.24 cm) by 4 in. (10.2 cm) to 54 in. (137.2 cm) by 22 in. (55.9 cm), each 0.25 in. (6.35 mm) thick. The tooling on the glass de-edging station has three stops that must be positioned within 5 mils (0.13 mm). In this position a Versatran FA Series robot with 660 control transfers the panels from the washer conveyor to the de-edging station on demand. The robot selects the appropriate de-edging machine based on input signals from either machine. To optimize cycle time, the robot is equipped with a dual hand. The robot's hand tooling is adjustable to handle the full range of the 22 different parts required in this application. The transfer's cycle time is 5.5 seconds.

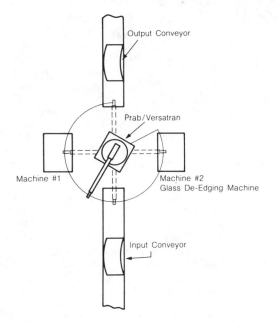

A Versatran FA Series robot is used here to transfer automobile windshield and window glass in a parallel process.

transferring, steel forgings (machinery). The problem is to transfer steel forgings through two successive machining operations. The parts are six kinds of forged steel housings that

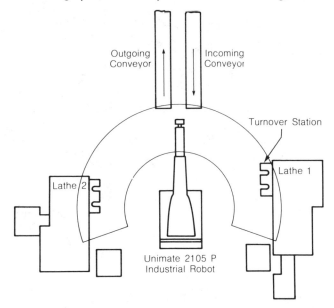

A Unimate 2000 Series robot transfers steel forgings in a serial process.

weigh from 2 to 40 pounds (0.9 to 18.2 kg) each. The outer diameters of the parts are about 14 in. (35.6 cm), and their thicknesses are about 3 in. (7.6 cm). This application uses a Unimate 2000 Series robot. The Unimate accepts raw parts from an incoming conveyor and preloads the parts on a positioning table in front of a Jones and Lamson turning machine. When the J&L machine has completed this cycle, it signals the Unimate. The robot extracts the semifinished part, places it on a second rest stand, and loads another raw part into the first J&L. When the raw part is correctly positioned in the first J&L, the robot retracts and signals the machine to begin its cycle. The robot then transfers the semifinished part to a third rest stand for preload into the second J&L. Upon receiving a signal that the second J&L has completed its cycle, the robot extracts a finished part and places it on a fourth rest station. As in the first operation, the robot loads the semifinished part into the second J&L, retracts, initiates the machining cycle, and deposits the finished part on an outgoing conveyor.

transferring, steering knuckles (automotive). A process that combines serial and parallel operations is shown in the diagram. Steering knuckles for large off-the-road earthmoving equipment must be processed through a numerically controlled (NC) turning machine, a gauge station and a dedicated transfer line for drilling and counterboring. Because of the NC machine's cycle time, three are required to maintain throughput. The steering knuckles weigh 78 pounds (35.4 kg), are 7 in. (17.78 cm) high, 8 in. (20.3 cm) wide, and 3 in. (7.6 cm) thick. A Series 4000 Unimate robot moves the steering knuckles through available NC turning machines, then takes the finished parts through the gauge and subsequent transfer machining operations. The Unimate is equipped with a dual hand to optimize cycle time. Ten seconds before the completion of a machine cycle on the NC turning machine, it sends a preinitiate signal. This allows the robot to position itself in a "ready" position just outside the NC machine. Cycle time for this operation is 8 seconds for each part transfer to the turning machine and 6 seconds for the gauge station cycle.

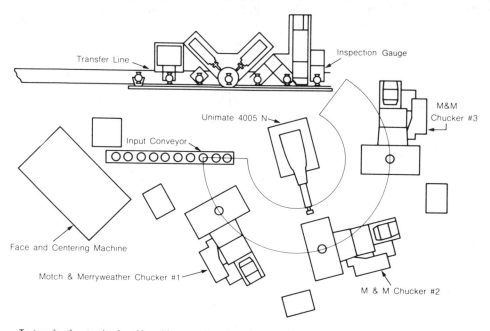

To transfer the steering knuckles of large earthmoving equipment, a Series 4000 Unimate robot is configured to combine serial and parallel process.

transferring, transmission cases (Ford Motor Co.). This was the first application of Universal Transfer Devices (UTD) in the Transmission and Chasis Division of Ford Motor Company in the Livonia plant. The system consists of a very simple network of limit-switch sensors, which control the logic system through the use of a step programmer. Transmission cases, after being loaded automatically onto a roller conveyor from an air test transfer, flow by gravity to an orientor. When a limit switch senses pressure, the orientor cycle orients and pushes the part into the load position. At this location another switch tells the robot that a part is ready for pick-up. At this time the robot arm will extend and clamp onto the case. If an empty monorail carrier is sensed, the robot will pick up the case and position it at a preload location where still another limit switch will sense the moving monorail carrier. At this time, the robot will proceed to load the part to the carrier. If a "successful load" sensor is triggered, the unit will then repeat these motions. If the "successful load" switch is not made, the unit will stop cycling and a warning light is triggered to alert personnel. Clamping is done on two symmetrical part surfaces facing the robot unit in the orientor. There are three models of cases, two are high-volume parts and the third is a service part of which only 300 are required per year. The service case configuration is much different than that of the other two and is not handled by the robot, but is manually loaded. The distance between the clamping surfaces on the other two cases are different by 1½ in. (3.8 cm), but is not a problem in gripping as the hydraulic cylinder stroke is adequate for both dimensions.

unloading, jars (Chesebrough-Pond Inc.). A Pacer I robot removes plastic Vaseline jars from cases and places them on the infeed end of a jar-filling line. Cases of empty jars are manually transferred from a pallet to the system infeed conveyor. This job is done by the same employee who palletizes the filled and sealed cases. The cases of unfilled jars are conveyed through a right angle transfer and then into a standard four flap opener where all four unsealed top flaps are opened. The case is then discharged onto an indexing conveyor, which is equipped with flap hold down rails. Various stops and photoelectric eyes on the conveyor signal the robot when the case is in position so the jar unloading cycle can begin. The Pacer robot is a two-axis, hydraulically operated, computer-controlled machine, equipped with a multiple-fingered vacuum gripper. The gripper removes an entire layer of jars at a time by reaching down into the jars and applying vacuum to the jar bottoms. The jars are then placed on a standard single filling machine and are conveyed to a filler. Each finger of the gripper is equipped with a spring-loaded detent so that it will push upward if it encounters an obstacle. In this way, the occasional upside down jar will not damage the gripper. In addition, the vacuum system is equipped with a pressure sensor that stops the robot if an entire layer of jars is not acquired for any reason.

valve body manufacturing cell (Lunkenheimer Co.). Once a cell is set up and turned over to a loader operator, the cell may be viewed as a single manufacturing unit. The advantages can readily be seen (cost, control, throughput) in substituting a robot for the load operator in a production cell. In the example illustrated, of an actual operation, the cell takes advantage of various control elements (manual, numerical control, auto-cycle) and links numerical control and auto-cycle controlled units with a robot to create a cell with both robot and operator participation. Equipment within the dotted line area is robot controlled; equipment outside this area is under the control of the operator. Part progress through the cell is as follows: (1) fill loading chute (manual); (2) pick part from loading chute (robot); (3) load/unload NC chucker; (4) wash part (robot); (5) load/unload gun drill (robot); (6) place piece on semifinished bench (robot); (7) remove part from semifinished bench (manual); (8) load/unload milling machine (manual); (9) place part on out-station skid (manual). All inspection and in-process adjustments are performed by the operator. The establishment of this cell with the use of a robot permitted the joining of various auto-cycle elements into a controlled process, whereas the previous manufacturing employed manual control only, with process control being established by production scheduling between operations.

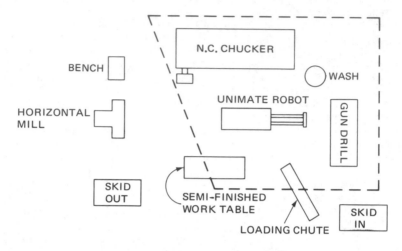

Lunkenheimer valve body manufacturing cell.

weave function (arc welding). If a weld joint width becomes excessive, it is often desirable to weave the weld gun from side to side in the seam. Weaving can be accomplished using a robot without the use of a mechanical oscillator. The weave function can be programmed between any two taught points. The operator teaches a point that includes the weave function at the beginning of the weld seam where the weaving will start, and then teaches the end point of the seam where the weaving will stop. Five parameters are involved in specifying the weave function: (1) Number of cycles (weaves) per inch. (2) Magnitude on the left (inches). (3) Magnitude on the right (inches). (4) Percent dwelling on the right. (5) Percent dwelling on the left.

weaving wiring harnesses (Lansing-Bagnall Ltd.). A Puma (Unimation) robot inserts pins into a universal wire mesh grid to suit the desired wire-bundle configuration. The robot selects a tool for pin placement, takes pins from a bowl feeder, and inserts the pins until the pin pattern is complete. Then, selecting a tool it lays rubber disks on predetermined pins to support the wires as needed. It then selects a wire-laying tool, picks up the wire that is fed out automatically and cut to length by a wire dispenser, inserts it, and lays the wire to a programmed pattern, tying each wire off at the end. Once all wires are laid, the robot changes tools and tapes the bundle at predetermined places. On completion, the board turns over and ejects the finished harness.

welding, respot (Chrysler Corp.). As pretacked bodies approach the automatic respot line on the body build trucks, the latches that hold them to the trucks are manually released. Here a stacker crane waits to pick up the body, move it about 34 ft (10.4 m) and position it on a respot car. The cars, which move and stop every 58 seconds as the robots weld the bodies, are part of an SI Cartrac conveyor within the respot line. The Load System stacker crane moves in all planes. It waits as the pretacked body approaches; a floor-mounted pusher synchronizes the stacker to the body truck speed to a lift point while automatic controls extend rack-and-pinion driven forks under the body. The body is lifted, traversed to the respot car, and positioned on it precisely. The forks are retracted and the stacker returns to its waiting position for the next body. The "respot" welding line is on a mezzanine level. The center of this line is an SI Cartrac conveyor, which receives the car bodies and advances them through the five automatic spot welding stations and then positions them for pick-up by the unload stacker at the output end of the line. When the body has been removed from the car, a hydraulic lift table will lower the car and return it beneath the respot line to the beginning for positioning of another body by the stacker. At the beginning of the respot line a hydraulic lift table will lower with its section of track and receive the Cartrac car. It will then raise and align with the respot line at the mezzanine level. When the load stacker has positioned a body onto the cart and withdrawn, the car will be powered into the first station of the respot line. The robots wait in a "pounce" position, which is low and a few quick motions away from their first weld point. When the car has positioned the body precisely and the Unimate robots change programs according to the body to be welded (either two-door or four-door), the Unimate welders will go through their complete program of welds. The body is advanced by the Cartrac to the next two welders for a repeat of the performance making a completely different set of welds. At one station an overhead robot will perform the spot welds around the rear window. When all welds have been completed, the body will be moved out onto a hydraulic lift table and await transfer by the American Monorail unload stacker.

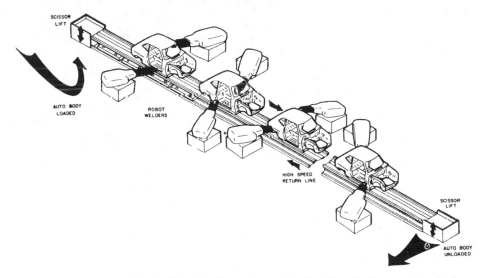

A sketch of the automatic welding line. The scissor lifts at each end are to lift and lower the body cars to transfer them to and from the high-speed return line.

welding, robot (Volvo, Sweden). Designed for production of 50 Volvo 242 car bodies an hour. The Volvo welding line contains 27 Unimate robots, the installation being fully automatic, including loading and unloading stations, and intermediate assembly of all body parts. The bodies are tacked at the second station without the use of the traditional multispot welding jigs. Lining up and clamping is by a system of swinging gates at both sides and two for the front and rear windscreens. These provide 36 centering and clamping points and ensure correct positioning, while seven robots perform 128 tack welds at structurally important locations. There is the use of four roller welding guns mounted on pendulum-type arms (two on each side of the body) to weld the roof to the drip channel. These welding guns provide overlapping spot welds to form a continuous seam along the line of the roof and down the windshield pillars. The guns are guided by a cam having the same shape as the outline of the top of the car. Formerly this work was carried out by hand. The line is composed of 10 stations, the first and last of which are used for loading and unloading. The bodies are mounted on pallets at all times and are conveyed from station to station by a sophisticated conveyor system. The pallets revolve on two levels. The upper used for welding, the lower for returning the pallets to the starting point. The pallets on the upper (working) level are moved step-by-step by a central pull bar, which hooks onto the pallets to move them to succeeding stations where they are positioned for welding and are held firm by special devices. The pallets are returned by a chain rotating continuously at 49 rpm (about 15 mpm). Special spring arrangements on the chain hook up the empty pallets one at a time. All robot operations are coordinated by two 8K programmable controllers. A main supervision panel gives full indication of working start/stop, cycle time, overload, bodies in position, etc. For easy fault finding the central panel indicates which station is in trouble.

wheel production (Goodyear Tire and Rubber Co.). At the Luckey, Ohio, plant an operation not well suited for humans requires the lifting of some 44,000 lb (19,958 kg) per day. A semifinished, styled wheel that weighs some 25 lb (11 kg) had to be picked out of a mold that's mounted on an intermittently advancing pour conveyor, then deposited on a takeaway/trim conveyor. To perform the job, a worker had to pry the wheel loose, pick it up and carry it, then place it on a conveyor approximately 5 ft (1.5 m) away, once every 15 seconds. It was a job suited for a robot, and after an engineering study was made, a Prab Model 4200 was selected and installed. The robot cycle initially used was: reach, drop, grasp, raise, retract, pivot, extend, release, retract, and reposition to starting point. The cycle time just met that of the wheel production unit. Later production requirements changed, and the robot had to be repositioned to serve a more productive unit than the original. However, a new requirement was introduced by a different wheel design. The wheel had to be inverted before it was placed on the conveyor. This presented no problem because the robot control facilitated reprogramming. An optional gripper assembly permits the turning of the part 180°. No modifications were required to the boom when the gripper was changed since the robot is designed to accept various hydraulically operated gripper or holding devices. There was an initial problem in that the cycle time of the robot exceeded the cycle time of the pour conveyor by a second or more. The robot's versatile programmable drum controller and the ruggedness of the robot provided the solution in that the robot cycle was reprogrammed to: reach, drop, grasp, pivot and rotate, release, and reposition to starting point. Two steps were eliminated from the original program. The pivot and rotate step could have presented a problem, because the arm is fully extended with 25 lb (11 kg) on the gripper during those moves, but the equipment had sufficient strength to make them without any hangups.

Robotics Glossary and Computer-Control Terminology

absolute address. An address in a computer language that identifies a storage location or a device without the use of any intermediate reference. An address that is permanently assigned by the machine designer to a storage location.

absolute order. In computer graphics, a display command in a computer program that causes the display devices to interpret the data bytes following the order as absolute data rather than as relative data.

acceleration time. That part of access time required to bring the auxiliary storage device, typically a tape drive, to the speed at which data can be read or written.

access. The manner in which files or data sets are referred to by the computer.

access time. The time interval between the instant at which data are called for from a storage device and the instant delivery is completed, that is, the read time. Also, the time interval between the instant at which data are requested to be stored and the instant at which storage is completed, that is, the write time.

accumulator. A register in which the result of an operation is stored.

accuracy. Quality, state, or degree of conformance to a recognized standard. Difference between the actual position response and the target position desired or commanded of an automatic control system.

ACK (acknowledge). Communication by the addressee of a message informing the originator of a communication that the message has been received and understood. In computer communication systems the computer or terminal sends an ACK to indicate that the message has been received without detected transmission errors and has passed any validity checks in the system.

acoustic coupler. An electronic device that sends and receives digital data through a standard telephone handset. To transmit data, the digital signals are converted to audible tones that are acoustically coupled to a telephone handset. To receive data, the acoustically coupled audible signals are converted to digital signals.

active accommodation. Integration of sensors, control, and robot motion to achieve alternation of a robot's preprogrammed motions in response to felt forces. If a wrist force sensor and resolved motion rate control are employed, then the felt force vector can be used as stimulus to create quite general changes in the velocity vector of the end point. This technique can be used to stop a robot when forces reach set levels or perform force feedback tasks like insertions, door opening, and edge tracing.

active illumination. Illumination that can be varied automatically to extract more visual information from a scene; for example, by turning lamps on and off, by adjusting brightness, by projecting a pattern on objects in the scene, or by changing the color of the illumination.

actuator. A motor. A transducer that converts electrical, hydraulic, or pneumatic energy to effect motion of a robot.

ADA. A Defense Department mandated programming language. It was invented by a team led by a French expert. The software development system that will provide the support for all phases of a system's life cycle is the ADA Program Support Environment (APSE) now in progress. Programmers are already using ADA to write applications programs for robotics, radar, and payroll disbursal.

adaptable. Multipurpose; capable of being redirected, retrained, or used for new purposes. Refers to the reprogrammability or multitask capability of robots. Capable of making self-directed corrections. In a robot, this is often accomplished with the aid of visual, force, or tactile sensors.

adaptive control. A control method in which control parameters are continuously and automatically adjusted in response to measured process variables to achieve near-optimum performance.

ADCCP. Advanced Data Communication Control Procedures; an ANSI standard protocol for communication that is becoming increasingly popular in the United States; closely compatible with the HDLC protocol.

addend. In an addition operation a number or quantity added to the augend.

adder. A device whose output data are a representation of the sum of the numbers represented by its input data.

address. A character or a group of characters that identifies a register, a particular part of storage, or some other data source or destination.

addressability. The characteristic of certain storage devices in which each storage area or location has a unique address. The address is then usable by the programmer to access the information stored at that location.

address format. The arrangement of the address parts of an instruction. The expression "plus one" is frequently used to indicate that one of the addresses specifies the location of the next instruction to be executed, such as one-plus-one, two-plus-one, three-plus-one, four-plus-one. The arrangement of the parts of a single address such as those required for identifying channel, module, track, etc., in a magnetic disk system.

address modification. The process of changing the address part of a machine instruction by means of coded instruction.

address register. A register in which an address is stored.

adjacency. In character recognition a condition in which the character spacing reference lines of two consecutively printed characters on the same line are separated by less than a specified distance.

ADP. Automatic data processing.

algebraic language. An algorithmic language many of whose statements are designed to resemble the structure of algebraic expression; examples are ALGOL and FORTRAN.

ALGOL (Algorithmic Language). It resembles FORTRAN and PL/1; a scientific language noted for its conciseness in expressing arithmetic and logical statements. It requires compiler translation.

algorithm. A set of well-defined rules for the solution of a problem in a finite number of steps, for example, a full statement of an arithmetic procedure for evaluating $\sin x$ to a stated precision. Contrast with **heuristic**.

alphabet. An ordered set of all letters used in a language, including letters with diacritical signs where appropriate, but not including punctuation marks.

alphabetic character. A letter or other symbol, excluding digits, used in a computer language. In COBOL, a character that is one of the 26 characters of the alphabet, or a space. In FORTRAN, a character of the set A, B, C, . . ., Z, $.

alphabetic character set. A character set that contains letters and may contain control characters, special characters, and the space character, but not digits.

alphabetic character subset. A character subset that contains letters and may contain control characters, special characters, and the space character, but not digits.

alphabetic string. A string consisting solely of letters from the same alphabet.

alphanumeric. Pertaining to a character set that contains letters, digits, and usually other characters, such as punctuation marks. Synonymous with alphameric.

alphanumerical code. A system in which characters may be either letters of the alphabet, numerals, or special symbols.

alphanumeric character set. A character set that contains both letters and digits and may contain control characters, special characters, and the space character.

American Standard Code for Information Interchange (*see* ASCII)

AML. *A Manufacturing Language*; an IBM-developed robotics language for programming robots.

analog. Pertaining to representation by means of continuously variable physical quantities.

analog communications. Transfer of information by means of a continuously variable quantity, such as the voltage produced by a strain gage or air pressure in a pneumatic line.

analog computer. A computer in which analog representation of data is mainly used.

analog control. Control involving analog signal-processing devices (electronic, hydraulic, pneumatic, etc.).

analog data. Data represented by a physical quantity that is considered to be continuously variable and whose magnitude is made directly proportional to the data or to a suitable function of the data.

analogic control. Pertaining to control by communication signals that are physically or geometrically isometric to the variables being controlled, usually by a human operator. A device for effecting such control. Compare to **symbolic control**.

analog-to-digital converter (A/D). A hardware device that senses an analog signal and converts it to a representation in digital form.

analog transmission. Transmission of a continuously variable signal as opposed to a discretely variable signal, such as digital data. Examples of analog signals are voice calls over the telephone network, facsimile transmission, and electrocardiogram information.

AND. A logic operator having the property that if *P* is a statement, *Q* is a statement, *R* is a statement, . . ., then the AND of *P, Q, R,* . . . is true if all statements are true, false if any statement is false. *P* and *Q* is often represented by *P•Q, PQ, P∧Q.* Synonymous with logical multiplying.

android. A robot that approximates a human in physical appearance.

annunciator. A light or sound signal designed to attract attention.

aperture. One or more adjacent characters in a mask that causes retention of the corresponding characters.

APL. *A Programming Language.* A programming language with an unusual syntax and character set, primarily designed for mathematical applications.

APT. *Automatically Programmed Tool.* A high-level or simplified programming language.

arbitrary sequence computer. A computer in which each instruction explicitly determines the location of the next instruction to be executed.

architecture. Physical and logical structure of a computer or manufacturing process.

arithmetic, decimal. Computers perform decimal arithmetic on signed packed decimal numbers using the storage-to-storage concept employed by most business-oriented second-generation computers. In the storage-to-storage concept, variable-length data fields are brought out of main storage and are operated on by the arithmetic logic unit, and the results are placed back into main storage.

arithmetic, fixed point. A method of calculation in which the computer does not consider the location of the decimal point. Fixed-point arithmetic uses the storage-to-accumulator or the accumulator-to-accumulator concepts that were used by most scientific-oriented second-generation computers. Fixed-point arithmetic operations are performed using fixed-length binary data fields. The results of either the storage-to-accumulator or the accumulator-to-accumulator operation will be stored in either one or two general registers. Addition, subtraction, multiplication, division, and comparison operations take one operand from a register and another from either a register or storage and return the result to the general register.

arithmetic, floating point. For certain arithmetic operations, typically those in the scientific and engineering areas, it is helpful or even essential to let the computer assume the task of keeping track of decimal points. It is a great convenience to let the computer take over the clerical details of a complete accounting for number sizes and decimal point alignment. Floating-point arithmetic saves programming time and makes possible the solutions of complex problems that would otherwise be almost impossible. The basic idea of floating-point arithmetic is that each quantity is represented as a combination of two items; a numerical fraction and a power of 16 by which the fraction is multiplied to get the number represented. Floating-point operations are performed with one operand from a floating-point register and another one from either a floating-point register or storage, with the result placed in a floating-point register.

arithmetic logic unit. The part of the computer processing section that does the adding, subtracting, multiplying, dividing, and/or logical tasks (comparing).

arithmetic overflow. That portion of a numeric word expressing the result of an arithmetic operation by which its word length exceeds the word length provided for the number representation.

arithmetic register. A register that holds the operands or the result of operations such as arithmetic operations, logic operations, and shifts.

arithmetic shift. A shift applied to the representation of a number in a fixed radix numeration system and in a fixed-point representation system, in which only the characters representing the absolute value of the numbers are moved. An arithmetic shift is usually equivalent to multiplying the number by a positive or a negative integral power of the radix except for the effect of any rounding.

arm. An interconnected set of links and powered joints comprising a manipulator and supporting or moving a hand or end effector.

array. An arrangement of elements in one or more dimensions.

artificial intelligence. The mode of programming that allows a computer to operate on its own, for example, to learn, adapt, reason, or correct and improve itself.

ASCII. American Standard Code for Information Interchange. A common coding scheme for alphanumeric characters and terminal control interfacing.

assemble. To translate a program expressed in an assembly language into a computer language and perhaps to link subroutines. Assembling is usually accomplished by substituting the computer language operation code and by substituting absolute addresses, immediate addresses, relocatable addresses.

assembler. A software program that translates assembly language instructions into machine language form. It translates symbolic codes into machine language and assigns memory locations for variables and constants.

assembly language. A programming language that is similar to machine language, but which makes extensive use of mnemonic codes and names as an aid in programming. Assembly languages have a special format. Assembly languages are used to write source programs which the high-level languages are also used to write. The source program is translated into an object program by an assembler program. The object program is written in machine code and can be immediately located into the computer's memory.

associative storage. A storage device whose storage locations are identified by their contents or by part of their contents, rather than by their names or positions.

asynchronous computer. A computer in which each event or the performance of each operation starts as a result of a signal generated by the completion of the previous event or operation, or on the availability of the parts of the computer required by the next event or operation.

asynchronous operation. Describes machine operations that are triggered successively, not by a clock but by the completion of an operation.

asynchronous processing. The opposite of synchronous processing. Each step is dependent on the completion of the previous step.

audio-response systems. Computer data-processing systems wherein audible answers are generated in response to keyed input questions. Bank teller operations are among the most common users of audio systems.

augend. In an addition operation, a number or quantity to which numbers or quantities are added.

automatic data processing (ADP). Data processing largely performed by automatic means.

automatic programming. The process of using a computer to perform some stages of the work involved in preparing a program.

automation. The theory, art, or technique of making a process automatic, self-moving, or self-controlling.

auxiliary memory. The storage area that is supplementary to main memory. No manipulation of data can take place in auxiliary memory. This kind of memory is usually much slower than main memory.

auxiliary operation. An operation performed by equipment not under continuous control of the central processing unit.

azimuth. Direction of a straight line to a point in a horizontal plane, expressed as the angular distance from a reference line, such as the observer's line of view.

background processing. The automatic execution of lower-priority programs when higher-priority programs are not using the system resources Contrast with **foreground processing.**

balanced merger. An external sort that places strings created by an internal sort phase or half of the available storage devices and their merger strings by moving them back and forth between an equal number of devices until the merging process is complete.

band. (1) A group of tracks on a magnetic drum or on one side of a magnetic disk. (2) In data communications, the frequency spectrum between two defined limits.

bandwidth. (1) A communications term that refers to the speed and carrying capacity of a communication channel. (2) The difference expressed in the number of cycles per second between the two limiting frequencies of a band.

bang–bang control. Control achieved by a command to the actuator that at any time tells it to operate either in one direction or the other with maximum energy.

bang–bang–off control. Control achieved by a command to the actuator that at any time tells it to operate either in one direction or the other with maximum energy, or to do nothing.

base. The platform or structure to which a robot arm is attached; the end of a kinematic chain of arm links and joints opposite to that which grasps or processes external objects.

base address. A numeric value that is used as a reference in the calculation of addresses in the execution of a computer program.

base number. That number which is the basis for counting in a particular number system; e.g., 10 is the base number for the decimal number system.

BASIC. *B*eginners *A*ll *P*urpose *S*ymbolic *I*nstruction *C*ode. A mathematical-problem-oriented programming language. BASIC resembles FORTRAN in its problem-solving orientation and is easy to use by those who are not versed in computing. It is often used in time-sharing systems where a number of remote terminals are linked up to one computer for business and commercial purposes. With BASIC, program statements can be written in any order because each statement is given a number for identification purposes.

batch manufacture. The production of parts in discrete runs or batches, interspersed with other production operations or runs of other parts.

baud. A unit of signaling speed equal to the number of discrete conditions or signal events per second. For example, one baud equals one-half dot cycle per second in Morse Code, one bit per second in a train of binary signals, and one three-bit value per second in a train of signals each of which can assume one of eight different states.

BEL character (BEL). A control character that is used when there is a need to call for human attention and that may activate an alarm or other attention devices.

binary. Pertaining to a selection, choice, or condition that has two possible values or states. Pertaining to a fixed radix numeration system having a radix of two.

binary arithmetic operation. An arithmetic operation in which the operands and the result are represented in the pure binary numeration system.

binary code. A code that makes use of exactly two distinct characters, usually 0 and 1.

binary coded decimal (BCD). A decimal notation in which the individual decimal digits are represented by a pattern of ones and zeros. This code is one of the most common variations of the binary system. It employs only the first four binary positions with respective values of 1, 2, 4, and 8. Any decimal digit from 0 to 9 can be represented by a combination of these four values. In this system a separate binary equivalent is required for each digit of the decimal number being expressed.

binary coded decimal system. One way in which information is represented in electronic computers is the binary coded decimal system. In this method each digit in a number is symbolized by a four-bit binary number. The manner in which information is represented within a computer has a very strong influence on its design. A piece of equipment is often referred to as a binary machine or a binary coded decimal machine. Binary machines are usually regarded as more useful than binary coded decimal machines for scientific and engineering calculations, and lends itself to faster arithmetic speeds. Another advantage of binary machines is that in the binary mode four bits can represent all of the decimal digits from 0 to 15, whereas in the binary coded decimal system four bits can represent only the numbers from 0 to 9. In this respect the binary coded decimal mode is less efficient.

binary coded notation. A binary coded notation in which each of the decimal digits is represented by a binary numeral.

binary data. Data that are written in binary, octal, or hexadecimal forms and that can indicate various codes to be used for computer operations.

binary digit (bit). In the binary system, a bit can represent either 0 or 1; to a computer a bit will indicate an off or on signal. Bits are the units of information that, when combined in certain configurations, will signal to the computer what it is to do.

binary element. A constituent element of data that takes either of two values or states. The term bit, originally the abbreviation of the term binary digit, is misused in the sense of binary element or in the sense of **shannon**.

binary notation. Any notation that uses two different characters, usually the binary digits 0 and 1, e.g., the gray code. The gray code is a binary notation but not a pure binary numeration system. Fixed-radix notation where the radix is two.

binary number system. A number system using the base 2, as opposed to the decimal number system which use the base 10. The binary system is comparable to the decimal system in using the concepts of absolute value and positional value. The difference is that the binary numbering system employs only two absolute values, 0 and 1. Because there are only two digits, the binary system has a base number of 2; the positional significance of a binary number is based on the progression of powers of 2. The numbers are expressed in binary notation as a series of 0's and 1's, commonly referred to as bits. The 0 is described as no bit and represents an "off" position. The 1 is described as a bit and represents an "on" condition. The lowest-order position in the binary system is called the 1-bit. The next position is called the 2-bit; the next, 4-bit; the next, 8-bit; and so on.

binary numeral. A numeral in the pure binary numeral system; e.g., the binary numeral 101 is equivalent to the Roman numeral V. A binary representation of a number.

binary picture. A digitized image in which the brightness of the pixels can have only two different values, such as white or black or zero or one.

binary search. A dichotomizing search in which, at each step of the search, the set of items is partitioned into two equal parts, some appropriate action being taken in the case of an odd number of items.

Binary Synchronous Communication Protocol (*see* **BISYNC**)

biquinary code. A notation in which a decimal digit n is represented by a pair of numerals, a being 0 or 1, b being 0, 1, 2, 3, or 4, and $(5a + b)$ being equal to n. The two digits are often represented by a series of two binary numerals.

bistable. Describes that which is able to assume one of two stable states; a flip-flop circuit is bistable.

BISYNC. Binary Synchronous Communication Protocol. An early standard protocol for half-duplex communication, developed by IBM about 1965 and in wide use today.

bit. In computer logic, a single number equivalent to 0 or 1. A series of bits can denote a binary number or word. A robot instruction or program step comprises a series of words and is called a byte. The capacity of a robot's memory depends on the number of bits it can carry or register. With solid-state devices this is increasing rapidly; memory chips can hold 2000, 4000, and more bits, or using the electrical notation for 1000: 2K and 4K (64K chips are now produced).

bit string. A string of binary digits (bits) in which the position of each binary digit is considered as an independent unit.

blank column detection. The collator function of checking for and signaling error conditions if a blank column is found in a particular data field.

block. A group of machine words considered or transported as a unit. In flow charts, each block represents a logical unit of programming.

block diagram. A diagram of a system, instrument, or computer, in which the principal parts are represented by suitably associated geometrical figures to show both the basic functions of the parts and the functional relationships among them.

block sort. A sort of one or more of the most significant characters of a key to serve as a means of making groups of workable size from a large volume of records to be sorted.

Boolean. Pertaining to the processes used in the algebra formulated by George Boole.

Boolean algebra. A process of reasoning or a deductive system of theorems using a symbolic logic and dealing with classes, propositions, or on-off circuit elements such as AND, OR, NOT, EXCEPT, IF, THEN, etc., to permit mathematical calculations.

Boolean function. A switching function in which the number of possible values of the function and each of its independent variables is two.

bootstrap. A technique for loading the first few instructions of a routine into storage, then using these instructions to bring the rest of the routine into the computer from an input device. This usually involves either the entering of a few instructions manually or the use of a special key on the console.

borrow digit. A digit is generated when a difference in a digit place is arithmetically negative and that is transferred for processing elsewhere. In a positional representation system, a borrow digit is transferred to the digit place with the next higher weight for processing them.

branch. A set of instructions that are executed between two successive branch instructions. In a data network, a route between two directly connected nodes. In the execution of a computer program, to select one from a number of alternative sets of instructions.

branch (jump). A means of departing from the sequence of the main program to another routine or sequence of operations as indicated by a branch instruction whose execution is dependent on the conditions of the results of computer operations.

branching. Transfer of control program execution to an instruction other than the next sequential instruction. If the next instruction selected is predetermined, the branch is an unconditional branch; if the next instruction is selected on the basis of some sort of test, it is a conditional branch. A robot must possess the ability to execute conditional branches in order to react intelligently to its environment. The wider the variety of tests it can perform, the better it can react.

branching, adaptive. Computer-controlled robot systems can easily be connected to other computer-based systems since facilities to accomplish this communication are provided in all computer system architectures. This more-complex type of external equipment in an industrial robot system can then easily supply more than the on/off signals that are typically available from other equipment in the system configuration. A higher level of robot decision making is therefore possible with computers that are part of a supervisory system or are an element in more-complex sensor systems employing vision, force, or tactile transducers. The data comprising a complete branch sequence in the robot control can be rewritten with data from the external computer system. If the position or orientation of a workpiece varies, the robot movements and functions can be adjusted by the external device to properly pick up or perform the required operations on the work. If an emergency situation is detected, a branch can be replaced with other branch data to handle the specific condition. The speed with which these data can be transmitted to the robot control is fast enough to complete the communication in a fraction of a second, so this type of branching alteration could be called "adaptive branching."

branching, conditional. Standard branches are the simplest way to alter a robot's path program, but they are limited in the sense that each branch is associated with one particular input signal to the robot control; any robot program is limited to 32 standard branches. Some applications can also have simpler installations and lower wiring costs if an external decision-making element is available to look at the number of signals simultaneously as a condition for branching; that is, if another computer system is supervising the total robot system installation, then 8 lines can provide 256 conditions for branching. This extension of the standard branch is called a conditional branch.

branching, offset. In many applications it is desirable for the robot system to have a method for creating a branch that can be used at a number of points in the robot cycle, a branch that can effect its sequence relative to the physical location of the robot arm when the branch is requested. In other words, the entire branch is offset about the robot's position and/or the wrist orientation. A standard offset branch is programmed into the cycle in similar fashion to a standard branch. At each point where the offset branch is programmed, the proper input signal is checked and the branch is entered if the input is active. The

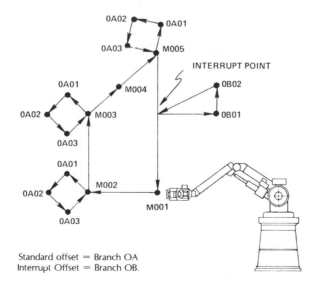

Standard offset = Branch OA
Interrupt Offset = Branch OB.

standard branch OA in the accompanying illustration is programmed at M002, M003, and M005. Such a branch type could be used where the same sequence of operations is to be performed at a number of points in the application, two examples being drilling and material pick-up from a palletized configuration. Some applications require another kind of offset branch where the branch can be entered not only at specifically programmed points but anywhere in the cycle. An input signal from the surrounding equipment causes the robot to enter this interrupt offset branch whenever the input is activated; branch OB is such a branch. One possible use of this branch type would be in spot welding to allow the robot system to recover from instances where the welding tips have welded themselves to the workpiece; the interrupt offset branch would be programmed as a set of twisting movements that would loosen the spot weld gun tips from the stuck position. The interrupt signal would be generated by external equipment supplied by the user when this condition occurs.

branching, standard. Truly general-purpose industrial robot systems must have some way of selecting or altering the programmed path and function based on changes in the environment around them. The name given to such a facility may vary, but the purpose is the same. The robot reaches some point and interrogates an input signal to determine whether it is electrically active, or the robot is interrupted by activation of another input signal. In either case, the robot path "branches" to a section of the path/function program; if no signal is present at this decision point, or no interrupt occurs, the robot continues in a normal path sequence. The accompanying figure displays a top view of a simplified "mainline" cycle (M001 through M005) that has been programmed to execute a sequence of events to perform routine housekeeping, inspection, etc. The "branch" routine symbolizes the actions the robot must take to pick up a new part for matching. A "part

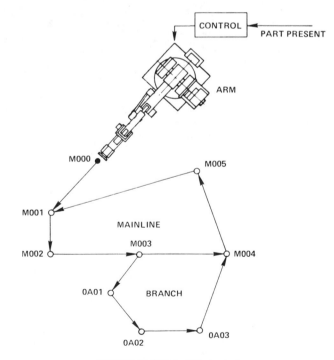

Simplified machine loading sequence.

present" signal is shown coming into the robot control that may originate as a limit switch closure when the part is present at the raw part conveyor. When the robot arm reaches point M003 (the decision point), the control examines the "part present" signal; if the signal is on, the part sequence passes through OA01, OA02, OA03, and then returns to M004; if no part is present, the robot continues in the mainline routine directly to point M004 and the housekeeping cycle continues through M005 and then back to M001. In actual application, a number of these standard branches may be included in the program.

branch instruction. Instructions that cause the computers to switch from one point in a program to another point, thereby controlling the sequence in which operations are performed.

breadboard. Describes the rough model for constructing another device, usually referring to a circuit board that has a specific configuration on it.

breakpoint. A point in a computer program specified by the computer user when the program is to stop running so that the user can check it for error and change it if necessary.

broadband. Data transmission facilities capable of handling frequencies greater than those required for high-grade voice communications, i.e., greater than 300 characters per second.

bubble sort. An exchange sort in which the sequence of examination of pairs of items is reversed whenever an exchange is made.

buffer storage. A storage device that is used to compensate for differences in the rate of flow of data between components of an automatic data processing system or for the time occurrence of events in the components.

burst. In data communication, a sequence of signals counted as one unit in accordance with some specific criterion or measure.

bus. (1) One or more conductors used for transmitting signals or power. (2) An information coding scheme by which different signals can be coded and identified when sharing a common data channel.

byte. Usually 8 bits of information. Eight bits of information are assembled together to make a word or an instruction. In general 8 bits is enough to characterize one word, and this is called a byte. A sequence of adjacent binary digits operated upon as a unit.

calibration. The act of determining, marking, or rectifying the capacity or scale graduations of a measuring instrument or replicating machine. To determine the deviation from standard so as to ascertain the proper correction factors.

call. The action of bringing a computer program, a routine, or subroutine into effect, usually by specifying the entry conditions and jumping to an entry point.

card code. The combination of punches used to represent alphabetical and numerical data on a punched card.

card field. The card column or consecutive columns used to store a particular piece of information.

carry. The action of transferring a carry digit. One or more digits produced in connection with an arithmetic operation on one digit place of two or more numerals in positional notation that are forwarded to another digit place for processing there.

carry bit. A conditional status flag bit contained in a CPU accumulator.

carry digit. A digit that is generated when a sum or a product in a digit place exceeds the largest number that can be represented in that digit place and that is transferred for processing elsewhere. In a positional representation system, a carry digit is transferred to the digit place with the next higher weight for processing.

Cartesian coordinate system. A coordinate system whose axes or dimensions are three intersecting perpendicular straight lines and whose origin is the intersection.

cathode-ray tube (CRT). A device that presents data in visual form by means of a controlled electron beam impinging on a phosphorescent surface.

CCD camera. A solid-state camera that uses a CCD (charge-coupled device; also call a bucket-brigade device) to transform a light image into a digitized image. A CCD camera is similar to a CID camera, except that its method of operation forces readout of pixel brightnesses in a regular line-by-line scan pattern. There is only one readout station, and charges are shifted along until they reach it.

cell. An ICAM manufacturing unit consisting of a number of work stations and the materials transport mechanisms and storage buffers that interconnect them.

cell control. A module in the ICAM control hierarchy that controls a cell. The cell control module is controlled by a center control module, if one exists. Otherwise, it is controlled by a factory control level.

center. An ICAM manufacturing unit consisting of a number of cells and the materials transport and storage buffers that interconnect them.

center control. A module in the ICAM control hierarchy that controls a center. The center control module is controlled by the factory control level.

centralized control. Control decisions for two or more control tasks at different locations made at a centralized location.

central processing unit (CPU). The heart or brain of a computer system, composed of at least three units: the arithmetic logic unit, the control unit, and a console unit. The first unit performs the arithmetic and logic operations as programmed. (Logical operations are those that enable the computer to decide among alternatives.) The control unit has the task of maintaining over-all control of the various units of the system; although main memory is a separate functional part of the computer system, it is frequently housed within the central processing unit.

chain printer. Printers that use a type chain or print chain as their printing mechanism.

channel. A path over which information is transmitted, generally from some input–output device to storage. With reference to magnetic or punched tape, a channel is one of the parallel tracks in which data are recorded.

character. A member of a set of elements upon which agreement has been reached and that is used for the organization, control, or representation of data. Characters may be letters, digits, punctuation marks, or other symbols often represented in the form of a spatial arrangement of adjacent or connected strokes or in the form of other physical conditions in data media. A letter, digit, or other symbol that is used as a part of the organization, control, or representation of data.

character recognition. The identification of characters by automatic means.

character set. A set of unique representations called characters such as the 26 letters of the English alphabet or the decimal digits, 0 through 9.

character subset. A selection of characters from a character set, comprising all characters that have a specified common feature. For example, in the definition of character set, digits 0 through 9 constitute a character subset.

check digit. One or more redundant digits in a character or word which depend on the remaining digits in such a fashion that if a change of digits occurs in data transfer operations, the malfunction of equipment can be detected.

chip. Describes the semiconductor material on which integrated circuits are imprinted. A rectangular or square silicon chip is cut from a circular silicon wafer in mass production; the chip can range in size from less than $\frac{1}{10}$ in. (2.54 mm) on a side to more than ¼ in. (6.4 mm).

CID camera. A solid-state camera that uses a charge-injection imaging device (CID) to transform a light image into a digitized image. The light image focused on the CID generates minority carriers in a silicon wafer, which are then trapped in potential wells under metallic electrodes held at an elevated voltage. Each electrode corresponds to one pixel of the image. To register the brightness of one pixel of the image, the voltage on the electrode that corresponds to that pixel is changed to inject the charge stored under that electrode into the substrate. This produces a current flow in the substrate that is proportional to the brightness of the image at that pixel location, and is therefore capable of producing a gray-scale image. In a CID camera, pixels of the image can be read out in an arbitrary sequence. This is not possible with a CCD camera. In some CID cameras, the same image can be read out hundreds or thousands of times (nondestructive readout capability).

circuit. (1) A system of conductors and related electrical elements through which electrical current flows. (2) A communication link between two or more points.

clear. To remove all information from a storage device or machine and restore it to a prescribed state, usually that denoting zero or blank.

clock. A device that initiates pulses for the synchronization of a computer operation.

closed loop. A loop that has no exit and whose execution can be interrupted only by intervention from outside the computer program in which the loop is included.

closed-loop control. Control achieved by a closed feedback loop, i.e., by measuring the degree to which actual system response conforms to desired system response, and utilizing the difference to drive the system into conformance.

closed subroutine. A subroutine that can be stored at one place and can be linked to one or more calling routines.

CMOS *(see* **complementary metal-oxide semiconductor**)

COBOL. The name COBOL is derived from Common Business Oriented Language. It was the first major attempt to produce a truly common business-oriented programming language. The COBOL character set is composed of the 26 letters of the alphabet, the numerals 0 through 9, and 12 special characters. The COBOL language consists of names to identify things; constants and literals; operations that specify some action or relationship; key words essential to the meaning of a statement; expressions consisting of names, constants, operators, or key words; statements containing a verb and an item to be acted on; sentences composed of one or more statements properly punctuated. COBOL programs are devided into four divisions: (1) the identification division is used to attach a unique identification such as program name, program number, program version, etc., to the program; (2) the environment division is used to acquaint the processor with the computer on which the program is to be compiled and executed; (3) the data division is used to define the characters and format of the data to be processed; (4) the procedure division is used to describe the internal processing that is to take place.

code. A set of rules that is used to convert data from one representation to another. Although a variety of coding techniques are used, most codes are constructed by using numerals to represent the original data. The use of codes to express many classifications of data not only saves space, but also increases efficiency by reducing the number of card columns to be processed for certain items of data.

coded character set. A set of unambiguous rules that establish a character set and the one-to-one relationship between the characters of the set and their coded represetations.

codes, block. Method involving the assignment of numbers in sequence by groups of various sizes other than tens, hundreds, and thousands. Instead, a block can consist of any quantity of numbers necessary to cover the items in a particular classification. In the original design of the code, a few blank numbers may be left in each block to provide for later additions.

code set. The complete set of representations defined by a code or by a coded character set.

codes, group classification. In this system, major and minor classifications are coded in groups of thousands, hundreds, and tens. Various categories under each classification are represented by the assignment of succeeding digits. The method is suitable for coding all classes of products, accounts, and items in which division of groups under a major heading is the primary objective.

codes, sequence. In sequence coding, numbers are assigned to a list of items in a straight sequence, starting with one, without regard to classification or order of the subjects being coded. It is useful for any short list of names, products, or accounts where the only object is the application of simple code numbers and where the arrangement of data is not important.

codes, significant digit. In this type of coding all or part of the numbers are related to some characteristic of the data such as weight, dimension, distance, capacity, or other significant factors. This type of coding reduces the work of decoding by providing a code number that can be read directly. This method is suitable for coding long lists of items where complete decoding would be laborious or impractical.

collate. To take two or more sets of related information already arranged according to the same sequence and to merge them in sequence into a single set.

collator. Collators can be used to perform the following types of operations: (1) *Sequence checking.* After the sorter has been used to place a file of cards in a desired sequence, the file can be checked on the collator to determine if the sequence is correct. The collator does this by comparing each card with the one ahead of it. (2) *Merging.* In merging, two files of cards already in sequence can be combined into one file. (3) *Matching.* In matching, instead of merging the two files, cards in either file that do not match the other can be separated, and cards that do match remain in the two original groups. (4) *Card selection.* The collator also has the ability to select certain types of cards from a file without disturbing the sequence of the others. The selecting task of the collator is similar to that of the sorter, except that the collator can select on more than one card column.

color. In optical character recognition the spectral appearance of the image. It is dependent on the spectral reflectance of the image, the spectral response of the observer, and the spectral composition of incident light.

column binary. Pertaining to the binary representation of data on punched cards in which adjacent positions in a column correspond to adjacent bits of data; e.g., each column in a 12-row card may be used to represent 12 consecutive bits of a 36-bit word.

combinational logic element. A device having at least one output channel and zero or more input channels, all characterized by discrete states, such that at any instant the state of each output channel is completely determined by the states of the input channels at the same instant.

command. A group of signals or pulses initiating one step in the execution of a computer program. Also called instruction.

command language. A source language consisting primarily of procedural operators, each capable of involving a function to be executed.

common field. A field that can be accessed by two or more independent routines.

common language. A coded structure that is compatible with two or more data processing machines or families of machines, thus allowing them to communicate directly with one another.

communication control program (CCP). In an IBM System/3 a control program that provides the services needed to operate a communication-based information processing system.

communications link. Any mechanism, usually electrical, for the transmission of information. It may be serial or parallel, synchronous or asynchronous, half duplex or full duplex, encrypted or clear, or point-to-point, multidrop, or broadcast; it may transmit binary data or text; it may use standard character codes to represent text and control information, such as the ASCII, EBCDIC, or BAUDOT (tty) codes; or it may use a handshaking protocol to synchronize operations of computers or devices at opposite ends of the link such as BISYNC, HDLC, or ADCCP.

comparator. A device that compares two items of data and indicates the result of that comparison.

compensation. Logical operations employed in a control scheme to counteract dynamic lags or otherwise to modify the transformation between measured signals and controller output to produce prompt stable response.

compiler. A program that converts a program written in a high-level language such as FORTRAN into binary-coded instructions that the machine can interpret.

complement. In a fixed radix numeration system, a numeral that can be derived from a given numeral by operations that include subtracting each digit of the digital representation of the given number from the corresponding digit of the digital representation of a specified number.

complementary metal-oxide semiconductor (CMOS). An integrated circuit logic family characterized by very low power dissipation, moderate circuit density per chip, and moderate speed of operation.

complete carry. In parallel addition a procedure in which each of the carries is immediately transferred.

complex number. A number consisting of a real and an imaginary part, expressible in the form $a + bi$, where a and b are real numbers and $i = \sqrt{-1}$.

computed path control. A control scheme wherein the path of the manipulator end point is computed to achieve a desired result in conformance to a given criterion, such as an acceleration limit or a minimum time.

computer-aided design (CAD). Describes the more demanding and elaborate preparation of complex schematics and blueprints, typically those of industry. In these applications, an operator constructs a highly detailed drawing on-line, using a variety of interaction devices and programming techniques. Facilities are required for replicating basic figures; achieving exact size and placement of components; making lines of specified length, width, or angle to previously defined lines; satisfying varying geometric and topological constraints among components of the drawing; etc. A primary difference between interactive plotting and design drafting lies in the amount of effort the operator contributes, with interactive design drafting requiring far more responsibility for the eventual result. In interactive plotting, the computation is of central importance and the drawing is typically secondary. A second difference is that design drawings tend to have structure, i.e., to be hierarchies of networks or mechanical or electrical components. These components must be transformed and edited. If, in addition to nontrivial layout, the application program involves significant computation of the picture and its components, we speak of the third and most complex category, that of interactive design. In addition to a pictorial datum base, or data structure, that defines where all the picture components fit on the picture and also specifies their geometric characteristics, an application datum base is needed to describe the electrical, mechanical, and other properties of the components in a form suitable for access and manipulation by the analysis program. This datum base must naturally also be editable and accessible by the interactive user.

computer-aided manufacture (CAM). The use of computer technology in the management, control, and operation of manufacturing.

computer classification. Depending on their flexibility in operation, computers are either special purpose or general purpose. A special-purpose computer is one designed to solve a restricted class of problems. Examples include computers in such industries as oil refining, chemical manufacture, steel processing, and power generation. General-purpose computers are designed to solve a wide variety of problems. Theoretically, a general-purpose computer can be adopted by means of an easily alterable set of instructions to handle any problem that can be solved by computation. Computers are classified as small, medium, or large. A small computer generally consists of a central processing unit, storage capacity up to 65,000 positions, a card input–output device, perhaps two to four magnetic tape units, and a high-speed printer. The medium-scale computer has more storage with faster access, and more and faster input–output devices. Large computers are much faster and provide more storage than the medium-size computers. Large-scale computers may contain up to several million positions of storage capacity. These computers as well as medium-scale computers may also provide for simultaneous operation of three or four input–output devices, along with program monitoring and data transmission. Electronic computers are basically of two types, analog and digital, according to the manner in which they represent data. An analog computer is so named because it performs by setting up physical situations that are analogous to mathematical situations. An analog computer operates on data in the form of continuously variable quantities such as pressure, temperature, revolutions, speed of sound, or voltage. Thus an analog computer is essentially a measuring device. Digital computers operate in representations of real numbers or other characters coded numerically. The digital computer has a memory and solves problems by counting precisely, adding, subtracting, multiplying, dividing, and comparing.

computer console. The general term applied to the unit(s) through which the operator can communicate with the combined system. Usually, the console consists of (1) a typewriter unit and (2) appropriate lights and switches.

computer control. Control involving one or more electronic digital computers.

computer graphics. Defined as the input, construction, storage, retrieval, manipulation, alteration, and analysis of pictorial data. Computer graphics, in general, includes both off-line input of drawings and photographs via scanners, digitizers, or pattern-recognition devices, and output of drawings on paper or (micro) film via plotters and film recorders. Interactive graphics is a term used to emphasize human–machine dialog, which takes place in real time using an on-line display console with manual input devices. Among such input devices are the alphanumeric and function keyboards for typing text and activating preprogrammed subroutines, respectively, and the lightpen and data tablet for identifying and entering graphic information by means of pointing and drawing. For various technological reasons, most of today's graphics concerns line drawings of two- and three-dimensional abstractions such as electronic and mechanical circuits; structural components of buildings, cars, ships, and planes; chemical diagrams; functional plots of mathematical formulas; and flow charts. In addition to line-drawing graphics, there is now an increase in interest in on-line manipulation of solid pictures with gray scale, color, and hidden line-surface representation of three-dimensional scenes.

computer language. The computer is organized to follow instructions by the way it is programmed. It can follow only very clear instructions. Thus, languages have been developed which help the programmer describe what the computer should do in a clear and precise manner.

computer-managed parts manufacture (CMPM). Computer-aided manufacture of discrete parts, usually when a number of processing and product transport operations are coordinated by computer.

computer numerical control (CNC). The use of a dedicated computer within a numerical control unit with the capability of local data input. It may become part of a DNC system by direct link to a central computer.

computer output microfilmer (COM). A CRT device that takes computer output and writes it onto microfilm.

computer word. A sequence of bits or characters treated as a unit and capable of being stored in one computer location.

conditional jump. A jump that occurs if the criteria specified are met.

conjunction. The Boolean operation whose result has the Boolean value 1 if and only if each operand has the Boolean value 1.

constant. Data with a fixed value or meaning that are available for use throughout a program.

contact sensor. A device capable of sensing mechanical contact of the hand or some other part of the robot with an external object.

continuous-path control. A control scheme whereby the inputs or commands specify every point along a desired path of motion. Continuous-path-control techniques can be divided into three basic categories based on how much information about the path is used in the motor control calculations, as illustrated in the accompanying illustration. The first is the conventional or servo-control approach. This method uses no information about where the path goes in the future. The controller may have a stored representation of the path it is to follow, but for determining the drive signals to the robot's motors all calculations are based on the past and present tracking error. This is the control design used in most of today's industrial robots and process control systems. The second approach is called preview control, also known as "feed-forward" control, since it uses some knowledge about how the path changes immediately ahead of the robot's current location, in addition to the past and present tracking error used by the servo controller. The last category of path control is the "path planning" or "trajectory calculation" approach. Here the controller has available a complete description of the path the manipulator should follow from one point to another. Using a mathematical–physical model of the arm and its load, it precomputes an acceleration profile for every joint, predicting the nominal motor signals that should cause the arm to follow the desired path. This approach has been used in some advanced research robots to a achieve highly accurate coordinated movements at high speed.

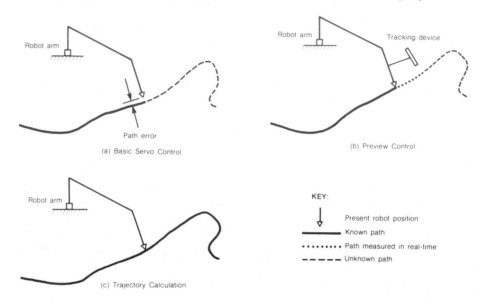

Three categories of continuous path control. In (a), the controller uses present and past error to determine motor drive signals. In (b), future path information is added to improve tracking. In (c), nominal motor drive signals are precomputed for the entire path, and modified in real time if tracking errors occur.

control. The process of making a variable or system of variables conform to what is desired. A device to achieve such conformance automatically.

control character. A character whose occurrence in a particular context initiates, modifies, or stops a control operation. A control character may be recorded for use in a subsequent action. A control character is not a graphic character, but may have a graphic representation in some circumstances.

control hierarchy. A relationship of control elements whereby the results of higher-level control elements are used to command lower-level elements.

controlled path system (CPS). Basically the CPS method takes advantage of the computational capability of the computer to give the operator coordinated control of the robot axes when teaching the device, and total position, velocity, and acceleration control of the robot end effector along a desired path between programmed points in the replay or automatic mode of operation. This capability combines desirable characteristics of both the point-to-point and continuous-path-control systems. This control provides two important functions. First, when teaching the robot, the axes are coordinated in a manner that allows the operator to position and orient the end effector at desired points without having to individually command each robot axis. This feature provides the ease of instinctively teaching without having to physically grasp the robot. Second, when teaching, the operator is not required to generate the desired path; he or she only programs end points. When in the replay or automatic mode, the computer automatically generates the controlled path at the desired velocity including acceleration and deceleration. This feature requires only the storage of path end points and does not require "real-time" teaching of the desired path data. The importance of the coordinated axes and controlled path features of the new control system is best understood by first reviewing typical physical configuration of robots. The operation of a particular controlled path system may be explained using the control system block diagram illustrated. During teaching, the operator depresses the position and orientation buttons to cause the tool center point (TCP) to move in a coordinated manner in the teach coordinate system selected, for example, rectangular or cylindrical. As long as the buttons are depressed, continuously changing position signals are generated. The "teach coordinates" are then transformed into "rectangular coordinates" in the first operation performed within the computer. (If the teach coordinate system used is rectangular, this operation is not necessary.) The "rectangular coordinates" are transformed in the second operation into the "robot coordinate" system. These coordinate values are then output to the axis servo systems. The six servo loops will then drive all axes simultaneously to provide the desired changes in position and orientation of the end effector. Since these operations in the computer are very fast, the operator will see an immediate motion of the TCP in the direction he or she commanded it to move. Once the TCP is in the desired position, the operator depresses the program button on the pendant causing the current values of the "rectangular coordinates" to be stored in computer memory. The operator also uses other buttons on the pendant and the keyboard to enter functional data, such as velocity, tool length, and the functions to be performed at the programmed point. The CRT displays the information being programmed or for editing purposes can display previously programmed data. During the auto cycle of operation the points stored in memory are recalled. Within the path generation operation, these path end points along with the velocity information are used to compute points incrementally along the path. These intermediate points on the path are generated in a proper time sequence to cause the robot TCP to move at the programmed speed and also to generate the proper acceleration and deceleration spans. The path data are in "rectangular coordinates" and must be transformed into "robot coordinates" before being output to the axis servos. The path generation is an on-line calculation done in real time.

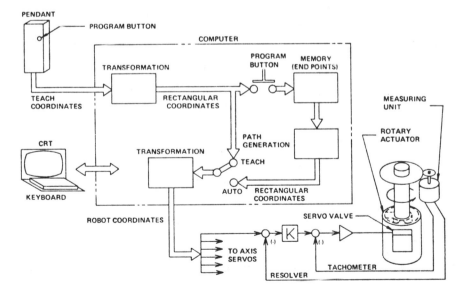

Control system diagram.

There is no buffering of path data before their immediate use. Thus, on-line measurements of position sensor data, such as conveyor or part position, may be dynamically added to the computed path data making such features as tracking a moving part easily implemented. While the robot may have a machine coordinate system, the control system itself makes all calculations in the basic rectangular coordinate system. Since all the end points are stored in rectangular coordinates and all path generation calculations are also made in this same coordinate system, many new features not easily implemented with the other control systems are practical.

controller. An information processing device whose inputs are both the desired and the measured position velocity or other pertinent variables in a process and whose outputs are drive signals to a controlling motor or actuator. The controller has a threefold function: first, to initiate and terminate motions of the manipulator in a desired sequence and at desired points; second, to store position and sequence data in memory; and third, to interface with the "outside world." Robot controllers run from simple step sequencers through pneumatic logic systems, diode matrix boards, electronic sequencers, and microprocessors to minicomputers. The controller may be either an integral part of the manipulator or housed in a separate cabinet. The complexity of the controller both determines and is determined by the capabilities of the robot. Simple nonservo devices usually employ some form of step sequencer. Servo-controlled robots use a combination of sequencer and data storage (memory). This may be as simple as an electronic counter, patch board, or diode matrix and series of potentiometers or as sophisticated as a minicomputer with core memory. Other memory devices employed include magnetic tape, magnetic disk, plated wire, and semiconductor (solid-state RAM). Processor- or computer-based controller operating systems may be hardwired, stored in core memory, or programmed in ROM (read-only memory). The controller initiates and terminates the motions of the manipulator through interfaces with the manipulator's control valves and feedback devices and may also perform complex arithmetic functions to control path, speed, and position. Another interface with the outside world provides two-way communications between the controller and ancillary devices. This interface allows the manipulator to interact with whatever equipment is associated with the robot's task.

control punch. The most common method used to differentiate master cards from detail cards when the decks are run through punched-card equipment is by means of a control punch. The majority of the machines are designed so that, with proper board wiring, they can recognize an 11-punch in a particular card column of a numeric field. The 11-punch, more commonly known as an x-punch, is usually used to signal the machine that a master card is passing through as opposed to a detail card (a NO X card). Board wiring then causes the particular machine to initiate one set of operations for the master card and another set for the detail card.

control unit. The part of a computer system that effects the retrieval of instructions in proper sequence, the interpretation of each instruction, and the application of the proper signals to the arithmetic unit and other parts of the system in accordance with this interpretation. The performance of these operations requires a vast number of "paths" over which data and instructions may be sent. Routing data over the proper paths in the circuitry, opening and closing the right "gates" at the right time, and establishing timing sequences are major functions of the control unit. All of these operations are under the control of a stored program.

converter. A unit that changes the representation of data from one form to another so as to make it available or acceptable to another machine, for example, from punched cards to magnetic tape.

convex programming. In operations research, a particular case of nonlinear programming in which the function to be maximized or minimized and the constraints are appropriately convex or concave functions of the controllable variables.

coordinated axis control. Control wherein the axes of the robot arrive at their respective end points simultaneously, giving a smooth appearance to the motion. Control wherein the motions of the axes are such that the end point moves along a prespecified type of path (line, circle, etc.). Also called **end-point control.**

core memory. The most commonly used main memory storage device at this time; the term core has become synonymous with main memory.

core plane. A grid of wires upon which small iron cores are strung. A series of core planes are stacked to make up main memory.

counter. (1) A programming device used to control the number of times a program loop is executed. (2) A device, register, or storage permitting these integers to be increased or decreased. (3) A device used to represent the number of occurrences of an event.

CPU (central processing unit). The center of the computer through which the information flows. It is the place where the program is realized; it is the place where the information is obtained through programming instructions. (*See also* **central processing unit.**)

cross-assembler. A computer program to translate instructions into a form suitable for running on another computer.

crosstalk. The unwanted energy transferred from one circuit, called the "disturbing" circuit, to another circuit, called the "disturbed circuit."

CRT (*see* **cathode-ray tube**)

cursor. A marker or pointer that indicates to the operator the exact position on a CRT screen where the next key stroke will be entered.

cycle. An interval during which one set of events or phenomena is completed. A set of operations that is repeated regularly in the same sequence.

cylindrical coordinate system. A coordinate system consisting of one angular dimension and two linear dimensions. These three coordinates specify a point on a cylinder.

damping. (1) The absorption of energy, as viscous damping of mechanical energy or resistive damping of electrical energy. (2) A property of a dynamic system that causes oscillations to die out and makes the response of the system approach a constant value.

data. A general term used to denote any facts, numbers, letters, and symbols, or facts that refer to or describe an object, idea, condition, situation, or other factors.

data acquisition system (DAS). The DAS scans digital and analog inputs in an order and at a rate controlled by a program. The input signals are first scaled and corrected. The resulting values may be compared against stored limits. Out-of-limit values can result in attentional alarms, or they may be logged. In a special-purpose implementation, the conversion, print-control, and limit-testing functions are wired in. Programming is then limited to simple selection techniques, often provided by patch cords or a fixed program on paper tape. In more-sophisticated applications, measured values are used in computation of process performance parameters. In such a case the need for a general-purpose machine, which can clearly also perform the rote functions, is also indicated. The DAS with general-purpose computation provides an industrial control capability that can be used in process optimization and in control of very complex industrial systems.

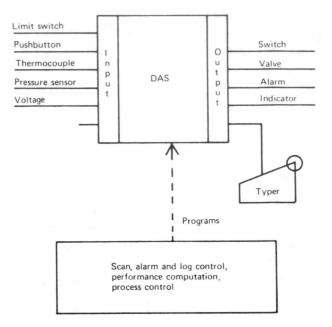

Descriptive schematic of data acquisition system (DAS).

data bank. A centralized computer storage facility containing extensive and detailed data on individuals, groups, corporations, etc. A collection of libraries of data. Specifically, one line of an invoice may form an item; a complete invoice may form a record; a complete set of such records may form a file; the collection of inventory control files may form a library; and the libraries used by a business organization are known as its data bank.

data base. A collection of data fundamental to an enterprise; the data are comprised of comprehensive files of information having predetermined structure and organization and suitable for communication, interpretations, or processing by humans or by automatic means.

data base management system. A combination of hardware and software that controls and processes all requests for data in data bases.

data cell. The IBM unit that stores data in the form of magnetic strips.

data channels. Highly specialized central processing units that manage and control one or more I/O control units.

data code. In data communication, rules and conventions according to which the signals representing data should be formed, transmitted, received, and processed.

data element. The smallest unit of data stored in some medium to which a reference or name may be assigned.

data file. A collection of data records usually organized on a logical basis. For example, all the records pertaining to one month's transactions would comprise a monthly data file.

data flow chart. A flowchart that represents the path of data in the solving of a problem, and that defines the major phases of the processing as well as the various data media used.

data link. The assembly of parts of two data terminal pieces of equipment that are controlled by a link protocol, together with their interconnecting data circuit, which enables data to be transferred from a data source to a data link.

data set. The major unit of data storage and retrieval in the operating system, consisting of a collection of data in one of several prescribed arrangements and described by control information to which the system has access.

data word. A unit of data to be operated on by a computer.

dead band. A range within which a nonzero input causes no output.

debug. To detect, locate, and remove all malfunctions from a robot and its controls or all metastables from a computer routine.

decimal. Pertaining to a selection, choice, or condition that has 10 possible different values or states.

decimal digit. In decimal notations, or in the decimal numeration system, one of the digits 0 through 9.

decimal notation. A notation that uses 10 different characters, usually the decimal digits, for example, the character string 196912312359 construed to represent the date and time one minute before the start of the year 1970; the representation used in the Universal Decimal Classification.

decimal numeration system. The fixed radix numeration system that uses the decimal digits and the radix 10 and in which the lowest integral weight is 1; for example, in this numeration system the numeral 576.2 represents the numbers: $5 \times 10^2 + 7 + 10^1 + 6 \times 10^0 + 2 \times 10^{-1}$.

decimal point. The radix point in the decimal numeration system. The decimal point may be represented according to various conventions, by a comma, by a period, or by a point at the mid-height of the digits.

decision table. A table that combines contingencies to be considered in the description of a problem, along with the action to be taken. Decision tables are sometimes used instead of flow charts to describe and document problems.

deck. A collection of punched cards; commonly, a complete set of cards that have been punched for a specific purpose.

decode. To apply a code so as to reverse some previous encoding. In machine operation, to translate data and/or instructions to determine exactly how and where signals are to be sent.

decoder. A device that decodes. A matrix of switching elements that selects one or more output channels according to the combination of input signals present.

default value. A value that is used until a more valid one is found.

deferred addressing. A method of addressing in which one indirect address is replaced by another to which it refers a predetermined number of times or until the process is terminated by an indicator.

degree of disorder. Robots cannot operate in a disorderly environment. Parts to be handled or worked on must be in a known place and have a known orientation. For a simple robot, this must always be the same position and attitude. For a more complex robot, parts might be presented in an array; however, the overall position and orientation of the array must always be the same. On a conveyor, part position and orientation must be the same and conveyor speed must be known. Sensor-equipped robots (vision, touch) can tolerate some degree of disorder; however, there are definite limitations to the adaptability of such robots today. A vision system, for example, enables a robot to locate a part on a conveyor belt and to orient its hand to properly grasp the part. It will not, however, enable a robot to remove a part incorrectly oriented from a bin of parts or from a group of overlapping parts on a conveyor belt. A touch sensor enables a robot to find the top part on a stack. It does not, however, direct the robot to the same place on each part if the stack is not uniform or is not always in the same position relative to the robot.

degree of freedom. One of a limited number of ways in which a point or a body may move or in which a dynamic system may change, each way being expressed by an independent variable and all required to be specified if the physical state of the body or system is to be completely defined.

delay. The time between input and output of a pulse or other signal that undergoes normal distortion.

derivative control. Control scheme whereby the actuator drive signal is proportional to the time derivative of the difference between the input (desired output) and the measured actual output.

destructive read. Reading that erases the data in the source location.

detail card or deck. A card usually containing changeable information as opposed to a master card or deck. Information from a master card is often transferred into a detail card at machine speed rather than by rekeypunching.

detail printing. (1) Printing information from each punched card passing through the machine. (2) A method of printing in which the accounting machine prints one line per card.

diagnostic check. A specific routine designed to locate a malfunction in the computer or a mistake in coding.

diagnostic program. A computer program that recognizes, locates, and explains either a fault in equipment or a mistake in a computer program.

dichotomizing search. A search in which an ordered set of items is partitioned into two parts, one of which is rejected; the process being repeated in the accepted parts until the search is completed.

differentiator. A device whose output function is proportional to the derivative of the input function with respect to one or more variables; for example, a resistance–capacitance network used to select the leading and trailing edges of a pulse signal.

digit. A graphic character that represents an integer, for example, one of the characters 0 to 9. A symbol that represents one of the nonnegative integers smaller than the radix. For example, in decimal notation, a digit is one of the characters from 0 to 9.

digital communications. Transfer of information by means of a sequence of signals called bits (for **binary digits**), each of which can have one of two different values. The signals may, for example, take the form of two different voltage levels on a wire or the presence or absence of light in a fiber-optic light guide. It can be made arbitrarily insensitive to external disturbances by means of error control procedures.

digital computer. A computer in which discrete representation of data is mainly used. (1)

A digital computer uses 1 and 0 as symbols and operates on the fact of the direct relationship between these numbers and the on and off condition at a specific place in the computer circuitry. An "analog" computer operates on a wide range of conditions one of which is the amount of voltage. (2) The digital computers operate on representations of real numbers or other characters coded numerically. The digital computer has a memory and solves problems by counting precisely, adding, subtracting, multiplying, dividing, and comparing. The ability of digital computers to handle alphabetical and numerical data with precision and speed makes them best suited for business applications.

digital control. Control involving digital logic devices that may or may not be complete digital computers.

digital data. Data represented by digits, perhaps with special characters and the space character.

digital data acquisition system (DDAS). Used in plant floor automation to collect digitized data, occasionally from limit switches, but most often from information inserted in work stations by means of punched cards and readable tags, as well as information inserted by the operator, using dials or a keyboard. The collected information is used on dynamic inventory control, for work-flow monitoring and control, for work measurement, and for pay determination. The DDAS is different from the data acquisition system (DAS) in that the input–output system is not noise limited but is bandwidth limited. A single installation may be spread over many buildings including thousands of input stations and many miles of

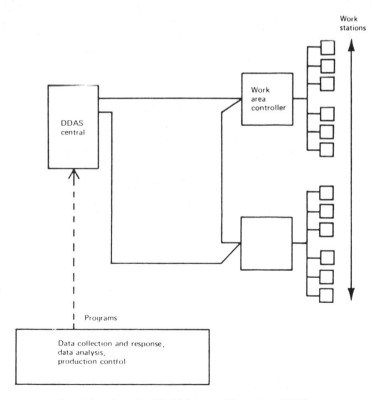

Descriptive schematic of digital data acquisition system (DDAS).

cabling. Data-handling requirements of 100K bit/sec to several megabits/sec are not unusual. Another difference is that the DAS application is based on a set of semistandardized operations; for example, signal scaling and correction limit comparison, logging, and recording. In the DDAS applications the type of data collected and the use to which they are put are less well defined, thus demanding complete freedom in programming. As a result while the local work stations are very simple special-purpose digital devices, a general-purpose central computer is clearly needed.

digital punch. Any of the punches made in the 0 or 1 through 9 rows of the **Hollerith card.** The 1 through 9 digit punches are combined with the zone punches to make alphabetic characters.

digital-to-analog convertor (D/A). A device that transforms digital data into analog data.

direct access. An addressing scheme or random access storage medium that permits direct addressing of data locations.

direct digital control (DDC). Use of a digital computer to provide the computations for the control functions of one or multiple control loops used in process control operations.

direct digital controller. A special-purpose machine that replaces an analog set-point controller, such as a flow-rate or temperature controller. Such controllers compare a measured value to a set value and compute a correction signal. The desirability of a digital implementation is indicated by the need for accuracy, for a means to change set points dynamically, and for the ability to modify algorithms easily. Since the cost of even a special-purpose digital machine would be greater than that of the analog device, all designs for DDCs have been based on the capability of one processor to handle at least 16 and as many as a thousand control loops.

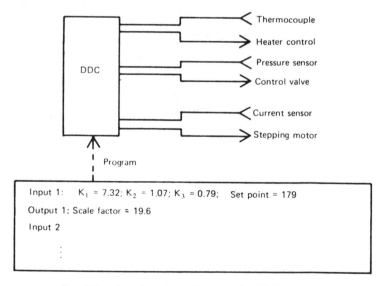

Descriptive schematic of direct digital controller (DDC).

direct memory access (DMA). A procedure used to access data stored in a high-speed storage device, for example, magnetic tape, without involving the CPU.

direct numerical control (DNC). The use of a computer for distribution of part program data via data lines to a plurality of remote numerically controlled machine tools.

discrimination instruction. One of the class of instructions that comprise branch instructions and conditional jump instructions.

disjunction. The Boolean operation whose result has the Boolean value 0 if and only if each operand has the Boolean value 0.

disk. The computer stores its bits on a variety of materials, one of which is a recordlike surface called a disk. The computer can then play the disk and find the information just as you would play a record for a specific song.

disk memories. Millions of bits can be stored on horizontally stacked disks that look like records in a juke box. Each disk contains a number of tracks, in each of which thousands of bits can be recorded. A comb of vertical arms moves in and out of every disk simultaneously, stopping at the desired track, and reading or writing information from whatever disk is specified.

disk pack. A removable assembly of magnetic disks. A portable set of flat, circular recording surfaces used on a disk storage device.

display console. In computer graphics, a console consisting of at least one display device (CRT) and usually one or more input devices such as an alphanumeric keyboard, functions key, a tablet, a joy stick, a control ball, or a light pen.

display device. An output device that stores results from computer operations and translates them into graphic, numerical, or literal symbols to be seen by the computer user.

display station. A device that provides a visual representation of data on the face of a CRT.

distal. Away from the base, toward the end effector of the arm.

distributed control. A control technique whereby portions of a single control process are located in two or more places.

distributed function. In data communication, the use of programmable terminals, controllers, and other devices to perform operations that were previously done by the processing unit, such as managing data links, controlling devices, and formation of data.

distributed processing. A system that assigns tasks in a large organization to smaller computers on the basis of location of type of task. These smaller computers may augment or replace a large, centralized computer.

DOS. Disk operating system.

DOS/VS. Disk operating system/virtual storage.

double precision. Pertaining to the use of two computer words to represent a number.

double rail logic. Pertaining to self-timing asynchronous circuits in which each logic variable is represented by two electrical lines that together can take three meaningful states — zero, one, and undecided.

double word. A contiguous sequence of bits or characters that comprises two computer words and is capable of being addressed as a unit.

drift. The tendency of a system's response to move gradually away from the desired response.

drop in. An error in the storage into or in the retrieval from a magnetic storage device, revealed by the reading of a binary character not previously recorded. Drop ins are usually caused by defects in or the presence of particles on the magnetic surface layers.

drop out. An error in the storage into or the retrieval from a magnetic storage device, revealed by a failure to read a binary character. Drop outs are usually caused by defects in or the presence of particles on the magnetic surface layer.

drum memory. A storage device generally used for auxiliary memory. The unit resembles a drum and information is stored magnetically on its surface.

drum sequencer. A mechanical programming device that can be used to operate limit switches or valves to control a robot.

dual in-line package (DIP). A device on which a microprocessor chip is mounted to connect it with the rest of the computer.

dump. To write the contents of a storage, or of part of a storage, usually from an internal storage to an external medium, for a specific purpose such as to allow other use of the storage, as a safeguard against faults or errors, or in connection with debugging. Data that have been dumped.

duodecimal. Characterized by a selection choice or condition that has 12 possible different values of states.

duplex. In data communication pertaining to a simultaneously two-way independent transmission in both directions.

duty cycle. The fraction of time during which a device or system will be active or at full power.

dyadic Boolean operation. A Boolean operation on two and only two operands.

dyadic operator. An operator that represents an operation on two and only two operands. The dyadic operators are AND, equivalence, exclusion, exclusive OR, inclusion, NAND, NOR, OR.

dynamic accuracy. Deviation from true value when relevant variables are changing with time. Difference between actual position response and position desired or commanded of an automatic control system as measured during motion.

dynamic dump. Dumping performed during the execution of a computer, usually under control of that computer program.

dynamic programming. In operations research, a procedure for optimization of a multistage problem solution wherein a number of decisions are available at each stage of the process.

dynamic range. The range of any dynamic property of a system.

dynamic storage. A device storing data in a manner that permits the data to move or vary with time such that the specified data are not always available for recovery. Magnetic drum and disk storage are dynamic nonvolatile storage. An acoustic delay line is a dynamic volatile storage.

EBCDIC. Extended Binary Coded Decimal Interchange Code. A code used by most third-generation computers, employing eight binary positions to represent a single character. The use of eight binary positions allows 256 different bit configurations (2^8) versus 64 provided by the six-position BCD code (2^6). This increase in possible bit configuration provides capacity for both upper- and lowercase letters, numerals and many special characters as well as unused configurations for future use. In addition, each of the possible 256 bit combinations can be punched into one column of an 80-column card. This allows pure binary information to be punched into a card, with each column representing eight bits of binary information. The eight-bit field can also be used to store two decimal digits.

echo check. A method of checking the accuracy of transmission of data in which the received data are returned to the sending end for comparison with the original data.

edit. To rearrange information. Editing may involve the deletion of unwanted data, the selection of pertinent data, and the insertion of symbols.

editor program. A computer program designed to perform such functions as the rearrangement, modification, and deletion of data in accordance with prescribed rules.

EDP (*see* **electronic data processing**)

effective address. The contents of the address part of an effective instruction. The address that is derived by applying any specified indexing or indirect addressing rules to the specified address and that is actually used to identify the current operation.

effector. An actuator, motor, or driven mechanical device.

electronic data processing (EDP). The general term used to define a system for data processing by means of machines utilizing electronic circuitry at electronic speeds, as opposed to electromechanical equipment.

element. In a set, an object, entity, or concept having the properties that define a set.

emulation. The act of executing a program written for one computer on a different computer. Frequently, this is accomplished by read-only circuits.

encode. To apply a set of rules specifying the manner in which data may be represented such that a subsequent decoding is possible.

encoder. A type of transducer commonly used to convert angular or linear position to digital data.

end-around borrow. The action of transferring a borrow digit from the most significant digit place to the least significant digit place.

end-around carry. The action of transferring a carry digit from the most significant digit place to the least significant digit place. An end-around carry may be necessary when adding two negative numbers that are represented by their diminished radix complements.

end effector. An actuator, gripper, or driven mechanical device attached to the end of a manipulator by which objects can be grasped or otherwise acted upon.

end-medium character (EM). A control character that may be used to identify the physical end of the data medium, the end of the used portion of the medium, or the end of the wanted portion of the data recorded on the medium.

end of address code (EOA). One or more control characters transmitted on a line to indicate the end of nontext characters, for example, addressing characters.

end of arm speed. There are various opinions on arm speed, varying depending on the axes about which the arm is moving, its position in the work envelope, and the load being carried to name a few factors. Keeping that in mind, a reasonable, though somewhat simplistic question to ask is: How fast can the gripper get from an arbitrary point A to an arbitrary point B in the envelope, empty, and how fast can it move back from B to A fully loaded? The best answer that can be expected is a ballpark figure, unless there is a willingness to accept the answer in the form of a differential equation or something similar.

end-point control. Any control scheme in which only the motion of the manipulator end point may be commanded and the computer can command the actuators at the various degrees of freedom to achieve the desired result.

end-point rigidity. The resistance of the hand, tool, or end point of a manipulator arm to motion under applied force.

enquiry character (ENQ). A transmission control character used as a request for a response from the station with which the connection has been set up; the response may include station identification, the type of equipment in service, and the status of the remote station.

entry point. The address of the label of the first instruction executed upon entering a computer program, a routine, or a subroutine.

envelope. The working envelope is the total space that the robot arm can reach: up, out, down, and side-to-side. The envelope shown in the illustration is highly idealized. Numerous options are available to the manufacturer to tailor robots to specific tasks.

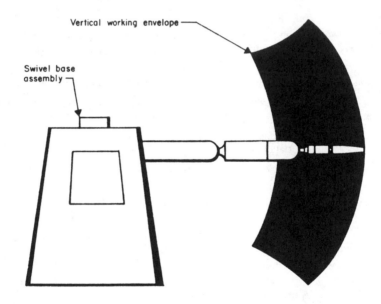

Vertical working envelope —

Swivel base assembly —

EPROM (erasable PROM). EPROM can be reprogrammed as many times as desired. It is erased by using ultraviolet light programmed in the same way as PROM (Programmable Read-Only Memory).

equivalence. A logic operator having the property that if P is a statement, Q is a statement, R is a statement, . . ., then the equivalence of $P, Q, R, . . .$, is true if and only if all statements are true or all statements are false.

equivalence operation. The dyadic Boolean operation whose result has the Boolean value 1 if and only if the operands have the same Boolean value.

equivalent-binary-digit-factor. The average number of binary digits required to express one radix digit in a nonbinary numeration system. For example, approximately 3⅓ times the number of decimal digits is required to express a decimal numeral as a binary numeral.

erase. To replace all the binary digits in a storage device by binary zeros. To remove data from a magnetic surface or other memory unit.

error burst. In data communication, a sequence of signals containing one or more errors but counted as only one unit in accordance with some specific criterion or measure.

error control procedure. The inclusion of redundant information in a message, for example, parity bits, check sums, cyclic redundancy check characters, Hamming codes, and fire, to permit the detection (and in some cases the correction) of errors that arise from noise or other disturbances in the transmission medium. May involve retransmission of messages until they are received correctly.

error correcting code. A code in which each acceptable expression conforms to specific rules of construction that also define one or more equivalent nonacceptable expressions, so that if certain errors occur in an acceptable expression, the result will be one of its equivalents and thus the error can be corrected.

error signal. The difference between desired response and actual response.

escape character (ESC). A code extension character used, in some cases, with one or more succeeding characters to indicate by some convention or agreement that the coded representations following the character or the group of characters are to be interpreted according to a different code or according to a different coded character set.

exception. An abnormal condition such as an I/O error encountered in processing data set or a file.

excess-three code. The binary coded decimal notation in which a decimal digit n is represented by the binary numeral that represents $n + 3$.

exclusion. The dyadic Boolean operation whose result has the Boolean value 1 if and only if the first operand has the Boolean value 1 and the second has the Boolean value 0.

execute. To carry out an instruction or to perform a routine.

execute phase. In a run, the logical subdivision that includes the execution of the target program.

exit. An instruction in a computer program, in a routine, or in a subroutine after the execution of which control is no longer exercised by that computer program, that routine, or that subroutine.

exponent. In a floating-point representation, the numeral that denotes the power to which the implicit floating-point base is raised before being multiplied by the fixed-point part to determine the real number represented; for example, a floating-point representation of the number 0.0001234 is 0.1234-3, where 0.1234 is the fixed-point part and -3 is the exponent.

Extended Binary Coded Decimal Interchange Code (*see* **EBCDIC**)

external devices. As applications grow increasingly more sophisticated, they eventually will exceed the computer-controlled robot's capacity for making decisions or its capacity for programmed points. A feature that helps solve these problems is the ability to communicate with external devices. This feature provides an external device (such as another computer) with the full capabilities for supplemental program management. Position, orientation, and velocity and the function associated with each point of a routine may be modified by the external device, and then sent to the robot over a data communication line for execution. Certain applications would require the robot to remember hundreds of routines. That many routines would exceed the memory and decision-making capacities of the robot. One solution is to store all the routines in another computer with sufficient memory. That computer would detect which type of part is presented to the robot and provide the robot with the appropriate routine. This external computer need not be dedicated to just communicating with one robot. It would be a computer that already exists within the application, in which case, its duties are expanded to include communicating with the robot. Communicating with external devices is important in terms of convenience. It is also important in terms of safety that these communications are performed with an error-prevention protocol. Without an established protocol, erroneous information could enter the robot and cause catastrophic results.

external sensor. A sensor for measuring displacements, forces, or other variables in the environment external to the robot.

external sort. A sort that requires the use of auxiliary storage because the set of items to be sorted cannot be held in the available internal storage at one time.

external storage. The storage of data on a device such as magnetic tape that is not an integral part of a computer but is in a form prescribed for use by a computer.

factory. An ICAM manufacturing unit consisting of a number of centers and the materials transport, storage buffers, and communications that interconnect them.

factory control. A module in the ICAM hierarchy that controls a factory. Factories are controlled by management personnel and policies.

fail-safe. Failure of a device without danger to personnel or major damage to product or plant facilities.

fail soft (*see* **graceful failure**)

false add. To form a partial sum, that is, to add without carries.

feedback. Use of the error signal to drive the control actuator. The process of returning portions of the output of a machine, process, or system for use as input in a future operation.

feedback control. A guidance technique used by robots to bring the end effector to a programmed point.

feedback devices. Installed to sense the positions of the various links and joints and transmit this information to the controller. These feedback devices may be simply limit switches actuated by the robot's arm or position-measuring devices such as encoders, potentiometers, or resolvers and/or tachometers to measure speed. Depending on the devices used, the feedback data are either digital or analog.

feedback loop. The components and processes involved in correcting or controlling a system by using part of the output as input.

ferromagnetics. In computer technology, the science that deals with the storage of information and the logical control of pulse sequences through the utilization of the magnetic polarization properties of materials.

fetch. In machine operation, to access data and/or instructions from memory and bring it to the CPU to be operated on.

field. A group of related characters treated as a unit in computer operations. A set of one or more columns of a punched card consistently used to record similar information. Punched cards are directed into segments called fields. Each field consists of one or more consecutive columns that are reserved for punching specific types of data. The length of a field is determined by the maximum length of the particular type of data to be recorded on it.

file. A collection of related records treated as a unit.

firmware. Fixed software (microprogram) by hardware manufacturer that is put into ROM and is not changeable.

first-ended, first-out (FEFO). A queuing scheme whereby messages on a destination queue are sent to the destination on a first-ended, first-out basis within priority groups. That is, higher-priority messages are sent before lower-priority messages; when two messages on a queue have equal priority, the one whose final segment arrived at the queue earliest is sent first.

first-generation computer. A computer utilizing vacuum tube components.

first-level message. Under time-sharing option (TSO) a diagnostic message that identifies a general condition; more specific information is issued in a second-level message if the text is followed by a ''+.''

fixed coordinate system. A coordinate system fixed in time.

fixed-length commands. Computer commands having the same length.

fixed-point part. In a floating-point representation, the number that is multiplied by the exponential implicit floating-point base to determine the real number represented; for example, a floating-point representation of the number 0.0001234 is 0.1234-3, where 0.1234 is the fixed-point part and -3 is the exponent.

fixed-point representation. A number system in which the position of the decimal point is fixed with respect to one end of the string of numerals, according to some convention.

fixed-radix numeration system. A radix numeration system in which all the digit places, except perhaps the one with the highest weight, have the same radix. The weights of successive digit places are successive integral powers of a single radix, each multiplied by the same factor. Negative integral powers of the radix are used in the representation of fractions.

fixed-word length. Pertaining to a storage device in which the capacity for digits or characters in each unit of data is a fixed length as opposed to a variable length.

flag. Any of various types of indicators used for identification, for example, a wordmark. A character that signals the occurrence of some condition, such as the end of a word.

flag bit. A bit which specifically indicates condition or status to be met by arithmetic operations, for example, carry, overflow, zero, sign, parity.

flexible manufacturing system (FMS). An arrangement of machines (usually NC machining centers with tool changers) interconnected by a transport system. The transporter carries work to the machines on pallets or other interface units so that accurate work–machine registration is rapid and automatic. A central computer controls machines and transport. It may have a variety of parts being processed at any one time.

flip-flop. A circuit or device containing active elements capable of assuming either one of two stable states at a given time.

floating point. A system of representing numerical quantities with a variable number of places in which the location of the point does not remain fixed.

floating-point base. In a floating-point representation system, the implicit fixed positive integer base, greater than unity, that is raised to the power explicitly denoted by the exponent in the floating-point representation or represented by the characteristic in the floating-point representation and then multiplied by the fixed-point part to determine the real number represented; for example, in the floating-point representation of the number 0.0001234, namely, 0.1234-3, the implicit floating-point base is 10.

floating-point representation. A representation of a real number in a floating-point representation system; for example, a floating-point representation of the number 0.0001234 if 0.1234-3, where 0.1234 is the fixed-point part and -3 is the exponent. The numerals are expressed in the variable-point decimal numeration system.

floor-to-floor time. The total time elapsed for picking up a part, loading it into a machine, carrying out operations, and unloading it (back to the floor, bin, pallet, etc.); generally applies to batch production.

fluerics. The area within the field of fluidics in which components and systems perform functions such as sensing, logic, amplification, and control without the use of mechanical parts.

fluidics. That branch of science and technology concerned with sensing, control, information processing, and actuation functions performed through the use of fluid dynamic phenomena.

font change character (FC). A control character that selects and makes effective a change in the specific shape or size or shape of the graphics for a set of graphemes, the character set remaining unchanged.

force feedback. A sensing technique using electrical or hydraulic signals to control a robot end effector.

force sensor. A sensor capable of measuring the forces and torques exerted by a robot at its wrist. Such sensors usually contain six or more independent sets of strain gages plus amplifiers. Computer processing (analog or digital) converts the strain readings into three orthogonal torque readings in an arbitrary coordinate system. When mounted in the work surface, rather than the robot's wrist, such a sensor is often called a pedestal sensor.

foreground processing. The automatic execution of programs that have been designed to preempt the use of computing facilities. Usually a real-time program. Contrast with **background processing**.

format. The arrangement of data on a form or in storage.

form feed (FF). A format effector character that causes the print or display position to move to the next predetermined first line on the next form, the next page, or the equivalent.

FORTRAN. The name FORTRAN is a derivative of the original title, Formula Translation. FORTRAN is a programming system that makes it possible to state a problem to be programmed in terms approximating mathematical notation. FORTRAN is a high-level problem-oriented language used for scientific and engineering problems. The FORTRAN source program is composed of a combination of mathematical and English statements. It has a character set of 26 letters, digits 0 through 9, and special symbols. It specifies five basic operations: addition, subtraction, division, multiplication, and exponentiation with certain symbols. Mathematical operations are defined by writing the mnemonic for the operation in front of the mathematical expression, for example, READ, END, PAUSE, DO, FORMAT. It is capable of using positive and negative integers (fixed-point numbers) and decimal numbers (floating-point numbers).

FORTRAN IV. A refinement of the original FORTRAN. It employs a wider range of symbols and instruction statements. It allows for more accuracy and flexibility because program statements and numbers can be longer. Its use also requires a compiler.

four-address. Pertaining to an instruction format containing four address parts.

four-plus-one address. Pertaining to an instruction that contains four operand addresses and the address of the next instruction to be executed.

frame buffer. An electronic device capable of storing a digitized image in a digital memory for later readout and processing.

frequency response. (1) The response of a dynamic system to a sinusoid. (2) The characterization of response of a dynamic system to any periodic signal according to the Fourier coefficients or the gain and phase at each frequency multiple of the period. (3) The characterization of dynamic response to a continuous spectral input according to a continuous plot of gain and phase as a function of frequency.

full adder. A combinational circuit that has three inputs that are an augend D, and addend E, and a carry digit transferred from another digit place F, and two outputs that are a sum without carry T and a new carry digit R, and in which the outputs are related to the inputs.

full duplex. In communications, pertaining to simultaneous two-way independent transmission.

full subtractor. A combinational circuit that has three inputs that are a minuend L, a subtrahend J, and a borrow digit K transferred from another digit place, and two outputs that are a difference W and a new borrow digit X, and in which the outputs are related to the inputs.

function. (1) A mathematical entity whose value, that is, the value of the dependent variable, depends in a specified manner on the values of one or more independent variables, not more than one value of the dependent variable corresponding to each permissible combination of values from the respective ranges of the independent variables. (2) A specific purpose of an entity or its characteristic action.

functions, computerized robot control. Each stored point in the computer contains the coordinate positions and orientations of the tool center point, velocity, tool length, and the functions to be performed at the point. The following are descriptions of some typical non-path-related functions: *Delay*: when this function is executed, robot motion is stopped for a defined period of time before moving to the next programmed point. *Wait*: robot motion is stopped until a signal is received on a defined terminal before proceeding to the next programmed point. This function may also be made "conditional" on a set of signals received on defined terminals. *Output*: this function causes robot motion to stop and an output signal to be sent to a defined terminal before proceeding to the next programmed point. This output may be defined as pulse or a level signal (on or off). *Continue*: with execution of this function, the robot motion is not stopped but continues to move to the next programmed point. An output signal may also be sent at the same time if desired. *Tool*: this is a specialized function that is used to signal one of two defined tools (end effectors) attached to the robot hand and to verify tool operation. Motion is stopped until the tool operation is complete before proceeding to the next programmed point. *Branch*: the sequence of points being followed may be changed through use of this function. Using this function, robot motion remains stopped, and if a signal is received on a defined terminal, another defined sequence of points, which is called a branch, is followed; otherwise, the previously programmed sequence of points and the last point on this branch may close upon another previously programmed point. If the branch is not closed on a specified point, it becomes a subroutine. Any time a subroutine is entered, the operation is always transferred back to the next point from which the branch function was first used to enter the subroutine.

function table. Two or more sets of data so arranged that an entry in one set selects one or more entries in the remaining sets — for example, a tabulation of the values of a function for a set of values of the variable; a dictionary.

gangpunching. The automatic punching of data read from a master card into the following detail cards.

gap character. A character that is included in a computer word for technical reasons, but does not represent data.

gate. A combinational circuit with only one output channel.

general-purpose computers. A computer that may be used to solve a wide variety of problems. A term used to describe the great bulk of digital computers, particularly those used in general business applications.

generated address. An address that has been formed as a result, during the execution of a computer program.

generating function. Pertaining to a given series of functions or constants, a mathematical function that, when represented by an infinite series, has those functions or constants as coefficients in the series.

generation. A differentiation of the ages to which the equipment belongs.

generator. A program for a computer that generates the coding of a problem.

giga. (1) Ten to the ninth power (10^9); 1,000,000,000 in decimal notation. (2) When referring to storage capacity, two to the thirtieth power (2^{30}); 1,073,741,824 in decimal notation.

GIGO. The term standing for garbage in–garbage out, meaning that if incorrect data are fed into the system, incorrect answers will result.

graceful degradation. Decline in performance of some component part of a system without immediate and significant decline in performance of the system as a whole and/or decline in the quality of the product.

graceful failure. Failure in performance of some component part of a system without immediate major interruption or failure of performance of the system as a whole and/or sacrifice in quality of the product.

graphic. A symbol produced by a process such as handwriting, drawing, or printing.

gray code. A binary code in which sequential numbers are represented by binary expressions, each of which differs from the preceding expression in one place only.

gray-scale picture. A digitized image in which the brightness of the pixels can have more than two values, typically 128 or 256; it requires more storage space and much more sophisticated image processing than a binary image, but offers potential for improved visual sensing.

grid. In optical character recognition, two mutually orthogonal sets of parallel lines used for specifying or measuring character images.

group indication. Printed information identifying a group of data.

groupmark. A mark that identifies the beginning or the end of a set of data, which may include blocks, characters, or other items.

group printing. A method of printing in which the accounting machine prints one line for each group of cards. Groups of cards are recognized by a comparison feature of the machine.

group technology. (1) A system for coding parts based on similarities in geometrical shape or other characteristics of the parts. (2) The grouping of parts into families based on similarities in their production so that the parts of a particular family could then be processed together.

half-adder. A combinational circuit that has two inputs, A and B, and two outputs, one being a sum without carry S and the other being a carry C and in which the outputs are related to the inputs.

half-adjust. To round by one-half of the maximum value of the number base of the counter.

half-duplex. In communications, pertaining to alternate, one-way-at-a-time transmissions.

half-subtractor. A combinational circuit that has two inputs that are a minuend G and a subtrahend H and two outputs that are a difference U and a borrow digit V, and in which the outputs are related to the inputs.

halfword. A contiguous sequence of bits or characters that comprise one-half a computer word; it is capable of being addressed as a unit.

hard automation. A production technique where equipment has specifically been engineered for a unique manufacturing sequence. "Hard" automation implies programming with hardware in contrast to "soft" automation, which uses software or computer programming.

hardwired. An electronics programming technique using soldered connections; hence, not readily reprogrammable. Hardwired memories in early robots employed a wire matrix to register voltages from feedback potentiometers.

hash total. A sum of numbers in a specified field of a record or batch of records used for checking or control purposes. The total may be insignificant except for audit purposes, as in the case of part numbers or customer numbers.

HDLC. High-Level Data Link Control Protocol. It is bit oriented, code independent, and suited to full-duplex communication. It has a potential of twice the throughput rate of **BISYNC** because it does not require immediate acknowledgments to each message frame. International Standard ISO 3309-1976 (E) defines in detail the frame structure to be used for each HDLC transmission as
1. An eight-bit sequence (01111110)
2. An eight-bit secondary station address field
3. An eight-bit control field containing
   a. commands from the primary station to the secondary
   b. responses from the secondary to the primary
   c. message sequence numbers
4. An optional information field of variable length
5. A 16-bit frame-checking sequence
6. An eight-bit flag sequence (01111110)

head. A device that reads, records, or erases data on a storage medium, for example, an electromagnet used to read, write, or erase data on a magnetic drum or tape, or the set of perforating, reading, or marking devices used to punch, read, or print on paper tape.

header card. A prepunched record of the basic information pertaining to a specific individual or firm that is used to create automatically the upper portion of a document.

heuristic. Pertaining to exploratory methods of problem solving in which solutions are discovered by evaluation of the progress made toward the final result. (*See also* **algorithm.**)

heuristic problem-solving. The ability to plan and direct actions to achieve higher-order goals.

hexadecimal numbering system. A numbering system using the equivalent of the decimal number 16 as a base. Most third-generation computers operate on a principle that utilizes the hexadecimal system as it provides high utilization of computer storage and an expanded set of characters for representing data. In base 16 (hexadecimal), 16 symbols are required. Because only a single character is allowed for each absolute value, the hexadecimal system uses the 10 symbols of the decimal system for the values, 0 through 9, and the first six letters of the alphabet to represent values 10 through 15 (A through F, respectively). The positional significance of hexadecimal symbols is based on the progression of powers of 16. The highest number that can be represented in the units position is 15.

hierarchical control. A distributed control technique in which the controlling processes are arranged in a hierarchy.

hierarchy. A relationship of elements in a structure divided into levels with those at higher levels having priority or precedence over those at lower levels. (*See also* **control hierarchy** and **sensory hierarchy**.)

high-level data link control protocol (*see* **HDLC**)

high-level language. Programming language that generates machine codes from problem- or function-oriented statements. ALGOL, FORTRAN, PASCAL, and BASIC are four commonly used high-level languages. A single functional statement may translate into a series of instructions or subroutines in machine language, in contrast to a low-level (assembly) language in which statements translate on a one-for-one basis.

high-order position. The leftmost position of a number or word.

HIPO. An abbreviation for Hierarchy plus Input-Process-Output. A design and documentation technique to describe systems function.

Hollerith card. The name given to the punched card developed by Dr. Herman Hollerith. It is also commonly known as an IBM card.

host computer. The primary or controlling computer in a multiple-computer operation.

housekeeping routine. That part of a program usually performed only at the beginning of machine operations which establishes the initial conditions for instruction addresses, accumulator setting, switch setting, etc.

ICAM. Integrated Computer-Aided Manufacturing. A U.S. Air Force project established to automate production in the aircraft industry.

identifier. A symbol whose purpose is to identify or name data in a programming language.

identity element. A logic element that performs an identity operation.

identity operation. The Boolean operation the result of which has the Boolean value 1 if and only if all the operands have the same Boolean value. An identity operation on two operands is an equivalence operation.

if-and-only-if element. A logic element that performs the Boolean operation of equivalence.

if–then element. A logic element that performs the Boolean operation of implication.

illegal character. A character or combination of bits that is not valid according to some criterion, for example, with respect to a specified alphabet, a character that is not a member.

image enhancement, computer. A picture is not always a satisfactory representation of the original object or scene; it may be geometrically distorted or it may be blurred or "noisy."

There are many cases in which one can reduce the difference between a picture and its original by operating on the picture; this is the goal of image restoration. One can sharpen a picture (increase local contrasts in it, deblur it) by emphasizing its high spatial frequencies. This can be done by multiplying the Fourier transform of the picture by a weighting function from the original, and then taking the inverse Fourier transform to obtain the sharpened picture. Similar effects can be obtained by performing a differencing operation on the picture and combining the results with the original picture. If the picture is not only blurred but also noisy, these methods make it still noisier. It is often possible to achieve a useful compromise by emphasizing only a selected band of spatial frequencies (or, analogously, using a difference between average gray levels rather than between the gray levels of single pixels). Similarly, one can smooth a picture by deemphasizing its high spatial frequencies or simply by locally averaging it, but this is usually undesirable because it blurs the picture. If the noise is random, and several copies of the picture are available in which the samples of the noise are independent, smoothing without blurring can be achieved by averaging the copies. A known geometrical distortion in a picture can be corrected by resampling it at an irregularly spaced array of positions and outputting the samples as a regular array. Gray levels can be assigned to the new samples by interpolation from the levels of the nearby pixels. To correct an unknown relative distortion between two copies of a picture, one can find matches between pairs of distinctive local patterns, measure the relative displacement of each pair, and construct a geometrical distortion function by interpolation from these displacements.

image processing. A wide variety of techniques exist for processing pictorial information by computer. The information to be processed is usually input to the computer by sampling and analog-to-digital conversion of video signals obtained from some type of two-dimensional scanner device. Initially the information is in the form of a large array in which each element is a number representing the brightness (and perhaps color) of a small region in the scanned image. A digitized image array is sometimes called a digital picture, its elements are called "points," "picture elements," or "pixels." The values of these elements are typically six-bit or eight-bit integers. They usually represent brightness (or gray color). A digital picture may contain millions of bits, but most of the classes of pictures encountered in practice are redundant and can be compressed without loss of information. One can take advantage of picture redundancy by using efficient encoding techniques in which frequently occurring gray levels or blocks or gray levels are represented by short codes and infrequent ones by longer codes. The pixels are encoded in a fixed succession. One can capitalize on the dependency of each gray level on the preceding ones by encoding differences between successive levels rather than by the levels themselves. If the dependency is very great, it may be even economical to represent the picture by the positions (or lengths) of runs of constant gray level or, more generally, to specify the positions and shapes of regions of constant gray level. Except for very simple classes of pictures, only a limited degree of compression can be achieved using efficient encoding. The digitization process itself, based on spatial sampling and gray-level quantization of a given real image, is a process of approximation. In designing approximation schemes, one can take advantage of the limitations of the human visual system, for example, quantization can be coarse in the vicinity of abrupt changes in gray level.

immediate access storage. A storage device whose access time is negligible in comparison with another's operating time.

immediate address. The contents of an address part that contains the value of an operand rather than an address.

immediate instruction. An instruction that contains within itself an operand for the operation specified, rather than an address of the operand.

impact printer. Any printing mechanism that employs some hitting or striking mechanism, such as a hammer.

implicator. The dyadic Boolean operation the result of which has the Boolean value 0 if and only if the first operand has the Boolean value 0 and the second has the Boolean value 1.

inclusive-or element. A logic element that performs the Boolean operation of disjunction.

incremental computer. A computer in which incremental representation of data is mainly used. A special-purpose computer that is specifically designed to process changes in the variables as well as the absolute value of the variables.

incremental integrator. A digital device modified so that the output signal is maximum negative, zero, or maximum positive when the value of the input is negative, zero, or positive.

index. In computer programming, a subscript, or integer value, that identifies the position of an item of data with respect to some other item of data.

index address. An address that is modified by the content of an index register prior to or during the execution of a computer instruction.

indexed sequential file. A file in which records are organized sequentially with indexes that permit quick access to undivided records as well as rapid sequential processing.

indexing. A method of address modification that is performed automatically by the data processing system.

index register. A register whose content may be added to or subtracted from the operand address prior to or during the execution of an instruction.

index word. A storage position or register, the content of which may be used to modify automatically the effective address of any given instruction.

indicators. Internal switches that are turned on or off depending on the results of arithmetical or logical comparisons.

indirect address. An address that designates the storage location of an item of data to be treated as the address of an operand but not necessarily as its direct address.

infix notation. A method of forming mathematical expression, governed by rules of operator precedence and using parentheses in which the operators are dispersed among the operands, each operator indicating the operation to be performed on the operands or the intermediate results adjacent to it.

information bits. In data communication, those bits that are generated by the data source and that are not used for error control by the data transmission system.

information separator (IS). Any control character used to delimit like units of data in a hierarchic arrangement of data. The name of the separator does not necessarily indicate the units of data that it separates.

information storage and retrieval (IS&R). A complex system in which information is placed on file in such a manner that future retrieval may be accomplished in a variety of ways. The methods and procedures for recovering specific information from stored data.

initialize. A programming term that refers to the act of establishing fixed values in certain areas of memory. Generally, the term applies to all the housekeeping that must be completed before the main part of the program can be executed.

initial program loader (IPL). The utility routine that loads the initial part of a computer program, such as an operating system or other computer program, so that the computer program can then proceed under its own control.

in-line procedures. In COBOL the set of statements that constitute the main or controlling flow of the computer program and that excludes statements executed under control of the asynchronous control system.

in-line processing. The processing of data in random order without preliminary editing or sorting.

input. Information transferred into the internal storage of a data processing system, including data to be processed or information to help control the process.

input channel. A channel for impressing a state on a device or logic element.

input–output controller (IOC). A functional unit in a data processing system that controls one or more units of peripheral equipment.

input–output (I/O) system. Communication with a computer data processing system is achieved through an input–output (I/O) device linked directly to the system. Data are entered into the system by means of an input medium that is sensed or read as it moves through an input device. This information is converted to a form usable by the system and is transmitted to main storage. Similarly, output involves converting processed data from main storage to a form or language compatible with an output medium and recording the data through the output device. All standard I/O devices have certain common characteristics. They are auxiliary machines connected to the computer and under control of the central processing unit. Most are automatic; once started, they continue to operate as directed by the stored program. These devices can transmit data to or receive data only from the main memory section of the central processing unit.

input–output unit. A device in a data processing system by which data may be entered into the system, received from the system, or both.

input signals. Input signals, determined by the presence or absence of a specific voltage at the input signal terminals, tell the robot when or where not to do something. A typical condition is "If Input Signal Three is present, put the part in chute one." The robot makes a programmed decision to perform the routine of placing the part in the chute based on the state of Input Signal Three. More complex applications may require decisions to be based on more than one condition. For example, "If a part is ready, and if the oven is up to temperature, and if the oven is empty, then put the part in the oven." Three conditions are required to make this decision, which normally means wiring three switches in series to an input signal terminal, or first wiring them to a relay panel or programmable controller if additional decisions are to be made with those same switches. It is this type of application that can bring out the cost effectiveness of a computer-controlled robot, because additional switching logic hardware is not required.

inquiry station. Data terminal station used for inquiry into a data processing system.

instruction. A set of characters that when interpreted by the control unit causes a data processing system to perform one of its operations.

instruction address. The address of an instruction word.

instruction address register. A register from which contents the address of the next instruction is derived.

instruction control unit. In a central processing unit the part that receives instructions in proper sequence, interprets each instruction, and applies the proper signals to the arithmetic and logic unit and other parts in accordance with the interpretation.

instruction cycle. That part of a machine cycle during which a computer instruction is transferred from a specified primary storage location to the instruction register in the control unit, where it is decoded before being executed.

instruction register. The register that stores the current instruction governing a computer operation.

instruction set. The set of the instructions of a computer, of a programming language, or of the programming languages in a programming system.

instruction word. A word that represents an instruction.

integer programming. In operations research, a class of procedures for locating the maximum or minimum of a function subject to constraints, where some or all variables must have integer values.

integral control. Control scheme whereby the signal that drives the actuator equals the time integral of the difference between the input (desired output) and the measured actual output.

integrated circuit (IC). An electronic circuit packaged in a small unit ranging from 0.3 to 2 in. (7.6 to 51 mm) square, varying in complexity and function from simple logic gates to microprocessors, amplifiers, and analog–digital converters. The circuit may be constructed on a single semiconductor substrate — a configuration called monolithic — or several such circuits can be connected in one package called a hybrid.

integrated data processing. A system that treats all data processing requirements as a whole to reduce or eliminate duplicate recording or processing while accomplishing a sequence of data processing steps or a number of related data processing sequences.

integrator. A device whose output function is proportional to the integral of the input function with respect to a specified variable, for example, a watt-hour meter.

intelligent terminal. A communication station containing storage and some of the components of a small computer, thus allowing batched data to be organized and edited before being transmitted to a central computer.

interactive plotting. The display console is used simply to "browse" through output of computational processes, typically in the form of a graph prepared by the host computer. Little interaction is required except for the real-time display of successive frames on operator command and simple "menu selection" (i.e., via labeled function key or lightpen identification of a command name displayed in a control area on the screen) to direct the browsing or further computation. Such applications as computer-assisted instruction and command and control operations fit into this category of primarily predefined pictures. It describes probably three-quarters of graphics application programs.

interconnection. Few, if any, industrial robots perform tasks that require no connection to equipment surrounding them. Typically it is necessary for the robot to receive such signals so that it can interface to a working environment. An example would include limit-switch signals to the robot when a part is in position. To illustrate this interconnection of equipment a diagram of a simple robot system is shown. This example is given to illustrate interconnections and does not represent an economical robot application. An industrial robot is servicing a milling machine, with raw (unfinished) parts arriving on one conveyor and finished parts leaving on another conveyor. A "ready for part" signal from the machine tool control to the robot control would inform the robot to pick up a raw part and load a fixture on the table. A "raw part available" signal to move the robot system would permit the arm to move to that conveyor and transfer the part to the milling machine. The robot then signals the machine tool control to begin its operations on the part. While waiting for completion, the robot could perform housekeeping functions such as chip removal, inspection of finished parts, placing of tools in a tool changer, and inspection of tools for breakage or excessive wear; in all of these chores, other interconnect signals could alter the functions performed by the robot depending on the outcome of these tests or the presence of any unusual situations during this housekeeping. If during these functions the milling machine control detects a malfunction or a tool breakage during a machine operation, the robot must abandon these routine tasks and take some action to either remedy the problem or initiate an emergency procedure for the total system. A "part finished" signal from the machine tool to the robot would request that the finished part be unloaded and transferred to the outgoing conveyor. The cycle could then be repeated. In the example illustrated the robot must respond to signals from the surrounding equipment and perhaps alter its movements and operation based on these inputs. Robot decision making can be defined as the ways an industrial system can respond to these changes in its working environment.

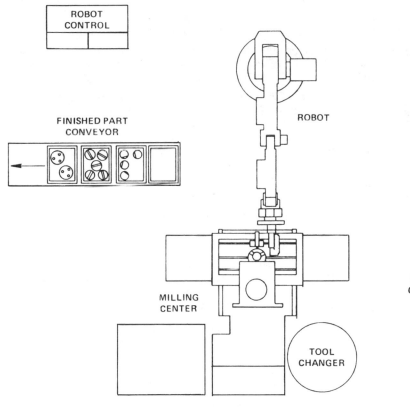

Milling machine/robot system.

interfacing. A shared boundary. Except in a few applications, most robots need to communicate and interact with the outside world. This can take the form of simple on/off signals by means of electrical, or pneumatic, contacts, or of more complex electronic signals. Inputs are the number of lines over which the robot will accept signals from the outside world, and outputs are the lines over which it will send signals to external equipment.

interlock. To prevent a machine or device from initiating further operations until the operation or some condition or set of conditions in process is completed.

internal sensor. A sensor for measuring displacements, forces, or other variables internal to the robot.

internal sort. A sort program or a sort phase that sorts two or more items within main storage.

internal storage. Usually referred to as main or primary storage, which is an integral physical part of the computer and is directly controlled by the computer. Thus, data in main storage are automatically accessible to the computer. An important characteristic of main storage units is that each position or word must be accessible on a random basis. It must also be possible to use the data as many times as desired without erasing it from storage until such time as it is no longer needed.

interoceptor. Internal sensor, usually used in physiology.

interpret. To translate into or restate in human language. To print at the top of a punched card the information punched on it using a machine called an interpreter.

interpreter. A program that translates and executes each source language expression before translating and executing the next one. A routine that decodes instructions and produces a machine language routine to be executed at a later time.

interpretive language. Interpretive language allows a source program to be translated by an interpreter for use in a computer. The interpreter translates the interpretive-language source program into machine code, and instead of producing an object program, lets the program be immediately operated on by the computer. Interpretive language programs are used for solving difficult problems and for running short programs.

interrecord gap (IRG). (1) A machine-generated space on magnetic tape that appears after each data block. Generally, the IRG is ¾ in. (19 mm) in length. (2) An area on a data medium that signals the end of a block or record.

interrupt. To stop a process in such a way that it can be resumed. To get a computer system's attention especially for the purpose of input–output of data, for making an inquiry or receiving a reply, or for carrying out interactive processes or procedures.

inverted file. In information retrieval, a method of organizing a cross index file in which a keyword identifies a record. The items, numbers, or documents pertinent to that keyword are indicated.

I/O (see **input/output system**)

item. One member of a group. A file may consist of a number of items, such as records, which in turn may consist of other items.

job. A set of data that completely defines a unit or work for a computer. A job usually includes all necessary computer programs, linkages, files, and instructions to the operating system.

job control statement (JCS). A statement in a program used to identify the job or describe its requirements to the operating system.

job shop. A discrete parts manufacturing facility characterized by a mix of products of relatively low-volume production in batch lots.

K. When referring to storage capacity, two to the tenth power (2^{10}); 1024 in decimal notation.

Karnaugh map. A rectangular diagram of a logic function of variables drawn with overlapping rectangles representing a unique combination of the logic variables such that an intersection is shown for all combinations.

key. One or more characters within a set of data that contain information about the set, including the identification.

keyboard. It is similar to a typewriter; the difference is that the information is translated by a device that transforms each word into a series of electrical signals that open and close the places in the computer in order to store information and instruction.

ladder diagram. An electrical engineering technique to illustrate schematically functions in an electrical circuit (relays, switches, timers, etc.) by diagramming them in a vertical sequence resembling a ladder.

lag. The tendency of the dynamic response of a passive physical system to respond later than desired. The time parameter characterizing the transient response of a first-order exponential system to a step. The phase difference between input and response sinusoids. Any time parameter that characterizes the delay of a response relative to an input. The time it takes a signal or an object to move from one location to another. (**Delay** is a more precise term for this.)

language. A set of representations, conventions, and rules used to convey data or information. The computer has several languages. One set that exists only internally is called machine language. This is usually in a binary form. Another set, computer language, is the language used to instruct and inform the computer concerning what is to be done. The computer makes the translation from the instructions given to the on/off states within the machine using machine language.

language processor. A computer program that performs such functions as translating, interpreting, and other tasks required for processing a specified programming language.

language translator. A general term for any assembler, compiler, or other routine that accepts statements in one language and produces equivalent machine language instructions.

large-scale integration (LSI). A classification for the complexity of an integrated electronic circuit chip. Other classes are medium-scale integration (MSI) and small-scale integration (SSI).

latency. The time interval between the instant at which an instruction control unit initiates a call for data and the instant at which the actual transfer of the data is started.

learning control. A control scheme whereby experience is automatically used to provide for future control decisions, which will be better than those in the past.

level. The degree of subordination of an item in a hierarchic arrangement.

level of automation. The degree to which a process has been made automatic. Relevant to the level of automation are questions of automatic failure recovery, the variety of situations that will be automatically handled, and the situation under which manual intervention or action by humans is required.

library. A collection of standard proven computer routines, usually kept on a library tape or random-access file, by which problems or portions of problems may be solved.

limit switch. An electrical switch positioned to be actuated when a certain motion limit occurs, thereby deactivating the actuator causing that motion.

line. On a terminal, one or more characters entered before a return to the first printing or display position.

linear-array camera. A TV camera (usually solid state) with an aspect ratio of 1:n; today, n is typically 128, 256, or 512.

linearity. (1) The degree to which an input–output relationship is proportional. (2) The degree to which a motion intended to be in a straight line conforms to a straight line.

linear language. A language that is automatically expressed as a linear representation. For example, FORTRAN is a linear language; a flowchart is not.

linear programming. The mathematical technique applied to management problems whose elements react in a straight line relationship.

line control block (LCB). A storage area containing control information required for scheduling and managing line operations. One LCB is maintained for each line in the data communication system.

line printer. A device that prints a line of characters as a unit.

link. In computer programming the part of a computer program, in some cases a single instruction or an address, that passes control and parameters between separate portions of the computer program; also in computer programming, to provide a link.

list. An ordered set of items of data.

list processing. A method of processing data in the form of lists. Usually chained lists are used so that the logical order of items can be changed without altering their physical limitations.

load. (1) To put data into a register or into internal storage. (2) To put a magnetic tape onto a tape drive or to put cards into a card reader.

load-and-go. An operating technique in which there are no stops between the loading and execution phases of a program, and which may include assembling or compiling.

logger. A functional unit that records events and physical conditions, usually with respect to time.

logical comparison. A logic operation to determine whether two strings are identical.

logical expression. In assembler programming a conditional assembly expression that is a combination of logical terms, logical operations, and paired parentheses.

logical operations. Nonarithmetical operations such as selecting, sorting, matching, comparing, etc.

logical record. A record whose scope, direction, or length is governed by the specific nature of the information or data that it contains rather than by some feature or limitation of the storage device that holds it. Such records differ in size from the physical records in which they are contained.

logical shift. A shift that equally affects all of the characters of a computer word.

logic elements. Various forms of electrical switches within the computer. The term is used interchangeably with switching elements.

long-term repeatability. Closeness of agreement of position movements, repeated under the same conditions during a long time interval, to the same location.

loop. A sequence of instructions that is executed repeatedly until some specified condition is met.

low-order position. The rightmost position of a number or word.

machine cycle. A set period of time in which the computer can perform a specific machine operation.

machine language. The instructions written in a form that is intelligible to the internal circuitry of the computer; it is not ordinarily comprehensible to persons without special training. Machine languages are written in binary code, using 1's and 0's. Binary machine code is what the computer understands immediately without any additional translation. Machine language can be used for writing programs for which another language does not seem appropriate. A machine language program is a personal choice and must conform specifically with the design of the computer hardware in use.

machine logic. All of the complex work that a data processing machine performs is based on four fundamental operations — AND, OR, NOT, and memory. In electronic computers these functions are executed by circuits called gates and triggers. The organization of these building blocks into circuits that can carry out programs is called machine logic or logical design. AND gates are devised so that they emit a 1 bit as output only when all the input bits are 1's. OR gates produce a 1 output whenever at least one of the inputs is a 1. A 0 output occurs only if both inputs are 0. The NOT operation is performed by a device called the inverter. This component reverses the signal that is applied at its input. If a 0 bit enters, a 1 output occurs. If a 1 bit enters, there is a 0 output. AND gate and OR gates may have more than two outputs. However, the same logical principles apply regardless of the number of inputs. An AND gate with three inputs performs a function equivalent to three relays in series. OR gates behave in the same way as relays in parallel.

macro. Programming with instructions (equivalent to a specified sequence of machine instructions) in a source language.

macrogenerator. A computer program that replaces macro instructions in the source language with the defined sequence of instructions in the source language.

macro instruction. A symbolic instruction in a source language that produces a number of machine language instructions. It is made available for use by the programmer through an automatic programming system. A macro instruction is a method of describing in a one-line statement a function, or functions, to be performed by the object program. Macro instructions enable the programmer to write one instruction such as ''read a tape'' and the processor will then automatically insert the corresponding detailed series of machine instructions. In this manner the programmer avoids the task of writing one instruction for every machine step.

magnetic card. A card with a magnetic surface on which data can be stored by selective magnetization of portions of the flat surface.

magnetic core. A small doughnut shaped piece of ferromagnetic material, about the size of a pin head, capable of storing one binary digit represented by the polarity of its magnetic field. Thousands of these cores strung on wire grids form an internal memory device. Cores can be individually charged to hold data and sensed to issue data.

magnetic core memory. A computer storage medium made up of thousands of magnetic cores, strung on a grid of fine wires. Each grid of wires and cores is called a plane. Cores are mounted with wires running through each core at right angles to each other, and magnetized by sending electrical current through the wires. By sending half the current needed to magnetize a core through each wire, only the core at the intersection of the wires is magnetized. The act of magnetizing one or more cores in a given line, called an address, causes all other cores in that address to be demagnetized. Cores are arranged so that combinations of charges representing data are instantly accessible. Cores are magnetized positively or negatively depending on the direction of the current. By reversing the flow of current, the magnetic state or polarity of a core can be changed.

magnetic delay line. A delay line whose operation is based on the time of propagation of magnetic waves.

magnetic disk storage. The magnetic disk is a thin metal disk resembling a phonograph record; it is coated on both sides with a magnetic recording material. Data are stored as magnetized spots arranged in binary form in concentric tracks on each face of the disk. A characteristic of disk storage is that data are recorded serially bit-by-bit, eight bits per byte, along a track rather than by columns of characters. Disks are normally mounted on a stack on a rotating vertical shaft. Enough space is left between each disk to allow access arms to move in and read or record data. A single magnetic disk unit is capable of storing several million characters. Usually more than one disk unit can be attached to a computer.

magnetic domain memory. An experimental memory method that uses magnetic bubbles to store data. The bubbles can also be read optically.

magnetic drum storage. The magnetic drum is a cylinder on which data are recorded serially in a series of bands around the drum in a manner similar to that utilized on disk storage. As the drum rotates at a constant speed, data are recorded or sensed by a set of read–write heads. The heads are positioned close enough to the surface of the drum to be able to magnetize the surface and to sense the magnetization on it. The heads contain coils of fine wire wound around tiny magnetic cores. There may be one or more heads for each drum track or one or more heads that can be moved to the various tracks. The drum may rotate up to 3500 revolutions per minute, and the data transfer rate to or from the processing unit may be up to 1,200,000 bytes per second. The rotational delay to a specific part of the track ranges from 0 to 17.5 milliseconds and averages 8.6 milliseconds. Data are stored in the form of minute magnetized spots, arranged in binary form on the individual recording track. Spots are magnetized by sending pulses of current through the wire coil. The polarity of a spot is determined by the direction of the current flow. Depending on their polarity, spots can represent either 1's or 0's, the two binary digits.

magnetic film storage. Magnetic film storage functions similarly to core storage; however, instead of individual cores strung on wires, magnetic film is made of much smaller elements in a form. One type of magnetic film, known as planar film (thin film), consists of very thin, flat wafers made of nickel–iron alloy. These metallic spots are connected by ultrathin wires and are mounted on an insulating base such as glass or plastic. Magnetic film may also be in the form of plated wire. This is a type of cylindrical film, essentially the same as planar film except that the film is wrapped around a wire. Another type of cylindrical film is the plated rod. This technique, known as thin film rod memory, consists of an array of tiny metal rods only 0.1 in. (2.54 mm) long. The operation of a magnetic film memory unit is similar in principle to that of a magnetic card unit as the storage elements in both are formed into planes that may be stacked.

magnetic head. An electromagnet that can perform one or more functions of reading, writing, and erasing data on a magnetic data medium.

magnetic ink. An ink that contains particles of a magnetic substance whose presence can be detected by magnetic sensors.

magnetic ink character readers. Magnetic ink character recognition (MICR) is a high-speed data input technique that reduces manual keystroke operations and allows source documents to be sorted automatically. Magnetic ink reading heads produce electrical signals when magnetic characters are passed beneath them. These signals are analyzed by special circuits and are compared with stored tables to determine what character has been sensed. The data are then transmitted to the memory of the computer for processing.

magnetic ink character recognition (MICR). The character recognition of characters printed with ink that contains particles of a magnetic material.

magnetic tape. A tape or ribbon of material impregnated or coated with magnetic material on which information may be placed in the form of magnetically polarized spots. The use of magnetic tape as a means of storing information is based on the same principles of magnetization and induction as are utilized in the magnetic drum. The tape is surfaced with a magnetizable material, and is moved past a reading and writing head that obtains or stores binary digits. The tape is wound around a reel. As the reel unwinds the tape passes the read–write station and is taken up by a second reel, like a roll of film in a camera. The physical end of the tape is sensed by a photoelectric cell near the read–write head. Special procedures are incorporated into programs to take care of the end-of-tape condition. An erase head is energized to remove previous information from the tape whenever the machine begins to "write" on the tape. Information on magnetic tape usually appears as a succession of characters written vertically. Records are demarcated by empty spaces called interrecord gaps. When writing on tape, the machine creates an interrecord gap at the end of each new record; information previously on the tape is erased as writing occurs. Additional instructions are available to backspace and to rewind the tape.

magnetic thin film. A layer of magnetic material, usually less than 1 micron thick, often used for logic or storage elements.

main control unit. In a computer with more than one instruction control unit, that instruction control unit to which, for a given interval of time, the other instruction control units are subordinated. An instruction control unit may be designated as the main control unit by hardware or by hardware and software. A main control unit at one time may be a subordinate unit at another time.

main frame. A term referring to the CPU (central processing unit) part of the hardware. The main frame does not encompass any of the input/output devices.

main memory. The storage area in which data can be manipulated arithmetically. Usually main memory is a magnetic core or thin-film device.

main storage. Program-addressable storage from which instructions and other data can be loaded directly into registers for subsequent execution or processing.

majority. A logic operator having the property that if P is a statement, Q is a statement, R is a statement, . . ., then the majority of P, Q, R, . . ., is true if more than one-half of the statements are true, false if one-half or less are true.

mantissa. The positive fractional part of the representation of a logarithm. In the expression, log 643 = 2.808, .808 is the mantissa and 2 is the characteristic.

map. To establish a set of values having a defined correspondence with the quantities or values of another set.

mark. A symbol or symbols that indicate the beginning or the end of a field, of a word, of an item of data, or of a set of data such as a file, a record, or a block.

Markov chain. A probabilistic mode of events, in which the probability of an event is dependent only on the event that precedes it.

mark sensing. An operation by which data in machine-readable form can be written or marked on special oblong areas called bubbles. The markings can then be sensed by a machine and converted into punches in the same card.

mask. A pattern of characters used to control the retention or elimination of portions of another pattern of characters.

mass production. The large-scale production of parts in a continuous process uninterrupted by the production of other parts.

mass storage. An auxiliary storage medium whereby data are magnetically recorded in tracks or channels on the surface of cards or strips stored in demountable cells or cartridges.

mathematical induction. A method of proving a statement concerning terms based on natural numbers not less than N by showing that the statement is valid for the term based on N and that, if it is valid for an arbitrary value of n that is greater than N, it is also valid for the term based on $(n + 1)$.

mathematical model. A mathematical representation of the behavior of a process, device, or concept.

matrix. (1) In mathematics, a two-dimensional rectangular array of quantities. Matrices are manipulated in accordance with the rules of matrix algebra. (2) In computers, a logic network in the form of an array of input leads and output leads, logic elements being connected at some of their intersections.

matrix-array camera. A TV camera (usually solid state) with an aspect ratio of $n{:}m$, where neither n nor m is 1; typically 128 by 128 today.

matrix printer. An output device that prints each character by means of a specially placed series of dots. Usually the dots are made by small wires that press against a ribbon and paper.

maximum speed. The greatest rate at which an operation can be accomplished according to some criterion of satisfaction. The greatest velocity of movement of a tool or end effector that can be achieved in producing a satisfactory result.

mean-time-between-failures (MTBF). The average time that a device will operate before failure.

mean-time-to-repair (MTTR). The average time that a device is expected to be out of service after failure.

mega (M). Ten to the sixth power (10^6); 1,000,000 in decimal notation. When referring to storage capacity, two to the twentieth power (2^{20}); 1,048,576 in decimal notation.

memory. (1) A device into which data can be entered, in which it can be held, and from which it can be retrieved at a later time. The robot memory is part of the controller. It stores the commands that have been programmed in and through the controller, tells the robot what to do and when. Since the type of memory determines how commands are stored, it gives an indication of the sophistication of the program it is possible to execute and the degree of flexibility in programming that is possible. Mechanical step sequencers include devices such as rotating drums. Other memory devices are pneumatic systems such as air logic controllers; electrical memories such as patch boards, and diode matrix boards, and step switches; and finally, electronic memories that include magnetic tape cassettes, floppy disks, and microprocessor-type devices (ROM, RAM, PROM). A combination of memory devices is often employed, such as tape cassettes in conjunction with a microprocessor. (2) In a computer it is the part that stores the program, holds intermediate results and various constant data. Same as storage. The memory consists of a series of bytes of information that have been assembled along two major themes: (i) the information as to how to use all the information that comes in and (ii) the new information that is to be used by the computer. The memory can be a disk, a tape, or some other device that can register and then return information.

memory address. Memory words are indicated by this address. The memory address specifies their location in memory. The memory address takes the form of a code number. In a program, memory addresses are referred to rather than the memory word itself. Accessing a memory word means obtaining its contents from memory by telling the computer the address of its location, which could be in one of several of the computer storage areas. The contents of the memory word are then taken electronically to the computer processing unit to be operated on. There are several kinds of memory location whose contents are another address. An indirect address specifies a memory location whose contents are another address. This is used in cases where an instruction contains many bits. A direct address specifies a memory location that contains the data to be operated on. An immediate address means that what would be an address in other addressing modes are the data and/or instructions to be operated on. (*See also* **direct address, immediate address,** and **indirect address.**)

memory dump. To copy the contents of all or part of a storage, usually from an internal storage into an external storage.

menu. A display of options on a terminal device for user selection.

merge. To combine items from two or more similarly sequenced files into one sequenced file without changing the order of the items.

merger sort. A sort program in which the items in a set are divided into subsets, the items in each subset are sorted, and the resulting sorted items are merged.

meta language. A language used to specify itself or another language.

metal-oxide semiconductor (MOS). A semiconductor used by manufacturing technology to produce integrated-circuit logic components.

MICR. Magnetic Ink Character Recognition. Machine recognition of characters printed with magnetic ink.

microcomputer. Microcomputers are systems based on the uses of microprocessors. They have limited flexibility but decided cost and operational advantages. Microcomputer memory is usually of two types. The first has a fixed content and is read only (ROM), which is used to store the microcomputer's operating program. The second type of memory has a variable content and is called read/write or random-access memory (RAM). It is generally used to store the variable data on which the microcomputer is to act. Random-access memory can also be used to store frequently changed programs.

microprocessor. A programmable large-scale-integrated-circuit chip containing all the elements required to process binary encoded data. A microprocessor can perform basic arithmetic and logical as well as control functions equivalent to the central processing unit of a conventional computer. The microprocessor differs from a conventional central processing unit by occupying only a single chip, or at most a few chips of silicon. Microprocessors have a wide range of actual and potential applications including control functions for automobiles, household appliances, and factory machinery. When a microprocessor is supplemented with power circuitry, input–output control interfaces, and memory, it becomes a fully operational microcomputer.

mnemonic. Assisting, or designed to assist, memory. A term used to describe the assignment of numbers and letters in a combination that is mnemonic or memory aiding to the eye or to the ear. Mnemonic symbols are used extensively for coding whenever it is deemed an advantage to be able to memorize code designations.

MODEM. A contraction of *MO*dulator–*DEM*odulator. Its function is to interface with data processing devices and convert data to a form compatible for sending and receiving on transmission facilities. (*See also* **modulator–demodulator**.)

modifier. A quantity used to alter the address of an operand.

modular. Made up of subunits that can be combined in various ways. In robots, a robot constructed from a number of interchangeable subunits, each of which can be one of a range of sizes or have one of several possible motion styles (prismatic, cylindrical, etc.) and number of axes. "Modular design" permits assembly of products or software or hardware from standardized components.

modulator–demodulator (MODEM). An electronic device that sends and receives digital data using telecommunication lines. To transmit data, the digital signals are used to vary (modulate) an electronic signal that is coupled into the telecommunication lines. To receive data, electronic signals are converted (demodulated) to digital data. (*See also* **MODEM**.)

modulo-n counter. A counter in which the number represented reverses to zero in the sequence of counting after reading a maximum value of $n-1$.

monadic operation. An operation with one and only one operand.

monitor. Software or hardware that observes, supervises, controls, or verifies the operations of a system.

Monte Carlo method. Method of obtaining an appropriate solution to a numerical problem by the use of random numbers, for example, the random walk method or a procedure using a random number sequence to calculate an integral.

multipass sort. A sort program that is designed to sort more items than can be in main storage at one time.

multiple-precision. Pertaining to the use of two or more computer words to represent a number in order to enhance precision.

multiplex. To interweave or simultaneously transmit two or more messages.

multiplexer. A hardware device that allows communication of multiple signals over a single channel by repetitively sampling each signal.

multiprocessing systems (MPS). A computer system employing two or more interconnected processing units to execute programs simultaneously.

multiprocessor. A computer that can execute one or more computer programs employing two or more processing units under integrated control of programs or devices.

multiprocessor control. Two or more control subtracks of the same overall control system accomplished simultaneously by more than one CPU.

multiprogramming. A technique whereby more than one program may reside in primary storage at the same time and be executed concurrently by means of an interweaving process.

MUM. Methodology for Unmanned Manufacturing. A Japanese program established to develop an unmanned factory by the mid-1980s. This will depend heavily on robots. The Japanese government has contributed $116 million and many private companies have donated funds and technical assistance. Planning includes a 250,000 ft^2 (232,250 m^2) factory that will produce 50 mechanical components such as gear boxes, motors, quills, etc.

Automatic technology will include forging, heat treat, welding press work, machining, inspection, assembly, and finishing as well as automated packaging and storage.

NAND. A logic operator having the property that if P is a statement, Q is a statement, R is a statement, . . ., then the NAND of P, Q, R, . . ., is true if at least one statement is false, false if all statements are true.

NAND element. A logic element that performs the Boolean operation of nonconjunction.

nanosecond. One-billionth (10^{-9}) of a second.

n-ary. Pertaining to a selection, choice, or condition that has n possible different values or states.

natural language. A language whose rules are based on current usage without being specifically prescribed.

natural number. One of the numbers, 0, 1, 2, ...

n-bit byte. A byte composed of n binary elements.

n-core-per-bit storage. A storage device in which each storage cell uses n magnetic cores per binary character.

negation. The monadic Boolean operation the result of which has the Boolean value opposite to that of the operand.

negative acknowledge character (NAK). A transmission control character transmitted by a station as a negative response to the station with which the connection has been set up.

neper. A unit of measuring power. The number of nepers is the base e logarithm of the ratio of the measured power levels.

nest. To incorporate a structure or structures of some kind into a structure of the same kind. For example, to nest one loop (the nested loop) within another loop (the nesting loop).

network analog. The expression and solution of mathematical relationships between variables using a circuit or circuits to represent these variables.

new-line character (NL). A formal effector that causes the print or display positions to move to the first position of the next line.

nines complement. The diminished radix complement in the decimal numeration system.

n-level address. An indirect address that specifies n levels.

node. In a data network, a point where one or more functional units interconnect data transmission lines.

noise. A spurious, unwanted, or disturbing signal. A signal having energy over a wide range of frequencies.

nonconjunction. The dyadic Boolean operation the result of which has the Boolean value 0 if and only if each operand has the Boolean value 1.

nondisjunction. The dyadic Boolean operation the result of which has the Boolean value 1 if and only if each operand has the Boolean value 0.

nonequivalence operation. The dyadic Boolean operation the result of which has the Boolean value 1 if and only if the operand has different Boolean values.

nonidentity operation. The Boolean operation the result of which has the Boolean value 1 if and only if all the operands do not have the same Boolean value. A nonidentity operation on two operands is a nonequivalence operation.

nonlinear programming. In operations research a procedure for locating the maximum or minimum of a function of variables that are subject to constraints, when the function or the constraints or both are nonlinear.

nonreturn-to-reference recording. The magnetic recording of binary digits such that the patterns of magnetization used to represent zeros and ones occupy the whole storage cell, with no part of the cell magnetized to the reference condition.

nontransparent. Pertaining to the mode of binary synchronous transmission in which all control characters are treated as control characters (that is, not treated as text).

no-operation instruction. An instruction whose execution causes a computer to do nothing other than to proceed to the next instruction to be executed.

NOR. A logic operator having the property that if P is a statement, Q is a statement, R is a statement, . . ., then the NOR of P, Q, R, . . ., is true if all statements are false, false if at least one statement is true. P NOR Q is often represented by a combination of OR and NOT symbols, such as $(P \vee Q)$. P NOR Q is also called neither P NOR Q.

NOT. A logic operator having the property that if P is a statement, then the NOT of P is true if P is false and false if P is true.

notation. A set of symbols, and the rules for their use, for the representation of data.

NOT element. A logic element that performs the Boolean operation of negation.

null. Empty. Having no memory. Not usable.

null character (NUL). A control character that is used to accomplish media-fill, or time-fill, and that may be inserted into or removed from a sequence of characters without affecting the meaning of the sequence; however, the control of equipment of the format may be affected by this character.

numerical analysis. The study of methods of obtaining useful quantitative solutions to problems that have been stated mathematically, and the study of the errors and bounds on errors in obtaining such solutions.

numerical control (NC). A technique that provides prerecorded information in a symbolic form representing the complete instructions for the operation of a machine.

numeric character set. A character set that contains digits and may contain control characters, special characters, and the space character, but not letters.

numeric code. A code according to which data are represented by a numeric character set.

numeric word. A word consisting of digits and possibly space characters and special characters.

object code. Output from a compiler or assembler that is itself executable machine code or is suitable for processing to produce executable machine code.

objective function. An equation defining a scalar quantity (to be minimized under given constraints by an optional controller) in terms of such performance variables as error, energy, and time. The objective function defines a tradeoff relationship between these cost variables.

object language. A language that is specified by a metalanguage. (*See also* **metalanguage**.)

object program. A program in machine language; generally, one that has been converted from a program written in symbolic language.

OCR. Optical Character Recognition. The machine recognition of printed characters.

octal. Pertaining to the number base of eight. In octal notation, octal 214 is 2 times 64 plus 1 times 8, plus 4 times 1, and equals decimal 140.

off-line. Pertaining to devices not under direct control of the central processing unit. Operation where the CPU operates independently of the time base of input data or peripheral equipment.

off-line storage. A storage device not under control of the central processing unit.

OMR. An abbreviation for optical mark recognition.

one-dimensional language. A language whose expressions are customarily represented as strings of characters, e.g., FORTRAN.

one-plus-one address instruction. An instruction that contains two address parts, the plus-one address being that of the instruction that is to be executed next unless otherwise specified.

ones complement. The diminished radix complement in the pure binary numeration system.

on-line. Pertaining to devices under direct control of the central processing unit. Operation where input data are fed directly from the measuring devices into the CPU, or where data from the CPU are transmitted directly to where it is used. Such operation is in real time.

on-line storage. A storage device under direct control of the central processing unit.

on-line system. A system in which the input data enter the computer directly from the point of origin or in which output data are transmitted directly to where they are used.

open code. In assembler program that portion of a source module that lies outside of and after any source macro definitions that may be specified.

open-loop control. Control achieved by driving control actuators with a sequence of preprogrammed signals without measuring actual system reponse and closing the feedback loop.

open subroutine. A subroutine of which a replica must be inserted at each place in a computer program at which the subroutine is used.

operand. (1) The part of a computer instruction that refers to data in storage. (2) That which is operated on.

operating system. Software that controls the execution of computer programs and that may provide scheduling, debugging, input–output control, accounting, computation, storage assignment, data management, and related services.

operating time. That part of available time during which the computer is operating and yielding correct results.

operation. A single defined action.

operational amplifier. A high-gain amplifier used as the basic element in analog computation.

operation table. A table that defines an operation by listing all permissible combinations of values of the operands and that indicates the result for each of these combinations.

operator. A symbol that represents the action to be performed in a mathematical operation.

optical character recognition (OCR). Machine recognition of printed characters through use of light-sensitive devices.

optical data recognition (ODR). The general term used to describe any form of optical recognition of data. Included in the ODR are optical mark readers, document readers, and page readers.

optical document reader. An optical reading device that scans or reads only a small portion of an input document and that is limited to a few type styles or fonts.

optical mark recognition (OMR). Machine recognition of marks on paper in the form of dots, checkmarks, or other recognizable symbols.

optical page reader. An optical reading device that can scan an entire page or document and that may have the capability of reading many type styles.

optical scanner. A device that optically scans printed or written data and generates its digital representations.

optimal control. A control scheme whereby the system response to a commanded input is optimal according to a specified objective function or criterion of performance, given the dynamics of the process to be controlled and the constraints on measuring.

optional pause instruction. An instruction that allows manual suspension of the execution of a computer program.

OR. A logic operator having the property that if P is a statement, Q is a statement, R is a statement, . . ., then the OR of P, Q, R, . . ., is true if at least one statement is true and false if all statements are false. P OR Q is often represented by $P + Q$, $P \vee Q$.

output contacts. Output contacts (switch contacts operated by the robot) provide a robot with some control over the application, such as, turning on or off motors, heaters, grippers, welding equipment, etc. Controlling output contacts becomes part of the robot routine. The robot is taught to close (or open) a contact at a particular point in the routine. Whenever that routine is replayed, that contact is closed (opened) at the same point at which it was taught. In addition to turning on or off individual output contacts, computer-controlled robots allow simultaneous operation of several contacts, pulsing of contacts, and "handshaking." The latter term means that after an output contact is turned on or off, the robot waits for a specific input signal to acknowledge that action before performing the rest of the routine. This is especially useful when controlling a tool.

outputs, analog. Not all processes can be controlled with contact closures. Some processes are of an analog nature and require a variable-type control. If the equipment is suitably adapted or manufactured to accept an external control voltage, then a computer-controlled robot with a programmable voltage source could be taught the appropriate settings, and they would become a part of the robot's routine. This greatly increases the versatility of the robot by eliminating the undesirable single or limited multiple set point compromise.

overflow. In an arithmetic operation, the generation of a quantity beyond the capacity of the register or location that is to receive the result.

overshoot. The degree to which a system response, such as change in reference input, goes beyond the desired value.

packed decimal. Representation of a decimal value by two adjacent digits in a byte. For example, in packed decimal, the decimal value 23 is represented by 0010 0011.

packed density. The number of storage cells per unit length, unit area, or unit volume; for example, the number of bits per inch stored on a magnetic tape track or magnetic drum track.

packet. A group of data and control bit sequences in a specified format, transferred as an entity determined by the process of transmission.

pad. To fill a block with dummy data, usually zeros or blanks.

page. In a virtual storage system, a fixed-length block that has a virtual address and that can be transferred between real storage and auxiliary storage.

paragraph. In COBOL a word followed by a period that identifies and precedes all paragraphs in the identification division and environment division.

parallel. (1) To handle simultaneously in separate facilities. (2) To operate on two or more parts of a word or item simultaneously.

parallel adder. A digital adder in which addition is performed concurrently on digits in all the digit places of the operand.

parallel communications. A digital communication method that transmits the bits of a message several at a time (usually 8 to 17 bits at a time); usually only used over distances of a few feet with electrical cables as the transmission medium.

parallel computer. A computer having multiple arithmetic or logic units that are used to accomplish parallel operations or parallel processing.

parallel processing. Concurrent or simultaneous execution of two or more operations, such as multiple arithmetic or logic units in devices.

parameter. A quantity to which arbitrary values may be assigned but which remain fixed for each program. In a program generator, parameters are used to specify certain machine hardware and data limits to be observed in the program being generated.

parameter word. A word that directly or indirectly provides or designates one or more parameters. (*See also* **word**.)

parity bit. A binary check digit inserted in an array of binary digits to make the arithmetic sum of all the digits including the check digit always odd or always even.

parity check. A check that tests whether the number of ones or zeros in an array of binary digits is even or odd. Such parity checks are widely used for paper tapes, magnetic tapes, and other computer memories.

part classification. A coding scheme, typically involving four or more digits, that specifies a discrete product as belonging to a part family.

part family. A set of discrete products that can be produced by the same sequence of machining operations. This term is primarily associated with group technology.

passive accommodation. Compliant behavior of a robot's end point in response to forces exerted on it. No sensors, controls, or actuators are involved. The remote center compliance provides this in a coordinate system acting at the tip of a gripped part. Use of the remote center compliance to achieve some of the capabilities of active accommodation.

passive mode. In computer graphics, a mode of operation of a display device that does not allow an on-line user to alter or interact with a display image.

patch. A section of coding inserted in a program in order to rectify an error in the original coding or to change the sequence of operation.

pattern recognition. Description or classification of pictures or other data structures into a set of classes or categories; a subset of the subject artificial intelligence.

pause instruction. An instruction that specifies the suspension of the execution of a computer program; a pause instruction is usually not an exit.

payload. The maximum weight or mass of a material that can be handled satisfactorily by a machine or process in normal and continuous operation.

perception. A robot's ability to sense by sight, touch, or some other means its environment and to understand it in terms of a task, for example, the ability to recognize an obstruction or find a designated object in an arbitrary location.

performance. The quality of behavior. The degree to which a specified result is achieved. A quantitative index of such behavior or achievement, such as speed, power, or accuracy.

peripheral equipment. Any unit of equipment, distinct from the central processing unit, that may provide the system with outside communication.

permutation. An ordered arrangement of a given number of different elements selected from a set.

phase modulation. Angle modulation in which the phase angle of a sinusoidal carrier is caused to vary from a reference carrier phase angle by an amount proportional to the instantaneous amplitude of the modulating signal.

photoresistor. A device for measuring light whose resistance changes as a function of incident light.

picosecond. One trillionth (10^{-12}) of a second. One thousandth of a nanosecond.

pinboard. A perforated board in which pins are manually inserted to control the operation of equipment.

pixel. A picture element. A small region of a scene within which variations of brightness are ignored. The pixel is assigned a brightness level that is the average of the actual image brightnesses within it. Pixels are usually arranged in a rectangular pattern across the scene, although some research has been done with hexagonal grids.

PL/1. Programming Language 1. Designed for solving problems that involve both science and business. It combines characteristics of FORTRAN and COBOL. It requires translation into machine code by a compiler program.

plasma panel. A part of a display device consisting of a grid of wires in a flat, gas-filled panel, where the energizing of a pair of intersecting wires causes the gas to be ionized and light to be emitted at that point.

playback accuracy. Difference between a position command recorded in an automatic control system and that actually produced at a later time when the recorded position is used to execute control. Difference between actual position response of an automatic control system during a programming or teaching run and that corresponding response in a subsequent run.

plotter. A graphic output device that draws digits, alphabetic characters, symbols, and lines on paper.

plugboard. A removable panel containing an array of terminals that can be interconnected by short electrical leads in prescribed patterns to control various machine operations. Synonymous with control panel.

point-to-point control. A control scheme whereby the inputs or commands specify only a limited number of points along a desired path of motion. The control system determines the intervening path segments.

polling. A technique by which each of the terminals sharing a communications line is periodically interrogated to determine whether it requires servicing. The multiplexer or control station sends a poll that, in effect, asks the terminal selected, "Do you have anything to transmit?"

polyphase sort. An unbalanced merge sort in which the distribution of sorted subsets is based on a Fibonacci series.

port. A functional unit of a mode through which data can enter or leave a data network.

position. In a string, each location that may be occupied by a character or binary element and that may be identified by a serial number.

position control. Control system in which the input (desired output) is the position of some body.

position error. In a servomechanism that operates a manipulator joint, the difference between the actual position of that joint and the commanded position.

positioning accuracy and repeatability. Accuracy is a measure of the robot's ability to move to a programmed position. Repeatability is its ability to do this time after time. With the pick-and-place robot, accuracy and repeatability are interchangeable. With a programmable robot, repeatability can be improved by fine tuning the controls.

postamble. A sequence of binary characters recorded at the end of each block on phase-encoded magnetic tape for the purpose of synchronization when reading backward.

potentiometer. An encoder based on tapping the voltage at various points along a continuous electrical resistive element.

power supply. The function of the power supply is to provide energy to the manipulator's actuators. In the case of electrically driven robots, the power supply functions basically to regulate the incoming electrical energy. Power for pneumatically actuated robots is usually supplied by a remote compressor, which may also service other equipment.

pragmatics. The relationship of characters or groups of characters to their interpretation and use.

preamble. A sequence of binary characters recorded at the beginning of each block on a phase-coded magnetic tape for the purpose of synchronization.

precision. The standard deviation or root-mean-squared deviation of values around their mean.

prefix notation. A method of forming mathematical expressions in which each operator precedes its operands and indicates the operation to be performed on the operands or the immediate results that follow it.

preset. To establish an initial condition, such as the control values of a loop, or the value to which a parameter is to be bound.

presumptive instruction. An instruction that is not an effective instruction until it has been modified in a prescribed manner.

problem-oriented language. A programming language that reflects the type of problem being solved rather than the computer on which the program is to be run.

procedure-oriented language. A problem-oriented language that facilitates the expression of a procedure as an explicit algorithm, for example, FORTRAN, ALGOL, PL/1.

processor. A machine language program that accepts a source program written in a symbolic form and translates it into an object program acceptable to the machine for which the source program was written. A processor frequently called a compiler or translator is a program usually supplied by the equipment manufacturer for creating machine language programs. A processor previously stored in the computer receives the source program written in symbolic language by the programmer and translates the instructions into machine language instructions that are acceptable to the computer. This machine language program is called an object program.

program. A set of instructions indicating to the computer the exact sequence of steps it must follow in processing a given set of data. Each instruction usually includes an operation code that specifies what is to be done, and one or more operands that designate the address or addresses of the data needed for the specified operations.

program diagnostics. The CRT may be used to display operator teaching errors or system errors. For example, an illegal entry of data will cause a corresponding error message to appear. System error messages reduce downtime by allowing quick isolation of operating problems that might occur. Stationary base line tracking is possible. The mathematical ability of the computer also allows many other features to be written into the software of the system without the necessity of changing the control hardware. Various software routines can be assembled to provide the user with a choice of features.

program editing. Through the use of a computer, a keyboard, and CRT, it is possible to implement easily a program editing feature. The CRT enables the operator to display the functional data stored at previously programmed points. The operator may delete or modify these data and restore them. He or she may also insert points between previously stored points by using the teach pendant.

program interrupt. The term applied to the automatic interrupting of regular program operation whenever an I/O unit becomes available. Processing is said to be asynchronous.

program loop. A series of instructions that may be executed repeatedly in accordance with the logic of the program.

programmable. Capable of being instructed to operate in a specified manner or of accepting set points or other commands from a remote source.

programmable logic controller (PLC). A stored program device intended to replace relay logic used in sequencing, timing, and counting of discrete events. Instead of physical wiring relay, pushbuttons, limit switches, etc., a PLC is programmed to test the state of input lines, to set output lines in accordance with input state, or to branch to another set of tests. The instruction sets of these machines generally exclude all arithmetic and Boolean operators, but do include vital decision instructions such as skip, transfer, unconditional, transfer conditional, and even transfer and link. (See illustration on p. 109.)

programmable read-only memory (PROM). A read-only memory that can be modified by special electronic procedures.

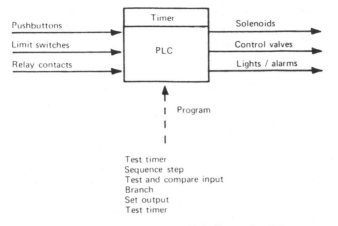

Descriptive schematic of programmable logic controller (PLC).

programming. In all industrial robots, it is necessary to program the robot to perform the required tasks. This can be accomplished in the following ways: (1) *Lead-Through.* The robot is placed in the "teach" mode of operation and points in space are recorded as the robot is lead through the desired sequence. (2) *Walk-Through.* The robot is placed in the "teach" mode of operation and manually walked through the desired sequence of movements and operations. The program is recorded and played back in the "operate" mode during actual operation. (3) *Plug-In.* A pre-recorded program is physically transferred into the robot control usually through the use of magnetic tape. (4) *Computer Programming.* These robots are programmed through the use of computer programs written especially for the computers being used to control the robot actions.

Programming Language 1 (PL/1). A procedure-oriented language that has some of the features of both FORTRAN and COBOL. (*See also* **PL/1.**)

program unit. Certain repetitive operations can be accomplished automatically by means of a device called the program unit, a simple and flexible device that permits programs for automatic card punching operations to be easily prepared and inserted. The program unit controls automatic skipping over columns not to be punched, automatic duplicating of repetitive information, and the shifting from numerical to alphabetic punching positions and vice versa.

PROM (*see* **programmable read-only memory**)

pronation. Orientation or motion toward a position with the back, or protected side, facing up or exposed.

proportional control. Control scheme whereby the signal that drives the actuator equals the difference between the input (desired output) and measured actual output.

proportional-integral-derivative control (PID). Control scheme whereby the signal that drives the actuator equals a weighted sum of the difference, time integral of the difference, and time derivative of the difference between the input (desired output) and the measured actual output.

protocol. The rules for controlling data communications between devices in computer systems.

proximal. Close to the base, away from the end effector of the arm.

proximity sensor. A device that senses that an object is only a short distance (e.g., a few inches or feet) away, and/or measures how far away it is. Proximity sensors work on the principles of triangulation of reflected light, lapsed time for reflected sound, and other principles.

pseudocode. A code that requires translation prior to execution.

pseudorandom number sequence. An ordered set of numbers that has been determined by some defined arithmetic process but is effectively a random number sequence for the purpose for which it is required.

punched card. A heavy stiff paper of uniform size and shape suitable for being punched with a pattern of holes to represent data for being handled mechanically. Standard cards measure 7⅜ in. (18.7 cm) by 3¼ in. (8.3 cm) and are divided into 80 vertical areas called card columns. These are numbered from 1 to 80, from the left side of the card to the right. Each column is then divided into 12 punching positions called rows, which are designated from the top to the bottom of the card. Each column of the card is used to accommodate a digit, a letter, or a special character. Digits are recorded by holes punched in the appropriate positions of the card from 0 to 9. The top three punching positions of the card (12, 11, and 10) are called the zone positions. In order to accommodate any of the 26 letters of the alphabet in one column, a combination of a zone and a digit punch is used. In accordance with the designated rows on a punched card, the top edge is known as the "12-edge" and the bottom edge is known as the "9-edge."

punched tape. A tape, usually paper, on which a pattern of holes or cuts is used to represent data. Since paper tape is a continuous recording medium, it can be used to record data in records of any length. Tapes using five, six, seven, and eight channels are available. The most popular types used are the five-channel and eight-channel codes. In the five-channel code, data are recorded (punched) in five parallel channels along the length of the tape. Each row of punches across the width of the tape represents one letter, digit, or symbol. Since the five punching positions allow only 32 possible combinations of punches, a shift system is used to double the number of available codes. In eight-channel code, data are recorded (punched) in eight parallel channels along with length of the tape.

pure binary numeration system. The fixed-radix numeration system that uses the binary digits and the radix 2; for example, in this numeration system, the numeral 110.01 represents the number "six and quarter," i.e., $1 \times 2^2 + 1 \times 2^1 + 1 \times 2^{-2}$.

pushdown list. A list that is constructed and maintained so that the next item to be retrieved and removed is the most recently stored item in the list, that is, last in–first out (LIFO).

pushup list. A list that is constructed and maintained so that the next item to be retrieved is the earliest stored item in the list, that is, first in–first out (FIFO).

quantization. The subdivision of the range of values of a variable into a finite number of nonoverlapping and not necessarily equal subranges or intervals, each of which is represented by an assigned value within the subrange.

quantized. To divide the range of a variable into a finite number of nonoverlapping intervals that are not necessarily equal, and to designate each interval by an assigned value within that interval.

quartet. A byte composed of four binary elements.

query. In data communication, the process by which a master station asks a slave station to identify itself and to give its status.

query language. A language for the terminal user, to retrieve and update data in a managed data base.

queuing. The mathematical technique that is applied to problems involving waiting lines or queues.

quintet. A byte composed of five binary elements.

quotient. The number or quantity that is the value of the dividend divided by the value of the divisor and that is one of the results of a division operation.

radix. The fundamental number in a number system, for example, 10 in the decimal system, 8 in the octal system, and 2 in the binary system. Synonymous with base. In a radix-numeration system, the positive integer by which the weight of the digit place is multiplied to obtain the weight of the next higher digit place — for example, in the decimal-numeration system, the radix of each digit place is 10; in a biquinary code, the radix of each position is 2.

radix complement. A complement obtained by subtracting each digit of the given number from the number that is one less than the radix of that digit place, then adding one to the least significant digit of the result and executing any carries required; for example, 830 is the tens complement, i.e., the radix complement of 170 in the decimal numeration system using three digits.

radix-numeration system. A positional representation system in which the ratio of the weight of any one digit place to the weight of the next lower digit place is a positive integer The permissible values of the character in any digit place range from zero to one less than the radix of that digit place.

radix point. In a representation of a number expressed in a radix numeration system, the location of the separation character associated with the fractional part.

RAM (*see*** random-access memory)**

random access. In COBOL an access mode in which specific logical records are obtained from a place in a mass storage file in a nonsequential manner.

random-access memory (RAM). An auxiliary memory device on which the programmer can directly access each separate data area without having to search through the whole data file. RAM has a larger memory space than ROM, commonly 4096 bits, often expressed as 4K bits. RAM is different from ROM because it can be changed; new data can be "written" in or stored. RAM can be static, where the contents of memory words will not disappear in computer operations, or dynamic, where the contents of memory words have to be constantly refreshed. RAM is used to store the macroprogram — the program designed by the computer programmer.

random-access storage. A storage device such as magnetic core, magnetic disk, and magnetic drum in which each record has a specific predetermined address that may be reached directly; access time in this type of storage is effectively independent of the location of the data.

random file. Data records stored in a file without regard to the sequences of the key or control field.

random number. A number selected from a known set of numbers in such a way that the probability of occurrence of each number in the set is predetermined.

raster. In computer graphics, a coordinate grid within a display space.

rate control. Control system in which the input is the desired velocity of the controlled object.

rated load capacity. A specified weight or mass of a material that can be handled by a machine or process that allows for some margin of safety relative to the point of expected failure.

rational number. A real number that is the quotient of an integer divided by an integer other than zero.

reach. Defines the robot's arm movement or work envelope. The work envelope usually has one of three shapes — cylindrical, spherical, and spheroidal — depending on the basic configuration of the arm and on the major axes of motion. For practical purposes, the description of the work envelope can be simplified by citing only its three major parameters: degrees of rotation about the center axis (horizontal arm sweep); vertical motion at both minimum and maximum arm extension; and radial arm extension, measured from the center axis.

read around ratio. The number of times a specific spot, digit, or location in electrostatic storage may be consulted before a spillover of electrons causes a loss of data stored in surrounding spots. The surrounding data must be restored before the deterioration results in any loss of data.

read-in. To sense information contained in some source and to transfer this information by means of an input device to internal storage.

read-only memory (ROM). The ROM often has a space of 1024 eight-bit data units. Once bits are stored in ROM they cannot be erased and will not disappear when the power running the computer is turned off. They are prefabricated circuitry and are acquired in a unit. Their configuration cannot be changed in computer operation. Generally ROM carries the basic instructions to control a robot.

read-only storage (ROS). Special circuitry in a computer that allows it to process commands written for some other type of computer. Some of the newer computers also use ROS as an integral part of their own command circuitry.

read-out. To transfer data from internal storage to an external storage device, or to display processed data by means of a printer, automatic typewriter, etc.

read/write head. A magnetic coil device that is capable of sensing or magnetizing a tiny spot on the surface of a magnetic storage device.

real constant. A string of decimal digits that must have either a decimal point or a decimal exponent, and may have both.

real number. A number that may be represented by a finite or infinite numeral in a fixed-radix numeration system.

real time. Pertaining to the processing of data by a computer in connection with another process outside the computer according to time requirements imposed by the outside process. The term "real time" is also used to describe systems operating in conversational mode and processes that can be influenced by human intervention while they are in progress.

recording density. The closeness with which data are stored on magnetic tape. The most common densities are 200, 556, 800, and 1600 characters per inch.

rectangular coordinate system. Same as Cartesian coordinate system, usually as applied to points in a plane (only two axes used). (*See also* **Cartesian coordinate system.**)

recursive. Pertaining to a process in which each step makes use of the results of earlier steps.

recursive function. A function whose values are natural numbers that are derived from natural numbers by substitution formulas in which the function is an operand.

redundancy. Duplication of information or devices in order to improve reliability.

reentrant program. A computer program that may be entered repeatedly and may be entered before prior executions of the same computer program have been completed, subject to the requirement that neither its external program parameters nor any instructions are modified during its execution. A reentrant program may be used by more than one computer program.

refreshable. The attribute of a load module that prevents it from being modified by itself or by any other module during execution. A refreshable load module can be replaced by a new copy during execution by a recovery management routine without changing either the sequence or results of processing.

regenerative track. Part of a track on a magnetic drum or magnetic disk used in conjunction with a read head and a write head that are connected to function as a circulating storage.

register. A device capable of temporarily storing a specified amount of data, usually one word, while or until it is used in an operation.

relation address. An address expressed as a difference with respect to a base address.

relation character. In COBOL a character that expresses a relationship between two operands.

relative coordinate system. A coordinate system whose origin moves relative to world or fixed coordinates.

relative data. In computer graphics, values in a computer program that specify displacements from the actual coordinates in a display space or image space.

relative error. The ratio of an absolute error to the true, specified, or theoretically correct value of the quantity that is in error.

relative order. In computer graphics, a display command in a computer program that causes the display device to interpret the data bytes following the order as relative data, rather than as absolute data.

reliability. The probability that a device will function without failure over a specified time period or amount of usage.

relocation factor. The algebraic difference between the assembled origin and the loaded origin of a computer program.

remote access. Pertaining to communication with a data processing facility by one or more stations that are at a distant point from that facility.

remote axis admittance (RAA). A device that performs the fine motions of parts mating. It can be mounted on the end of a robot arm and will perform the final phases of assembly when the parts are in close proximity and when they are in contact. The RAA can be adapted to a number of different types of tasks, including the simple insertion, such as the chamfered peg and hole, the insertion of edges in slots, the multiple insertion, and the chamferless insertion. The RAA has optional built-in sensing and actuation, depending on the task, and uses a microcomputer type of controller to monitor and switch its different modes of operation. The RAA also has built-in safety features and inherent internal damping. The RAA operated by projecting virtual axes of rotation to locations at or near the assembly interfaces. These axes permit the contact forces and torques induced by the mating parts to produce motions of rotation, translation, and tilting in directions to perform the assembly. In cases where straight-line motion is required, the corresponding axis is projected to a large distance (infinity). The motions of the various axes are sensed and are used to operate mechanical mode switching according to instructions from an optical microcomputer. In the case of more complex types of assembly tasks, it is also possible to power the axes to produce programmed motions. The RAA is also arranged to yield under overload conditions, preventing damage to the assembler and the parts. The RAA can be used together with many different types of robot arms to perform parts fetching and assembly.

remote batch processor. A terminal device located some distance from the central computer, used to process data by batches of records.

remote center compliance (RCC). A compliant device used to interface a robot or other mechanical workhead to its tool or working medium. The RCC allows a gripped part to rotate about its tip or to translate without rotating when pushed laterally at its tip. The RCC thus provides general lateral and rotational float and greatly eases robot or other mechanical assembly in the presence of errors in parts, jigs, pallets, and robots. It is especially useful in performing very close clearance or interference insertions.

remote job entry (RJE). Submission of a job through an input unit that has access to a computer through a data link.

repeatability. Closeness of agreement of repeated position movement, under the same conditions, to the same location.

repetitive addressing. A method of implied addressing, applicable only to zero-address instructions, in which the operation part of an instruction implicitly addresses the operands of the last instruction executed.

replica master. A teleoperator control mechanism that is kinematically equivalent to the slave manipulator or other device that is being controlled (i.e., the master has the same kind of joints in the same relative positions as does the slave). As a human operator moves the master by hand, the control system forces the slave to follow the master's motions. A replica master may be larger than, smaller than, or the same size as the slave device it controls. The control system may reflect back to the joints of the master any forces and torques that are applied to corresponding joints of the slave (bilateral force feedback) to allow the operator to "feel" objects remotely through the slave. The replica master (and the slave) may or may not have a geometry similar to that of a human arm.

report generator. A programming system for producing a complete report given only a description of the desired content and format of the output reports and certain information about the input file and hardware available.

reserved word. A word of a source language whose meaning is fixed by the particular rules of that language and cannot be altered for the convenience of any one computer program expressed in the source language; computer programs expressed in the source language may also be prohibited from using such words in other contexts in the computer program.

residue check. A validation check in which an operand is divided by a number to generate a remainder that is then used for checking.

resolution. (1) The least interval between two adjacent discrete details that can be distinguished from one another. (2) The smallest increment of distance that can be read and acted upon by an automatic control system.

resolved motion rate control. A control scheme whereby the velocity vector of the end point of a manipulator arm is commanded and the computer determines the joint angular velocities to achieve the desired result. Coordination of a robot's axes so that the velocity vector of the end joint is under direct control. Motion in the coordinate system of the end point along specified directions or trajectories (line, circle, etc.) is possible. Used in manual control of manipulators and as a computational method for achieving programmed coordinate axis control in robots.

resolver. A rotary or linear feedback device that converts mechanical motion to analog electric signals that represent motion or position.

return-to-reference recording. The magnetic recording of binary characters in which the patterns of magnetization used to represent zeros and ones occupy only part of the storage cell, the remainder of the cell being magnetized to a reference condition.

robot. A mechanical device that can be programmed to perform some task of manipulation or locomotion under automatic control.

rod memory. A thin-film memory in which the metallic film is deposited on short metallic rods. The rods are then strung into planes and stacked according to the coding structure of the system.

ROM (*see* **read-only memory**)

root segment. That segment of an overlay program that remains in main storage at all times during the execution of the overlay program; the first segment in an overlay program.

ROS (*see* **read-only storage**)

routing. In production, the sequence of operations to be performed in order to produce a part or an assembly. In telecommunications, the assignment of the communications path by which a message can reach its destination.

row binary. A method of encoding binary numbers on a card where each bit in sequence is represented by the presence or absence of punches in successive positions in a row as opposed to a series of columns. Row binary is especially convenient for 40 or fewer bit words, since it can be used to store 12 binary words on each half of an 80-column card.

RS-232-C, RS-422, RS-423, RS-449. Standard electrical interfaces for connecting peripheral devices to computers. EIA Standard RS-449, together with EIA Standards RS-422 and RS-423, are intended to gradually replace the widely used EIA Standard RS-232-C as the specification for the interface between data terminal equipment (DTE) and data circuit-terminating equipment (DCE) employing serial binary data interchange. Designed to be compatible with equipment using RS-232-C, RS-449 takes advantage of recent advances in integrated-circuit design, reduces crosstalk between interchange circuits, permits greater distance between equipment, and permits higher data signaling rates (up to 2 million bits per second). RS-449 specifies functional and mechanical aspects of the interface, such as the use of two connectors having 37 pins and 9 pins instead of a single 25-pin connector. RS-422 specifies the electrical aspects for wideband communication over balanced lines at data rates up to 10 million bits per second. RS-423 does the same for unbalanced lines at data rates up to 100,000 bits per second.

run-length encoding. A data-compression technique for reducing the amount of information in a digitized binary image. It removes the redundancy that arises from the fact that such images contain large regions of adjacent pixels that are either all white or all black (i.e., black–white transitions are relatively infrequent). The brightness information is replaced by a sequence of small integers that tell how many consecutive black and white pixels are encountered while traversing each scan line. For gray–white imagery, some compression can be achieved by considering the first *n* high-order bits of the brightness information to represent *n* different binary images and then transforming each into run-length format (the low-order bits will vary so much that there will be little redundancy to remove).

saturation. A range within which the output is constant regardless of input.

scale. To change the representation of a quantity, expressing it in other units, so that its range is brought within a specified language.

scaling. In assembler programming, indicating the number of digit positions in object code to be occupied by the fractional portion of a fixed-point or floating-point constant.

scanner. A device that examines a spatial pattern one part after another, and generates analog or digital signals corresponding to the pattern. Scanners are often used in mark sensing, pattern recognition, or character recognition.

scroll. (1) A graphic display technique whereby the generation of a new line of alphanumeric text at the bottom of a display screen automatically regenerates all other lines of text one line higher than before and deletes the top line. (2) In computer graphics, the continuous vertical or horizontal movement of the display elements within a window in a manner such that new data appear at one edge of the window as old data disappear at the opposite edge. The window may include the entire display surface.

search function. A robot system can adjust the position of data points within an existing

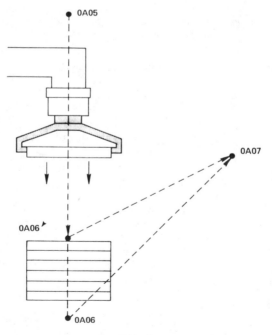

Search function.

cycle based on changes in external equipment and workpieces. The search function depicted is one example of this type of robot decision making. Three points, 0A05, 0A06, 0A07, have been taught to the industrial robot. In a "normal" cycle the center of the robot end effector (hand) would move in a straight-line path at a defined velocity from 0A05 to 0A06 with controlled acceleration and deceleration at the ends of the segment. After stopping and performing the programmed function at 0A06, the robot would similarly move to point 0A07. In the example, however, a search function has been programmed at 0A05. The robot end effector would accelerate from 0A05 and proceed to the normal cycle above, but in this case the robot control monitors an input signal that causes the robot to decelerate and stop when it is activated. This new stop point (called 0A06' in the figure) is treated as the "new" 0A06 point and the robot end effector moves from 0A06' to 0A07 during the next part of the program cycle. One use of the search function is in stacking operations, especially when the stacked items are fragile or have irregular thicknesses. The time delay inherent in deceleration from the input signal activation will permit some movement beyond the robot's receipt of the signal; so, if the signal originates through a limit switch that is closed upon contact with the stack, some compliancy must be built into the robot gripper. A fragile workpiece would also require a slow velocity during the search segment.

second-generation computer. A computer utilizing solid-state components.

section. (1) In COBOL, a logically related sequence of one or more paragraphs. A section must always be named. (2) In computer graphics, to construct and to position a bounded or unbounded intersecting plane with respect to one or more displayed objects and then generate and display the intersection on a display.

sector. That part of a track or band on a magnetic drum, a magnetic disk, or a disk pack that can be accessed by the magnetic heads in the course of a predetermined rotational displacement of the particular device.

segmentation. Partitioning of a scene into subregions; in "windowing," for example, the portion of the scene outside a rectangular subregion is ignored to speed up image processing.

sensor. A transducer or other device whose input is a physical phenomenon and whose output is a quantitative measure of that physical phenomenon.

sensors, contact. Contact sensing of force, torque, and touch can be usefully combined with visual sensing for many material-handling and assembly tasks. The function of contact sensors in controlling manipulation can be classified into the following basic material-handling and assembly operations: *searching* — detecting a part by sensitive touch sensors on the hand exterior without moving the part; *recognition* — determining the identity, position, and orientation of a part, again without moving it, by sensitive touch sensors with high spatial resolution; *grasping* — acquiring the part by deformable, roundish fingers, with sensors mounted on their surfaces; *moving* — placing, joining, or inserting a part with the aid of sensors.

sensors, electrooptical imaging. Until recently, electrooptical imaging sensors have provided the most commonly used "eyes" for industrial robots and visual inspection. Standard television cameras, using vidicons, plumbicons, and silicon target vidicons, have interfaced with a computer and have provided the least expensive and most easily available imaging sensors. These cameras scan a scene, measure the reflected light intensities at a raster of approximately 320×240 pixels (picture elements), convert these intensity values to analog electrical signals, and feed this stream of information serially into a computer, all within $\frac{1}{60}$th of a second. These signals may either be stored in the computer core memory for subsequent processing or be processed in real time "on the fly" with consequent reduction of memory requirements. Recently, solid-state area array cameras have become commercially available. These small, rugged, and potentially reliable cameras are fabricated using modern large-scale-integration silicon technology and may become the dominant electrooptical sensors for industrial applications. The photoactive chip of an area-array camera consists of photodiodes, usually charged-coupled devices, whose number at present varies from 32 X 32 to 320 X 512 for different requirements of resolution. These cameras operate in a raster-scan mode, similar to that of the vidicon television cameras, and produce two-dimensional images of scenes. A one-dimensional solid-state camera, using a linear array that varies from 16 to 1872 elements, is also available commercially. This device can perform a single linear scan and is very useful for sensing objects that are in relative motion to the camera, such as workpiece moving on a conveyor belt. Another large class of electrooptical sensors, which differ in several important characteristics from the above-mentioned cameras, has been used primarily in advanced "hand–eye" artificial intelligence research projects. These sensors include the image dissector camera, the cathode ray flying spot scanner, and the laser scanner. These electrooptical sensors can be programmed to image selected areas of the field of view in a random-access manner, as contrasted with the prescribed "raster-scan" acquisition of the ordinary television camera. In many instances this method of operation permits the acquisition, storage, and processing of only the relevant data in a field of view. The image dissector has low sensitivity requiring high levels of illumination and is relatively expensive.

sensors, force and torque. The force and torque acting on each point of a manipulator can be sensed directly. If the joint is driven by an electric dc motor, then sensing is done by measuring the armature current; if the joint is driven by a hydraulic motor, then sensing is done by measuring the back pressure. Sensing joint forces directly has the advantage of not requiring a separate force sensor. However, the force (or torque) between the hand and its environment is not measured directly. Thus the accuracy and resolution of this measurement are adversely affected by the variability in the inertia of the arm and its load and by the nonuniform friction of the individual joints.

sensors, photoelectric proximity (noncontact). A version of the photoelectric tube and light source, these sensors appear to be well adapted for controlling the motion of a manipulator. They consist of a solid-state light-emitting diode (LED), which acts as a transmitter of infrared light, and a solid-state photodiode, which acts as a receiver. Both are

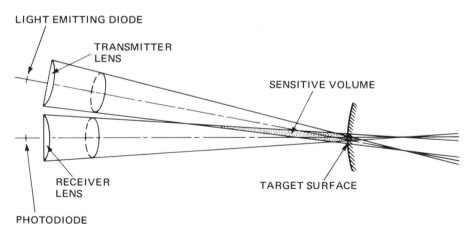

Proximity sensor.

mounted in a small package. The accompanying figure indicates that the sensitive volume is approximately the intersection of two cones in front of the sensor. This sensor is not a rangefinder because the received light is not only inversely proportional to the distance squared but is also propositional to the target reflectance and the cosine of the incidence angle, both of which may vary spatially. However, if the reflectance and incidence angle are fixed, then the distance may be inferred with suitable calibration. Usually, a binary signal is generated when the received light exceeds a threshold value that corresponds to a predetermined distance. Furthermore, the sensor will detect the appearance of a moving object in a scene by sensing the change in the received light. Such devices are sensitive to objects located from a fraction of an inch to several feet in front of the sensor.

sensors, proximity (noncontact). A device that senses and indicates the presence or absence of an object without requiring physical contact. Five of six major types of proximity sensors available commercially are radio-frequency, magnetic bridge, ultrasonic, permanent-magnet hybrid, and photoelectric. Noncontact sensors have widespread use, such as for high-speed counting, indication of motion, sensing presence of ferrous materials, level control, reading of coding marks, and noncontact limit switches.

sensors, range-imaging. Measures the distance from itself to a raster of points in the scene. Although range sensors are used for navigation by some animals (e.g., the bat), hardly any work has been done so far to apply range image to control the path of a manipulator. Difference range-imaging sensors have been applied to scene analysis in various research laboratories. These sensors may be classified into two types, one based on the trigonometry of triangulation and the other based on the time of flight of light (or sound). Triangulation range sensors are further classified into two schemes, one based on a stereo pair of television cameras (or one camera in two locations) and the other based on projecting a sheet of light by a scanning transmitter and recording the image of the reflected light by a television camera. Alternatively, the second scheme may transmit a light beam and record

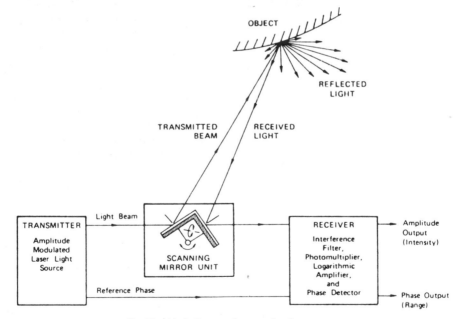

Simplified block diagram of a range imaging sensor.

the direction of the reflected light by a rocking receiver. The first scheme suffers from the difficult problem of finding corresponding points in the two images of the scene. Both schemes have two main drawbacks: missing data for points seen by the transmitter but not by the receiver and vice versa, and poor accuracy for points that are far away. These drawbacks are eliminated by the second type of range-imaging sensor using a laser scanner, which is also classified into two schemes, one based on transmitting a laser pulse and measuring the arrival time of the reflected signal and the other based on transmitting amplitude-modulated laser beams and measuring the phase shift of the reflected signal. The transmitted beam and the received light are essentially coaxial. Range-imaging sensors have been applied so far primarily to object recognition. They are also very suitable for other tasks, such as finding a factory floor or a road, detecting obstacles and pits, and inspecting the completeness of subassemblies.

sensors, touch. Touch sensors are used to obtain information associated with the contact between the finger(s) of a manipulator hand and objects in the workspace. They are normally much lighter than the hand and are sensitive to forces much smaller than those sensed by the wrist and contact sensors. Touch sensors may be mounted on the outer and inner surfaces of each finger. The outer sensor may be used to search for an object and possibly to determine its identity, position, and orientation. Outer sensors may also be used for sensing unexpected obstacles and stopping the manipulator before any damage can occur. The inner-mounted sensors may be used to obtain information about an object before it is acquired and about grasping forces and workpiece slippage during acquisition. Touch sensors may be classified into two types, binary and analog. A binary touch sensor is a contact device, such as a switch. Being binary, its output is easily incorporated into a computer controlling the manipulator. A simple binary touch sensor consists of two microswitches, one on the inner side of each finger. An analog touch sensor is a compliant device whose output is proportional to a local force. Analog touch sensors are usually mounted on the inner surface of the fingers to measure gripping force and to extract information about the object between the fingers.

sensors, wrist force. A wrist force sensor measures the three components of force and three components of torque between the hand and the terminal link of the manipulator. Basically, a wrist force sensor consists of a structure with some compliant sections and transducers that measure the compliant sections along three orthogonal axes as a result of the applied force and torque. There are different types of force transducers, such as strain gage, piezoelectric, magnetostrictive, magnetic, and others. One sensor, with seven-bit resolution, was built at Stanford Institute for the Stanford arm. This sensor is made of milled 3-in.-diameter (7.6-cm-diameter) aluminum tube, having eight narrow elastic beams with no hysteresis. The neck at the end of each beam transmits a small bending torque and thus increases the strain at the other end of the beam where two foil strain gages are cemented. The two strain gages are connected to a potentiometer circuit whose output is proportional to a force component normal to the strain-gage plane, and is automatically compensated for variation in temperature. The wrist sensor measures the three components of force and three components of torque in a Cartesian coordinate system (x, y, z) attached to the manipulator hand.

sensory control. Control of robot based on sensor readings. Several types can be employed: sensors used in threshold tests to terminate robot activity or to branch to another activity; sensors used in a continuous way to guide or direct changes in robot motions (*see also* **active accommodation**); sensors used to monitor robot progress and to check for task completion or unsafe conditions; and sensors used to retrospectively update robot motion plans prior to the next cycle.

sensory hierarchy. A relationship of sensory processing elements whereby the results of lower-level elements are utilized as inputs by higher-level elements.

sequence checking. Checking items in a file to ensure that they are all in ascending (or descending) order.

sequencing. Ordering in a series or according to rank or time.

sequential. Pertaining to the occurrence of events in time sequence, with no simultaneity or overlap of events.

sequential-access memory. An auxiliary memory device, which lacks any addressable data areas. A specific piece of data can only be found by means of a sequential search through the file.

sequential batch processing. A mode of operating a computer in which a run must be completed before another run can be started.

sequential control. A mode of computer operation in which instructions are executed in an implicitly defined sequence until a different sequence is explicitly initiated by a jump instruction.

serial. The handling of data in a sequential fashion such as to transfer or store data in a digit-by-digit time sequence or to process a sequence of instructions one at a time.

serial arithmetic operations. A method by which the computer handles arithmetic fields one digit at a time, usually from right to left.

serial communications. A digital communication method that transmits the bits of a message one at a time; the most common long-distance transmission method; suitable for use with cable, radio, or modulated light as the transmission medium.

serial operation. The flow of information through a computer in time sequence, using one digit, word, line, or channel at a time as opposed to parallel operation.

servomechanism. An automatic control mechanism consisting of a motor driven by a signal that is a function of the difference between commanded position and/or rate and measured actual position and/or rate.

servomotor, valve. These are controlled by feedback systems so that when the ultimate position is reached the valve or motor stops operating.

servovalve. A transducer whose input is a low-energy signal and whose output is a higher-energy fluid flow that is proportional to the low-energy signal.

sexadecimal. Pertaining to a selection, choice, or condition that has sixteen possible different values or states.

shaft encoder. An encoder used to measure shaft position.

shannon. In informational theory, a unit of logarithmic measure of information equal to the decision content of a set of two mutually exclusive events expressed by the logarithm to base 2, for example, the decision content of a character set of eight characters equals three shannons.

shared control. A facility that allows multiple concurrent interactions with a particular unit of data in a data base.

short-term repeatability. Closeness of agreement of position movements, repeated under the same conditions during a short time interval, to the same location.

sign bit. A bit or binary element that occupies a sign position and indicates the algebraic sign of the number represented by the numeral with which it is associated.

sign character. A character that occupies a sign position and indicates the algebraic sign of the number represented by the numeral with which it is associated.

significant digit. In a numeral, a digit that is needed for a given purpose; in particular, a digit that must be kept to preserve a given accuracy or a given precision.

significant digit arithmetic. A method of making calculations using a modified form of a floating-point representation system in which the number of significant digits in the result is determined with reference to the number of significant digits in the operands, the operation performed, and the degree of precision available.

silicon-controlled rectifier (SCR). An electronic device that is generally used in control systems for high-power loads such as electronic heating elements.

simulator. A computer program that represents certain features of the behavior of another program or system.

simultaneous computer. A computer that contains a separate unit to perform each portion of the entire computation concurrently, the units being interconnected in a way determined by the computation.

skeletal code. A set of instructions in which some parts, such as addresses, must be completed to the reference edge of a data medium.

slew rate. The maximum velocity at which a manipulator joint can move; a rate imposed by saturation somewhere in the servo loop controlling that joint (e.g., by a value's reaching its maximum open setting). The maximum speed at which the tool tip can move in an inertial Cartesian frame.

smart sensor. A sensing device whose output signal is contingent upon mathematical or logical operations and inputs other than from the sensor itself.

SNOBOL. A list-processing language used with large computers. A list-processing language helps to process data in terms of lists, for example, by recognizing patterns in a large group of data. Other list-processing languages are LSP, used for processing symbolic lists, and SLIP.

software. The programs and routines used to extend the capabilities of computers, such as compilers, assemblers, routines, and subroutines. Also, all documents associated with a computer, for example, manuals and circuit diagrams. All the instructions, programs, computer languages, and operations that happen between the user and the hardware.

solenoid. A cylindrical coil of wire surrounding a movable core, which, when energized, sets up a magnetic field and draws in the core.

solid-state camera. A TV camera that uses some type of solid-state integrated circuit instead of a vacuum tube to change a light image into a video signal. Solid-state cameras have the following advantages over vacuum-tube cameras: ruggedness; small size; no high voltages; insensitivity to image burn and lag (antibloom capability is possible with the proper readout technique); potentially very low cost, characteristic of solid-state technology; and a spatially stable, precise geometry that effectively superimposes a fixed, repeatable measurement grid over the object under observation without the pin-cushion or barrel distortion introduced by the deflection systems of tube cameras.

source document. The original paper on which are recorded the details of a transaction.

source language. A language from which statements are translated.

source program. In a language, a program that is an input to a given translation process.

space character (SP). A graphic character that is usually represented by a blank site in a series of graphics. The space character, though not a control character, has a function equivalent to that of a format effector that causes the print or display position to move one position forward without producing the printing or display of any graphics. Similarly, the space character may have a function equivalent to that of an information reporter.

spherical coordinate system. A coordinate system, two of whose dimensions are angles, the third being a linear distance from the point of origin. These three coordinates specify a point on a sphere.

stable state. In a trigger circuit, a state in which the circuit remains until the application of a suitable pulse.

staging. The moving of data from an off-line or low-priority device back to an on-line or higher-priority device, usually on demand of the system or on request of the user.

standard binary-coded-decimal interchange code. A computer code used by most second-generation computers, which is an expansion of the binary-coded-decimal system. The significant difference in the standard BCD code is the use of zone bits. The zone bits of an alphanumeric character perform a code function similar to the zone positions of a punched card. They are used in combination with digits to represent the letters of the alphabet or special characters.

standing-on-nines carry. In the parallel addition of numbers represented by decimal numerals, a procedure in which a carry to a given digit place is bypassed to the next digit place. If the current sum in the given digit place is nine, the nine is changed to zero.

start-of-message code (SOM). A character or group of characters transmitted by the polled terminal and indicating to the stations on the line that what follows are addresses of stations to receive the answering message.

statement. In a programming language, a meaningful expression that may describe or specify operations and is usually complete in the context of that programming language.

static accuracy. Deviation from time value when relevant variables are not changing with time. Difference between actual position response and position desired or commanded of an automatic control system as determined in the steady state, that is, when all transient responses have died out.

station control. A module in the ICAM control hierarchy that controls a work station. The station control module is controlled by a cell control module.

steady state. General term referring to a value that is not changing in time. Response of a dynamic system due to its characteristic behavior, that is, after any transient response has stopped; the steady-state response is either a constant or a periodic signal.

stepping motor. An electric motor whose windings are arranged in such a way that the armature can be made to step in discrete rotational increments (typically $\frac{1}{200}$th of a revolution) when a digital pulse is applied to an accompanying "driver" circuit. The armature displacement will stay locked in this angular position independent of applied torque, up to a limit.

storage tube. A CRT display device that retains a graphic image if no new signals are imposed.

stored program computer. A computer that has the ability to store, to refer to, and to modify instructions to direct its step-by-step operations.

straight-line coding. A set of instructions in which there are no loops.

strain gage. A sensor that, when cemented to elastic materials, measures very small amounts of stretch by the change in the material's electrical resistance. When used on materials with high modulus of elasticity, strain gages become force sensors.

strain-gage rosette. Multiple strain gages cemented in two- or three-dimensional geometric patterns such that independent measurements of the strain on each can be combined to yield a vector measurement of strain or force.

stratified language. A language that cannot be used as its own metalanguage, for example, FORTRAN. (*See also* **metalanguage**.)

string. A set of records in ascending or descending sequence according to a key contained in the records.

stroke edge. In character recognition, the line of discontinuity between a side of a stroke and the background, obtained by averaging, over the length of the stroke, the irregularities resulting from the printing and detecting process.

structure light. Illumination designed so that the three-dimensional pattern of light energy in the viewing volumes causes visible patterns to appear on the surface of objects being viewed, from which patterns that are the shape of the objects can easily be determined.

structured programming. A technique for organizing and coding programs that reduces complexity, improves clarity, and makes them easier to delay and modify. Typically, a structured program is a hierarchy of modules that each have a single entry point and a single exit point; control is passed downward through the structure without unconditional branches to higher levels of the structure.

subroutine. A subset of a routine, usually a short sequence of instructions designed to solve a specified part of a problem. Originally, these basic routines recorded in a computer input medium were included in the source program at the proper place and assembled along with the rest of the program. The subroutines had to be inserted at each point that they were needed in a routine. As a result they were included in the main operational sequence of the object program. These are known as open routines. A closed routine is one that requires programming only once, since it may be entered several times during a program.

summary records. Summary records are prepared as a result of totals accumulated by a punched card accounting machine. The totals are automatically punched into unit records by the summary punch machine. Summary records can subsequently be used to prepare other reports which do not require the detail that provided the basis for the totals.

supervisory control. A control scheme whereby a person or computer monitors and intermittently reprograms, sets subgoals, or adjusts control parameters of a lower-level automatic controller, while the lower-level controller performs the control task continuously in real time.

supervisory program. A computer program, usually part of an operating system, that controls the execution of other computer programs and regulates the flow of words in a data processing system.

swap. In systems with time sharing, to write the main storage image of a job to auxiliary storage and read the image of another job into main storage.

switch. A point in a programming routine at which two courses of action are possible, the correct one being determined by conditions specified by the programmer; a branch point.

switch control. Control of a machine by a person through movement of a switch to one or two or a small number of positions. The device used for such control.

switch core. A core in which the magnetic material generally has a high residual flux density and a high ratio of residual to saturated flux density with a threshold value of magnetizing force below which switching does not occur.

symbolic address. An address expressed in symbols that are convenient to the programmer.

symbolic control. Pertaining to control by communication of discrete alphanumeric or pictorial symbols that are not physically isomorphic with the variables being controlled, usually by a human operator. A device for effecting such control. (Compare to **analogic control.**)

symbolic language. A programming language that expresses addresses and operation codes of instructions in symbols convenient to humans rather than in machine language.

symbolic program. A program written in a language that makes use of mnemonic codes and in which names, characteristics of instructions, or other symbols convenient to the programmer are used instead of the numeric codes of the machine.

synchro. A shaft encoder based on differential inductive coupling between an energized rotor coil and field coils positioned at different shaft angles.

synchronous computer. A computer in which each event or the performiong of any basic operation is constrained to start on signals from a clock and usually to keep in step with them.

syntax. The relationship among characters or groups of characters, independent of their meanings or the manner of their interpretation and use.

tachometer. A rotational velocity sensor.

tactile sensor. A sensor that makes physical contact with an object in order to sense it, includes touch sensors, tactile arrays, force sensors, and torque sensors. Tactile sensors are usually constructed from microswitches, strain gages, or pressure-sensitive conductive elastomers.

tag. One or more characters attached to a set of data that contains information about the set, including its identification.

tape row. That portion of tape on a line perpendicular to the reference edge on which all binary characters may be either recorded or sensed simultaneously.

target language. A language into which statements are translated.

target program. A computer program in a target language that has been translated from a source language.

TCP (*see* **tool center point**)

teach. To guide a manipulator arm through a series of points or in a motion pattern as a basis for subsequent automatic action by the manipulator.

teaching interface. The physical configuration of the machine or the devices by which a human operator teaches a machine.

template matching. Pixel-by-pixel comparison of an image of a sample object with the image of a reference object, usually for purposes of identification, but also applicable to inspection.

tens complement. The radix complement in the decimal numeration system.

tera (T). Ten to the twelfth power (10^{12}), 1,000,000,000 in decimal notation. When referring to storage capacity, two to the fortieth power (2^{40}), 1,099,511,627,776 in decimal notation.

term. The smallest part of an expression that can be assigned a value.

ternary. (1) Pertaining to a selection, choice, or condition that has three possible different values or states. (2) Pertaining to a fixed-radix numeration system having a radix of 3.

ternary incremental representation. Incremental representation in which the value of an increment is rounded to one of three values, plus or minus one quantum or zero.

thin-film memory. A main memory device that uses a thin film of metal as its storage medium. Information is stored by magnetizing the thin-film material.

three-plus-one address instruction. An instruction that contains three address parts, the plus-one address being that of the instruction that is to be executed next, unless otherwise specified.

threshold. A logic operator having the property that if P is a statement, Q is a statement, R is a statement, . . ., then the threshold of $P, Q, R, \ldots$, is true if at least n statements are true, false if less than n are true, where n is a specified nonnegative integer called the threshold condition.

threshold function. A two-valued switching function of one or more not necessarily Boolean arguments that take the value of one if a specified mathematical function of the arguments exceeds a given threshold value, and zero otherwise.

thresholding. The process of quantizing pixel brightness to a small number of different levels (usually two levels, resulting in a binary image). A threshold is a level of brightness at which the quantized image brightness changes.

time constant. Any of a number of parameters of a dynamic function that have units of time. Parameters that particularly characterize the temporal properties of a dynamic function, such as the period of a periodic function or the inverse of the initial slope of a first-order exponential response to a step.

tool center point (TCP). The user of a robot is primarily concerned with the position of a given point on an end effector, such as the center of a pair of gripper jaws or the tip of an arc welding gun. Basically, the robot arm is a means of moving the TCP from one programmed point to another in space. The control philosophy of the robot is built up around TCP concept. The control directs the movement of the TCP in terms of direction speed and acceleration along a defined path between consecutive points. This method of control, termed a controlled-path system, utilizes the mathematical ability of a computer to give the operator coordinated control of the predefined TCP in a familiar coordinate system during the teaching operation. It also controls the TCP in terms of position, velocity, and acceleration between programmed points in the replay or automatic modes of operation. The TCP is predefined by the operator who enters a tool length into the control. This represents the distance between the end of the robot arm and the TCP. In the controlled-path system the coordinates of the TCP are stored as $x, y,$ and z coordinates in space and not as robot axis coordinates. During the automatic mode of operation the position of the TCP and the orientation of the end effector relative to the TCP are known at all times by the control system.

top-down programming. The design and coding of computer programs using a hierarchical structure in which related functions are performed at each level of the structure.

total-systems concept. The complete integration of all major operating systems within a business organization into the one functional organized system operating under the discipline of a data processing facility.

trace program. A computer program that performs a check on another computer program by exhibiting the sequence in which the instructions are executed and usually the result of executing the instruction.

tracking. Continuous position control response to a continuously changing input.

tracking, abort branches. A special software routine called "Abort Branch" is included in the controls for stationary base line tracking robots. This function constantly monitors the position of the tracking window. If, at any time during automatic operation, the robot's TCP coordinate in the tracking direction coincides with the coordinate of either limit of the tracking window, the robot control immediately initiates an abort branch. The abort branch will direct the robot to exit from the part along a pretaught safe path relative to the part. The abort branch is taught by the operator during the teaching operation and, depending on the configuration of the part on which the robot is working, can contain a number of smaller branch programs. This will ensure that the TCP of the robot will always follow a safe path and a quick exit path from its operating position on the part, regardless of its position in the taught program.

tracking, utility branch. Occasionally, during the execution of a tracking application, it will be necessary for the robot to take some form of corrective action in response to a signal that indicates the occurrence of some malfunction of the peripheral equipment. Such action may be taken with the computer-controlled robot by using a function called "utility branch." A utility branch is taught in a similar manner to abort branch, and if necessary, it can also contain a number of smaller branches. The utility branch is, however, initiated by an external signal from the peripheral equipment rather than by an internal signal from the control. As an example, if, during a spot welding sequence, the gun tip sticks to a flange, immediate correcting action is required. Upon receipt of the signal indicating the "stuck tip" condition, the control will immediately initiate the utility branch to take corrective action regardless of where the robot is in its sequence of operations. In this case the action taken may be, for example, a twisting motion to break the tip of the gun away from the flange.

tracking window. The diagram illustrates the robot's large tracking range, when used in

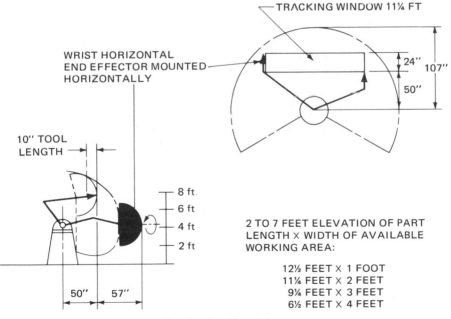

Examples of tracking windows.

tracking applications in which the y axis of the robot is set parallel to the moving line. As the diagram indicates, there are many parameters that influence the length of working range of the robot in the direction parallel to the moving line. This working range of the robot parallel to the line is termed the "tracking window." The height of the part on the conveyor, the distance of the robot from the conveyor, and the length and configuration of the end effector all play a part in determining the tracking window. Therefore, every tracking application must be considered separately in order that the robot is positioned correctly, relative to the conveyor, to ensure the optimum tracking window. Once the tracking window for a given operation sequence has been established, it is entered into the memory of the control. The tracking window basically defines in memory the two limits in the tracking direction beyond which the robot will not attempt to reach. More than one tracking window may be defined for different segments of a tracking operation. These tracking window limits cause two separate types of action by the control: (1) If the robot has just replayed a point, its control will check the position of the next point in the sequence. (2) If the next point in a sequence is outside the tracking window, but away from it, the robot will move with the line until such time that the position of the TCP coincides with the tracking window limit.

trailing zero. In positional notation, a zero in a less significant digit place than the digit place of the least significant nonzero digit of a numeral.

transaction file. A file containing transient data to be processed in combination with a master file.

transducer. A device that converts one form of energy into another form of energy.

transient. General term referring to a value that changes in time. Response of a dynamic system to a transient input such as a step or a pulse.

transistor–transistor logic (TTL). A common electronic logic configuration used in integrated circuits characterized by high speed and noise immunity.

triple length register. Three registers that function as a single register.

triple precision. Pertaining to the use of three computer words to represent a number in accordance with the required precision.

triplet. A byte composed of three binary elements.

truncate. To terminate a computational process in accordance with some rule, for example, to end the evaluation of a power series at a specified term.

truth table. An operation table for a logic operation. A table that describes a logic function by listing all possible combinations of input values and indicating for each combination the true output values.

two-out-of-five code. A binary-coded decimal notation in which each decimal digit is represented by a binary numeral consisting of five bits of which two are of one kind, conventionally ones, and three are of the other kind, conventionally zeros. The usual weights are 0-1-2-3-6 except for the representation of zero, which is then 01100.

two-plus-one address instruction. An instruction that contains three address parts, the plus-one address being that of the instruction that is to be executed next unless otherwise specified.

undershoot. The degree to which a system response to a step change, in reference to input, falls short of the desired value.

uniprocessing. Sequential execution of instructions by a processing unit or independent use of a processing unit in a multiprocessing system.

unpacked decimal. Representation of a decimal value by a single digit in one byte. For example, in unpacked decimal, the decimal value 23 is represented by xxxx 0010 xxxx 0011, where xxxx in each case represents a zone.

unstable state. In a trigger circuit, a state in which the circuit remains for a finite period of time at the end of which it returns to a stable state without the application of a pulse.

unstratified language. A language that can be used as its own metalanguage, for example, most natural language. (*See also* **metalanguage**.)

unwind. To state explicitly and in full, without the use of modifiers, all the instructions that are involved in the execution of a loop.

urnary operator. An arithmetic operator having only one term. The urnary operators that can be used in absolute, relocatable, and arithmetic expressions are positive (+) and negative (−).

utility program. Standard programs prepared and generally used to assist in the operation of data processing systems.

VAL. A proprietary robot-oriented language developed by Unimation Inc.

variable. (1) In computer programming, a character or group of characters that refers to a value and, in the execution of a program, corresponds to an address. (2) A quantity that can assume any of a given set of values.

variable-point representation. A positional representation in which the position of the radix point is explicitly indicated by a special character at that position.

Veitch diagram. A means of representing Boolean functions in which the number of variables determines the number of possible states, that is, two raised to a power determined by the number of variables.

vertical tabulation character (VT). A format effector that causes the print or display position to move to the corresponding position in the next of a series of predetermined lines.

V format. A data set format in which logical records are of varying length and includes a length indicator, and in which V-format logical records may be blocked, with each block containing a block length indicator.

virtual address. The address of a notational storage location in virtual storage.

virtual image. In computer graphics, the complete visual representation of an encoded image that would be displayed if a display surface of sufficient size were available.

virtual storage. A concept by which primary storage capacity is increased beyond that available in the computer by storing segments of programs and data on auxiliary devices. The program segments and data are brought into primary storage under control of the virtual operating system as they are needed for execution by the computer.

virtual storage access method (VSAM). An access method for direct or sequential processing of fixed and variable length records on direct access devices. The records in a VSAM data set or file can be organized in logical sequence by a key field (key sequence), in the physical sequence in which they are written on the data set or file (entry sequence) or by relative record number.

virtual storage management. Routines that allocate address spaces and virtual storage areas within address spaces and that keep a record of free and allocated storage within each address space.

virtual telecommunications access method (VTAM). A set of programs that control communications between terminals and application programs under DOS/VS, OS/VSI, and OS/VS2.

virtual unit address. In a mass storage system (MSS) an address for a virtual drive. The virtual unit address can be assigned to any staging drive group. Each staging drive can have more than one virtual unit address, but only one real address.

V-mode records. In COBOL, records of variable length, each of which is wholly contained within a block. Blocks may contain more than one record. Each record contains a record length field, and each block contains a block length field.

weight. In a positional representation, the factor by which the value represented by a character in the digit place is multiplied to obtain its additive contribution in the representation of a real number.

word. (1) A character string or a binary element string that is convenient for some purposes to consider as an entity. (2) A character string or a bit string considered as an entity.

word time. In a storage device that provides serial access to storage locations, the time interval between the appearance of corresponding parts of successive words.

working envelope (*see* **envelope**)

working range. Same as **working envelope**. The range of any variable within which a system normally operates.

working space or volume. The physical space bounded by a robotics system in operation.

work-in-process. Products in various stages of completion throughout the production cycle, including raw material that has been released for initial processing and finished products awaiting final inspection and acceptance for shipment to a customer.

work station. An ICAM manufacturing unit consisting of one or more numerically controlled machine tools serviced by a robot.

world coordinates. The coordinate system referenced to the earth or the shop floor.

wraparound. The continuation of an operation from the maximum addressable location in storage to the first addressable location. The continuation of register addresses from the highest register address to the lowest.

wrist. The manipulator arm joint to which a hand or end effector is attached.

wrist movement. Although wrist movement can make a minor contribution to the shape and size of the work envelope, its main significance is the ability to orient the gripper or any other end-of-arm tooling. Pitch refers to wrist movement in the vertical plane; yaw represents movement in the horizontal plane (swing); and the ability to rotate is denoted by roll.

yaw. An angular displacement left or right viewed from along the principal axis of a body having a top side, especially along its line of motion.

zero-address instruction. An instruction that contains no address part, and is used when the address is implicit or when no address is required.

zero suppression. The elimination from a numeral of zeros that have no significance in the numeral. Zeros that have no significance include those to the left of the nonzero digits in the integral part of a numeral and those to the right of the nonzero digits in the fractional part.

Section 4

Robotics Manufacturers
and
Typical Specifications

Most industrial plants in the future will use some robotic applications, but since there are certain advantages and limitations in industrial applications today, there are considerations that should be given before deciding on such an investment.

The first step is to become familiar with the basic capabilities and limitations of the equipment available. As stated previously, today's robots range from simple pick-and-place devices to multiaxis, computer-controlled machines, with handling capbilities from a few ounces to half a ton or more, and operating in fixed-stop, point-to-point, or continuous-path modes.

First, determine what kinds of operations are to be performed with robots and then concentrate your search on the machines that have capabilities to do those jobs. There is a great deal of specification information available from manufacturers (such as that in this chapter), which can serve as the primary source of data. In order to make the analysis easier, develop a matrix so that a direct comparison of such features as load capacity, control system, speed, price, options, and so forth can be made among suitable robots. More than 300 different models are available with total system prices ranging from $1500 to $250,000 each, depending on the options chosen.

Some Key Robot Manufacturers

Acco Industries Inc.
Babcock International
101 Oakview Drive
Trumbull, CT 06611

Acrobe Positioning Systems Inc.
3219 Doolittle Drive
Northbrook, Il 60062

Admiral Equipment Co.
305 W. North St.
Akron, OH 44303

Advanced Robotics Corp.
Newark Industrial Park
Building 8
Route 79
Hebron, OH 43025

Air Technical Industries
7501 Clover Ave.
Mentor, OH 44060

American Robot Corp.
354 Hookstown Rd.
Clinton, PA 15026

ASEA, Inc.
4 New King St.
White Plains, NY 10604

Automated Assemblies Corp.
Subsidiary of Nypro Inc.
Clinton, MA

Automation Corp.
Marathon Industries
23996 Freeway Pk. Dr.
Farmington Hills, MI 48024

Automatix, Inc.
1000 Technology Park Drive
Billerica, MA 01821

Bendix Corp.
Robotics Div.
21238 Bridge St.
Southfield, MI 48034

Binks Mfg. Co.
9201 W. Belmont Ave.
Franklin Park, IL 60131

Bra-Con Industries, Inc.
12001 Globe Rd.
Livonia, MI 48150

Cincinnati Milacron, Inc.
Industrial Robot Div.
215 S. West St.
Lebanon, OH 45036

Cognex Corp.
Boston, MA

Colortronic Robots Systems
Dayton, OH

Comet Welding Systems
900 Nicholas Blvd.
Elk Grove Village, IL 60007

Conair Inc.
Franklin, PA

Control Automation, Inc.
P.O. Box 2304
Princeton, NJ 08540

Copperweld Robotics
1401 East 14 Mile Rd.
Troy, MI 48084

Cybotech, Inc.
Div. of Ransburg Corp.
P.O. Box 88514
Indianapolis, IN 46208

Cyclomatic Industries Inc.
Robotics Div.
7520 Convoy Ct.
San Diego, CA 92111

DeVilbiss Co.
Div. of Champion Spark Plug Co.
300 Phillips Ave.
P.O. Box 913
Toledo, OH 43692

ESAB/Heath
P.O. Box 2286
Ft. Collins, CO 80522

Expert Automation, Inc.
40675 Mound Rd.
Sterling Heights, MI 48078

Gallaher Enterprises
2110 Cloverdale Ave., Suite 2B
Winston-Salem, NC 27103

GCA Corp.
PaR Systems
3460 Lexington Ave. No.
St. Paul, MN 55112

General Electric Co.
Automation Systems Operation
1285 Boston Ave.
Bridgeport, CT 06602

General Numeric Corp.
390 Kent Ave.
Elk Grove Village, IL 60007

Graco Robotics Inc.
Graco Inc.
12898 Westmore Ave.
Livonia, MI 48150

Hall Automation
c/o FARED Robot Systems, Inc.
3860 Revere St., Suite D
Denver, CO 80239

Hirata Corp. of America
8900 Keystone Crossing
Indianapolis, IN 46240

Hitachi America Ltd.
6 Pearl Ct.
Allendale, NJ 07401

Hobart Brothers Co.
600 W. Main St.
Troy, OH 45373

Hodges Robotics Int'l. Corp.
3710 N. Grand River Ave.
Lansing, MI 48906

International Business Machines Corp.
Advanced Manufacturing Systems
1000 N.W. 51st St.
Boca Raton, FL 33432

Int'l. Robomation/Intelligence
6353 El Camino Real
Carlsbad, CA 92008

C. Itoh & Co. America Inc.
21415 Civic Center Dr.
Suite 111
Southfield, MI 48076

The Lone Co.
Palo Alto, CA

Lloyd Tool & Manufacturing Corp.
2475 E. Judd Rd.
Burton, MI 48529

Lynch Machinery
Anderson, IN

Machine Intelligence Corp.
330 Potrero Ave.
Sunnyvale, CA 94086

Manca Inc.
Leitz Bldg.
Link Drive
Rockleigh, NJ 07647

Martin Industries Div.
Westover Air Park
Chicopee, MA 01022

Mentor Products, Inc.
7763 Mentor Ave.
Mentor, OH 44060

Microbot Inc.
453-H Ravendale Dr.
Mountain View, CA 94043

Midway Machine & Engineering Co.
2324 University Ave.
St. Paul, MN 55114

Mobot Corp.
2755 Kurtz St.
Suite 11
San Diego, CA 92110

Moog, Inc.
Industrial Div.
East Aurora, NY 14052

Nordson Corp.
Robotics Div.
555 Jackson St.
P.O. Box 151
Amherst, OH 44001

Pentel of America
1100 Arthur Ave.
Elk Grove Village, IL 60007

PickOmatic Systems, Inc.
Div. of Fraser Automation
37950 Commerce Drive
Sterling Heights, MI 48077

Planet Corp.
Robot Div.
27888 Orchard Lake Rd.
Farmington Hills, MI 48018

Prab Robots Inc.
5944 E. Kilgore Rd.
Kalamazoo, MI 49003

R2000 Corp.
804 Broadway
West Long Branch, NJ 07764

Reis Machines
1426 Davis Rd.
Elgin, IL 60120

Rob-Con Ltd.
12001 Globe Rd.
Livonia, MI 48150

Robot Systems, Inc.
Corporate Div.
50 Technology Parkway
Technology Park Atlanta
Norcross, GA 30092

Robotics, Inc.
RD 3, Rte 9
Ballston Spa, NY 12020

Sandhu Machine Design, Inc.
308 S. State St.
Champaign, IL 61820

Seiko Instruments USA Inc.
2990 W. Lomita Blvd.
Torrance, CA 90506

Scovill Manufacturing Co.
Schrader Bellows Div.
200 W. Exchange St.
Akron, OH 44309

Snow Mfg./Origa Corp.
928 Oaklawn
Elmhurst, IL 60126

Sterlong Detroit Co.
261 E. Goldengate Ave.
Detroit, MI 48203

Textron, Inc.
Bridgeport Machines Div.
500 Lindley St.
Bridgeport, CT 06606

Thermwood Corp.
P.O. Box 436
Dale, IN 47523

Tokico America, Inc.
3555 Lomita Blvd.
Suite E
Torrance CA 90505

Unimation, Inc.
Shelter Rock Lane
Danbury, CT 06810

United States Robots, Inc.
1000 Conshohocken Rd.
Conshohocken, PA 19428

United Technologies Corp.
Steelweld Robotics Div.
5200 Auto Club Drive
Dearborn, MI 48126

Westinghouse Electric Corp.
Industry Automation Div.
400 Media Drive
Pittsburgh, PA 15205

Yaskawa Corp. of America
305 Era Drive
Northbrook, IL 60062

Vision Systems

ASEA Inc.
White Plains, NY

Automated Vision Systems
Campbell, CA

Automatix, Inc.
Burlington, MA
   Robovision I
   Autovision II

Control Automation, Inc.
Princeton, NJ
   CA-V1000 Sembler

Copperweld Robotics
Troy, MI
   OPTO-SENSE

Diffracto Ltd.
Windsor, Ontario, Canada

General Electric Co.
Optoelectronic Systems Operation
Syracuse, NY
   Optomation II

Machine Intelligence Corp.
Sunnyvale, CA
   VS-100

Object Recognition Systems, Inc.
Princeton, NJ

Octek, Inc.
Burlington, MA

Perception, Inc.
Farmington Hills, MI

Robotic Vision Systems, Inc.
Melville, NY

Selecom, Inc.
Valdese, NC
   Optocator

Robot Manufacturing Companies

Acrobe Positioning Systems, Inc. (Acrobe AG-4).

Since the majority of assembled parts weigh less than 1 pound (0.45 kg), the AG-4 robot was specifically designed to handle this weight with both speed and accuracy. The base of the unit can easily fit on most equipment to be automated or can be "carried" by two people to where it is needed. The unit has a resolution of less than 0.001 in. (0.0254 mm) at maximum reach using direct all-electric drive.

The microcomputer used in the AG-4 controller is the 16-bit LSI-11/2 made by Digital Equipment Corporation to provide for the flexibility of the AG-4. This advanced computer allows for the addition of such senses as vision, touch, heat detection, voice command, and voice response. With the built-in sophistication it is possible to tap into any mainframe computer to allow control from a central location. This feature would enable large-scale plants to be controlled completely by a central planning computer. If production calls for batch runs of different parts, no resetting of robots would be necessary. A simple signal generated to the robots at the proper time would alter operations instantly.

The electronics are designed in a modular fashion, which permits an unlimited flexibility for future needs. An example of this would be image-sensing capabilities, which at this point could be achieved with the insertion of a single board.

The AG-4 automatically reinitializes itself after all power failures, and informs the operator of all momentary power outages. The AG-4 industrial robot is programmed manually by stepping it through the desired control sequence and instructing the controller to remember the current position and all the accompanying ancillary control functions, such as gripper control, delays, and interlocks. This sequence is repeated until the entire path to be traversed by the AG-4 has been described.

Once the programming is complete, the AG-4 robot can be instructed to "play back" the program. Typically, the AG-4 is cyclic in operation. The input and output interlocks facilitate synchronization of the robot with cooperating machines or processes. The palletizing feature of the controller allows the robot to increment the position of a particular point in space each time that point is traversed by the robot. The palletizing feature is available at each program step and is available for all axes (Cartesian).

In the event the sequence of operations performed by the robot needs to be corrected or modified, the program-editing functions provided by the AG-4 allow the operator to modify the program as needed. In addition, the program can be loaded into the controller from any external computer or device through the industry standard RS-232C serial port at the rate of 1920 bytes per second.

The path traversed by the AG-4 robot can be made arbitrarily precise by describing a greater number of points along the trajectory. Because of this precision, the AG-4 can easily function in environments where potential obstacles exist in the field of operation. As more points are described along the desired path, the AG-4 controller can adjust its operating speed to maintain the desired level of precision.

Acrobe AG-4 Robot

Base Rotation	280° max.
Horizontal Reach	32 in. (81 cm)
Vertical Reach	24 in. (61 cm)
Wrist Pitch	210° max.
Wrist Roll	360° max.
Number of Axes	Five standard, 10 possible
Repeatability	Under 0.001 in. (0.0254 mm)
Carrying Capacity	2 lb. (0.9 kg) avg.
Control	Micro
Floor Space	24 in. (61 cm) wide × 34 in. (86 cm) long × 15 in. (38 cm) high
Weight	120 lb (54 kg)
Program Capacity	500 points or more
Drive	All electric
Power Requirements	115 V, 60 Hz, 20 A
Speed	45°/s

Advanced Robotics Corp. (Cyro 750).

This is a five-axis robot, with horizontal travel, reach up and down, reach forward and back, torch rotation, and torch tilt. The wrist has a 120° torch rotation and 140° torch tilt. The process is integrated into the Cyro controls and mechanics. The robot can be equipped for Mig, Tig, fluxcore, subarc, or plasma welding. Special processes, including powdered plasma for wear surfacing applications, are available. Cyro is preprogrammed for auto radial welding, burnback, and oscillation. Programmable control of the weld process enables the unit to weld rapidly or slow down in critical areas to ensure weld quality. Limited manual overrides for changes in gas moisture and wire surface characteristics are security protected. The controls allow the robot to control the welding current and voltage, wire speed, weld speed, and oscillation width and speed for infinite versatility within the process. The workpiece can be manipulated continuously during the welding process. One-axis positioning robots rotate the part for continuous welding or for sequence welding to

Cyro 750 Robot Specifications

Motions
5 axes—powered by electric Servo Motors
Travel:
    X axis—80 in. (2032 mm.) expandable
    Y axis—30 in. (762 mm.)
    Z axis—30 in. (762 mm.)
    A axis—130°
    C axis—720°

Repeatability
Repeatable to ±0.008 in. (±0.20 mm.)

Maximum Speed
X, Y axis—600 in./min. (15240 mm./min.)
Z axis   —400 in./min. (10160 mm./min.)
A, C axis—90°/sec.

Floor Space
Robot Base: 27.5 sq. ft. (2.47 sq. m.)
Control Cabinet: 10 sq. ft. (0.9 sq. m.)

Power Requirements
480 Volts, 3 phase, 60 Hz, 10 KVA

Environments
40°F to 120°F (5°C to 50°C)

Weight
Robot —5740 lbs. (2613 kg.)
Control—1400 lbs. (636 kg.)

Programming Methods
Teaching with a pendant
Numerical programming via terminal

Programmable Features
Linear interpolation
Circular interpolation (3 types)
Acceleration/deceleration
Analog function (2 outputs)
Dwell
Inch/Metric units
Absolute/Incremental dimension
Program shift
Programmable tooling point
Oscillation
Program editor
8 I/O expandable to 32 I/O

Memory Capacity
64K Bytes
Permanent program storage on
  tape cassette

Options
Coordinated Positioning Robots
X axis expansion
Welding process packages including
  computer programmable weld
  parameters, voltage, wire speed,
  dwell, burnback
ArcScan™ welding seam tracker

Specifications subject to change without notice

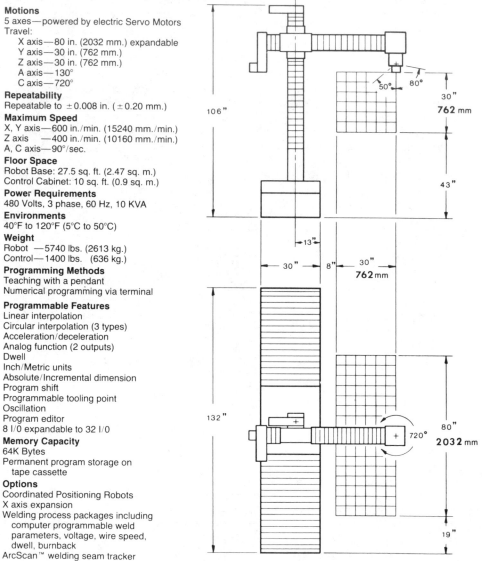

control distortion. They also enable the workpiece to be indexed for welding on all sides, reducing handling time and increasing arc time. Two-axis positioning robots provide coordinates of rotation and tilt, enabling the robot to reach the weld joint while positioning the workpiece for optimum control of the weld puddle.

The all-electric, rectilinear Cyro 750 is designed to handle a variety of jobs. The control system can be programmed to accommodate part changes. Multiple robot coordination enable dissimilar functions at multiple work stations. While performing its task at one station, parts can be loaded/unloaded at the next. Advanced control techniques offer a variety of programming features.

Advanced Robotics Corp. (Cyro 820).

This unit uses the same control techniques used by the Cyro 750 and Cyro 2000 robots. The Cyro control provides linear interpolation, increasing the memory capacity and reducing programming time. Process parameters are commanded from the robot and stored in the robot control for easy access and editing. Program storage is provided for up to eight immediate programs in memory or on cassette. The unit is particularly suited for intricate maneuvering in and around small workpieces. It can be equipped for arc welding processes, and process packages for inspection and assembly are to be introduced.

Cyro 820 Robot Specifications

Motions

Five axes — powered by electric
  servomotors
Movement
  Vertical motion   35 in. (890 mm)
  Horizontal motion   32 in. (820 mm)
  Horizontal sweep   240°
  Wrist/rotate   380°
      bend   200°

Repeatability

Repeatable to ± 0.012 in. (± 0.3 mm)

Maximum Speed

Vertical motion   39 in./sec (1 m/sec)
Horizontal motion   31 in./sec (0.78 m/sec)
Horizontal sweep   90°/sec
Wrist/rotate   150°/sec
      bend   100°/sec

Floor Space

Robot base: 20 in. × 28 in. (500 mm ×
    700 mm)
Control cabinet: 28 in. × 28 in. (700 mm
    × 700 mm)

Power Requirements

480 V, 30, 60 Hz, 3 kVA

Environment

32°F to 113°F (0°C to 45°C)

Weight

Robot   660 lb (300 kg)
Control   440 lb (200 kg)

Programming Methods

Teaching with a pendant

Programmable Features

Continuous-path or point-to-point
    operation (selectable)
Linear interpolation (five axes)
Cartesian coordinates
I/O — 15 inputs, 14 outputs
Program selector for eight programs
Digital/analog outputs 0-100/0-15 V
    (two provided)
Oscillation functions (three types)
Manual speed override ± 5%
Jump function
Call function
Automatic zero set
Programmable tooling point
Timer function
Diagnostics

Memory Capacity

1000 points

Permanent program storage on tape
cassette

Options

Welding process packages
Cassette recorder

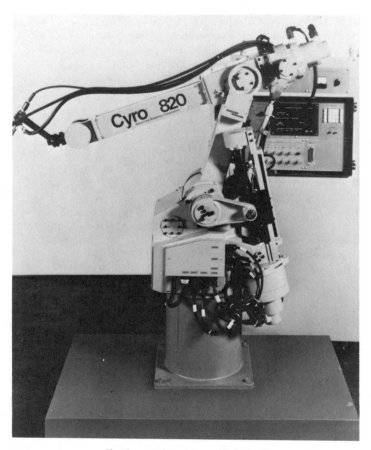

The Cyro 820 from Advanced Robotics Corp.

Advanced Robotics Corp. (Cyro 2000).

This is a rectilinear robot with a 6.6 ft × 6.6 ft × 6.6 ft (2 m × 2 m × 2 m) reach. Additional expansion of the horizontal axis enables the Cyro 2000 to handle even longer parts or to accommodate multiple work stations. The control of this robot enables on-site programming with a portable hand-held pendant, remote editing, and other techniques.

Cyro 2000 Robot Specifications

Motions
5 axes—powered by electric Servo Motors
Travel:
   X axis—80 in. (2032 mm.) expandable
   Y axis—80 in. (2032 mm.)
   Z axis—80 in. (2032 mm.)
   A axis—130°
   C axis—720°

Repeatability
Repeatable to ± 0.016 in. (± 0.40 mm.)

Maximum Speed
X, Y axis—300 in./min. (7620 mm./min.)
Z   axis—150 in./min. (3810 mm./min.)
A, C axis—90°/sec.

Floor Space
Robot Base: 54 sq. ft. (4.86 sq. m.)
Control Cabinet: 13 sq. ft. (1.17 sq. m.)

Power Requirements
480 Volts, 3 phase, 60 Hz, 15 KVA

Environments
40°F to 120°F (5°C to 50°C)

Weight
Robot —12000 lbs. (5454 kg.)
Control— 1800 lbs. (818 kg.)

Programming Methods
Teaching with a pendant
Numerical programming via terminal

Programmable Features
Linear interpolation
Circular interpolation (3 types)
Acceleration/deceleration
Analog function (2 outputs)
Dwell
Inch/Metric units
Absolute/Incremental dimension
Program shift
Programmable tooling point
Oscillation
Program editor
8 I/0 expandable to 32 I/0

Memory Capacity
64K Bytes
Permanent program storage on
tape cassette

Options
Coordinated Positioning Robots
X axis expansion
Welding process packages including
   computer programmable weld
   parameters, voltage, wire speed,
   dwell, burnback
ArcScan™ welding seam tracker

Specifications subject to change without notice

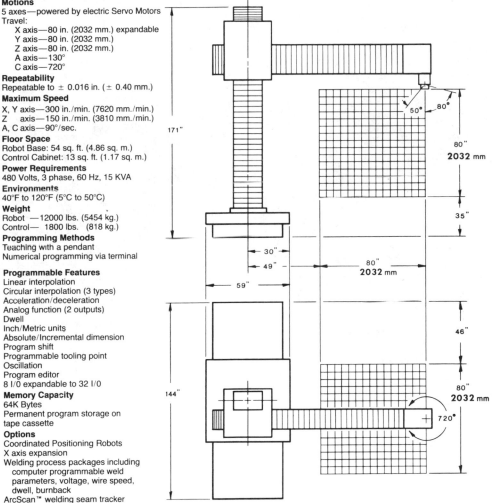

American Robot Corporation (MERLIN Robot).

This robot arm has excellent capabilities — repeatability of ±0.001 in. (0.0254 mm) and loads of 20 to 50 pounds (9 or 22.5 kg) (depending on the model) at speeds greater than 5 fps. This robot is well suited for a large range of applications: high-precision assembly, material handling, welding testing, inspection, and parts fabrication and processing. The robot arm is modular and configurable from three to six axes (upward compatible).

The robot controller integrates 32-bit computer hardware with powerful software, which includes AR-BASIC, a proprietary robotic version of the most popular, conversational easy-to-use programming language. The hand-held robot teach pendant incorporates a joystick and a keyboard with conversational software. At Level 2, a Cluster Controller is a marriage of a 32-bit computer system with a multitasking operating system and software for color graphics, robot simulation, data base management, and production reports. Hardware and software diagnostics are used at all levels.

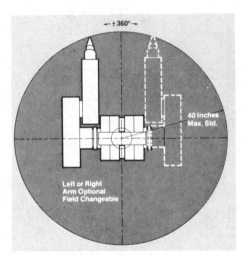

Elevation view of work envelope   Plan view of work envelope.

Robot Arm Specifications

Configurations
Modular, 3 axes to 6 axes, 20 pound or 50 pound maximum payload

Repeatability
±0.001" (±0.025 mm)

Maximum payload
20 pounds/50 pounds (9 kg/22 kg), depending on model selected

Straight-line Velocity
5 feet/second (1.5 m/sec)

Waist Rotation (Axis 1)
720° (±360°)

Shoulder Rotation (Axis 2)
720° (±360°)

Elbow Rotation (Axis 3)
300°

Wrist Rotation or Yaw (Axis 4)
Bidirectionally continuous

Wrist Bend or Pitch (Axis 5)
180°

Hand Rotation or Roll (Axis 6)
Bidirectionally continuous
Gripper Force
0-40 pounds variable

Environmental Range
50°-120° F (10°-50°C), 10%-80% RH
Work Envelope
See Diagrams

Robot Controller Specifications

Computer Hardware
Processor
32-bit (Motorola 68000)
Memory
128KB/256KB
Mass Storage
512KB Floppy Disk
Stepper Motor Control
Up to 6 axes
Interface Ports Available
3 × RS232 (serial), 1 × RS422 (serial), 2 × 16 bit parallel
External Inputs & Outputs
8 Binary Inputs/Outputs, 8 Analog Inputs, 2 Analog Outputs
Network Support
MAGICNET Local Area Network, HDLC Protocol, 19.2 Kilobaud
Teach Pendant
Keyboard
20 × 2 keys
Joystick
3-way joystick plus speed control

Display
16 characters (alphanumeric)
Software
Real-time Multi-tasking Operating System
VERSADOS (Motorola)
Teach Pendant Language
AR-SMART
Manufacturing Language
AR-BASIC
Diagnostics, Utilities
Extensive
Motion Control
Point-to-point and Continuous Path
Options
Color CRT (for teaching, programming, control or diagnostics)
Color Printer (for high-definition printouts)
Remote/Dial-up Management and Service Terminals
Additional Binary and Analog Input/ Output Modules
Line Isolation Transformer (240/480 V,3 Phase)

Level 2:

MERLIN Cluster Controller

The MERLIN Cluster Controller is intended for the support of up to sixteen robots, for off-line programming, robot simulation, color graphics, production reporting, and other optional functions and capabilities

Cluster Controller Specifications

Hardware
Processor
32-bit (Motorola 68000)
Memory
128KB to 1 MB
Mass Storage
Flexible or Hard Disks

CRT
High-resolution color
Printer
Color or black/white
Interface to Robot Controller
RS422

Network Support
MAGICNET Local Area Network, HDLC
Protocol, 19.2 kilobaud
Software
**Real-time Multi-tasking Operating
System**
UNIX® (Bell Labs)
Color Graphics System
MAGIGRAPH
Off-line Manufacturing Languages
AR-BASIC
AR-PASCAL
AR-''C''

Data-base Management System
MAGICDATA
Robot Simulator
MAGICSIM
Diagnostic, Utilities
Extensive
Options
**Remote Management and Diagnostic/
Service Terminals**
CRTs, Printers, Disks, Other Peripherals
Word Processing Software
Business Accounting Software

Anorad Corp. (Standard Anorad Products).

(1) *Anoride*. High-speed positioning tables of meehanite construction, single or multiple axes — X, Y, and Z — crossed roller, vee track, patented design for production applications. (2) *Anoround*. High-accuracy, high-speed rotary tables for production-automated applications, available in direct drive or geared versions. (3) *Anomatic*. Positioning Controller (CNC Microprocessor) with dc servo for automatic positioning of up to six axes (linear or rotary). (4) *Anotronic*. Positioning controller for direct real-time control by computer. (5) *Anoglide-5*. Very-high accuracy X-Y positioning tables, friction-free air-bearing glides, for production and inspection applications. (6) *Anoglide large travel*. Large-area-precision, high-speed positioning systems for X, Y, and Z axes. Granite construction with friction-free air-bearing glides, for production of large products for multiple operations. (7) *Anoscan*. Precision-measuring machine of granite construction with Z-axis-mounted sensors and laser-interferometer positioning. (8) X, Y, Z positioning system of granite construction for large or multiple production of products utilizing machine tool work spindles. (9) Optical sensor system for automatic focusing, tracking of objects, and centering of circles, dots, lines, etc. (10) *Ano Robots*. Combined linear and rotary stages for automated machining, assembly, and automatic adjustment of electronic and mechanical components or assemblies; robots use standard Anoride, Anoround, and Anomatic positioning systems with 1–40 in. (2.54–101.6 cm) motion and up to six axes.

Anorad Corp. (Anoscan)

A total X-Y-Z positioning system capable of automatically or semiautomatically performing ultraprecision linear dimensional measurements and of functioning over large areas. It incorporates laser interferometers with flat reference mirrors for the ultimate positioning accuracy. The X and Y stages are air-bearing-supported granite carriages that ride on highly stable granite guides and base structure. The Y carriage work tables on the PMMs can accommodate a measurement requirement up to an area of 30 in. (76.2 cm) by 40 in. (96 cm). The automatic sensors are mounted on the Z-axis carriage and provide scanning capabilities of the workpiece in the X or Y axis, or both. Major subsystems include (a) granite base with shock absorbers and leveling feet; (b) X and Y granite stages for positioning the work and the mechanical or electrooptical sensors, using air-bearing glide system; (c) Z-axis (vertical) carriage assembly cantilever mounted in the X carriage for positioning of the sensing system; (d) additional Z-axis stages can be provided; (e) closed-loop dc servo drive for X-Y-Z positioning; (e) laser interferometer with mirrors to measure directly the relative position between the sensing system and the carriage supporting the work; (f) custom-designed fixtures with optional vacuum holddown or rotary adjustment; (g) optical-sensing systems mounted on Z stage or performing such functions as autofocus, edge detector/scanner, edge tracking, TV camera, and TV monitor.

Anorobot X-Y-Z-$\theta 1$-$\theta 2$ with turret for one optics head and three tools.

Anorobot X-Y-Z-θ1 with three-tool turret head, sealed version.

ANOROBOT Standard Configurations

	User-Selectable Anorobot Features	Small Anorobot S1	Medium Anorobot M2	Large Anorobot L1
X-Axis (lower) Motion In Inches	2,4,6,8,10,12,16, 18,20,24,30,36,40	4	12	36
Y-Axis (upper) Motion in Inches	2,4,6,8,10,12,16, 18,20,24,30,36,40	4	12	30
Z-Axis (vertical) Motion In Inches	2,4,6,8,10,12,16, 18,20,24,30,36,40	4	8	12
θ A Diameter In Inches	6, 12, and Special Diameter	6	6	12
θ B Diameter In Inches	6, 12, and Special Diameter	6	6	6
Typical Weight Lifted Pounds	5 to 50	5 to 20	5 to 40	5 to 50
Typical Torque Inch-Pounds	3 to 50	3	50	50
Controller	Anomatic II Controller with Teach Mode. Optional point-to-point and interpolation. Can select up to eight added axes (eight positions each; control up to 48 added functions).			
Turret and Optics	Options: (1) optical sensor; (2) mechanical gripper; (3) vacuum gripper; (4) nut driver; (5) hex key, (6) screwdriver. One element on each head; up to four heads per system.			

ASEA, Inc. (IRb-6, IRb-60).

Basic system includes robots for 6 or 60 kg (13.2 or 132 pounds) handling capacity, together with control equipment and programming units. A battery back-up system is also included to maintain memory in the event of power failure. The robot has up to six degrees of freedom; rotary movement; arm movement, radial; arm movement, vertical; rotary wrist movement; wrist bend; wrist sweep (IRb-60); horizontal travel (IRb-6). The repeatability is better than ± 0.2 mm (0.008 in.) for the smaller robot and better than ± 0.4 mm (0.016 in.) for the larger robot. The electric-drive system enables the robot to operate quietly, and its design makes it insensitive to hostile workshop environments. The movements of the robot are programmed using a portable programming unit. Step by step, each position is stored in the memory. The robot's programming possibilities provide a good illustration of its versatility. (1) Point-to-point position control at a programmable speed. (2) Linear control permits the programming of curves at varying speeds. In this case, the curve is divided into a number of straight sections. (3) Linear-controlled search function allows picking from racks of varying heights or searching for corners. (4) Jump function permits simultaneous tending of machines that are not synchronized. Jumps can be made both within the same program and to another program. (5) Waiting function where times between 0.1 and 99 seconds can be selected at will. (6) Test-wait function, where the robot stops and waits until it receives a signal, via an input, before it continues executing the program. (7) Repeat function makes it possible to repeat a section of a program for a fixed number of times. (8) Pattern function simplifies programming for pattern picking and placing. (9) Correction function facilitates alterations, cancellations, and additions in existing programs. (10) Grip function for maneuvering one or two grippers. Compiled programs can be stored in a tape recorder cassette for future use. Complex programs can be compiled easily and rapidly with dissimilar items; different speed rates/items; addition or omission of steps; integration of the whole operating sequence. The electronic section is built up from plug-in units and this, together with the fully electrical drive and control system, makes servicing easier. To increase further the robot's capabilities there are: (1) Tape recorder for receiving and transmitting programs. (2) Additional memory increasing the capacity from 500 to 1000 positions. (Version with five degrees of freedom.) (3) Memory capacity increased up to 30 times by using a tape recorder and programmed automatic entry of programs from tape. This provides a total memory capacity of up to 15,000 positions. (4) Pneumatic unit for installation in the robot arm when a pneumatic gripper is used. (5) Grippers tailored to suit different applications. (6) Servo-powered travel motion [1.3–5.3 m (4.3–17.4 ft) for IRb-6]. (7) Servo-powered positioner that can be fitted to a robot with five degrees of freedom, providing it with a sixth. (8) Modified and extended servo system for torque measurement, for example, or soft servo which ensures that the force of application is proportional to the difference between the actual position and the programmed position. (9) Computer link that enables the robot to communicate with an overriding computer graphic display unit or other sophisticated electronic device. (1) Test panel for troubleshooting and servicing purposes. (11) Adaptive control that provides the user with several additional benefits.

ASEA, Inc. (IRb 6/2)

Robot is designed for operation in difficult environments. Designed for 13.2-lb (6-kg) handling capacity, and has up to six degrees of freedom: rotary movement; arm movement, radial; arm movement, vertical; rotary wrist movement; wrist bend; horizontal travel (option). The repetition accuracy is better than +0.001 in. (±0.2 mm). Complex programs can be easily and rapidly compiled with dissimilar items; different operating sequences for items; additional or omission of steps; integration of the whole operating sequence. Robot is programmed by means of a "dialogue" with the control system via a portable programming unit. The principle is that the control system poses questions in plain language on an alphanumerical display and the operator/programmer answers by pushing the button or buttons providing the correct answer. The robot can be ordered to move according to one of three different coordinate systems: (a) rectangular, (b) cylindrical, (c) wrist-orientated rectangular.

Dimensions and operating range

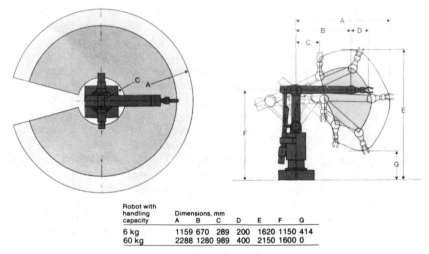

Robot with handling capacity	Dimensions, mm						
	A	B	C	D	E	F	G
6 kg	1159	670	289	200	1620	1150	414
60 kg	2288	1280	989	400	2150	1600	0

Working range.

ASEA Robots[a]

	IRb-6	IRb-60
Base Rotation	340°	330°
Horizontal Reach	37.8 in. (959 mm)	74.3 in. (1888 mm)
Vertical Reach	55.9 in. (1420 mm)	68.9 in. (1750 mm)
Wrist Bending	± 90°	+75°, − 120°
Wrist Turning	± 180°	± 180°
Number of Axes	3–6	
Repeatability	± 0.008 in. (± 0.20 mm)	± 0.016 in. (± 0.40 mm)
Carrying Capacity	13.3 lb (6 kg)	133 lb (60 kg)
Control	Microcomputer	
Program Capacity	500 points–15,000 points	
Computer Interface	Yes	
Drive	dc servo motors	
Total Power Consumption (equipment & robot)	2 kW	7 kW

[a]**Principle Applications:** Snag grinding, deburring, polishing, arc welding, spot welding, materials handling, machine loading, glueing, inspection.

ASEA, Inc. (IRb-6 Arc Welding).

There are several complete arc welding systems available, which mainly consist of three parts: IRb-6 with control equipment, a positioner with control panel, and a welding unit.

In the specific system illustrated in the figure the positioner or manipulator is to hold the workpiece at the correct angle during welding. Workpiece plus fixture can weigh anything up to 333 pounds (150 kg). The robot stands on the same base as the positioner. Six different positions guarantee the correct distance from the workpiece. When workpieces are to be changed, the table is turned automatically to 180°.

The welding equipment comprise standard components—welding rectifier, wire feed unit, welding hose with contact unit, cooling unit, fume extractor, and programmer. Together they form a system tailor made for robot welding. With the programmer you can prepare five different welding programs covering welding data, start/stop, gas preflushing, electrode feed, and nozzle cleaning. During operation the welding process is controlled by a central computer, which selects the program, starts and stops the welding, and actuates fume extraction and nozzle cleaning.

If the shielding gas or welding current fails, the system is blocked automatically. There is also an emergency stop control.

MHS 150 Handler with Robot

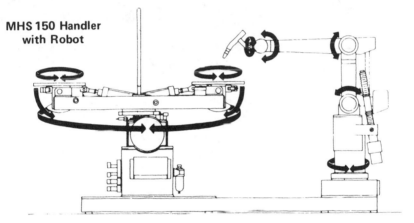

A typical robot positioner arrangement and the IRb-6.

Bendix Robotics Div. (ML-360 Robot).

The jointed arm (revolute) geometry of the ML-360 industrial robot provides dexterity and a large usable work envelope. The vertical reach of 165 in. (4.2 m) combined with an elbow extension of 98 in. (2.5 m) and a rotation at the base of 300° encompass a work envelope of 1200 ft³ (34 m³). Three wrist drives provide almost infinitely variable roll, pitch, and yaw movements at the tool nose, and there are few obstacles that cannot be negotiated and few places that cannot be reached by the ML-360 robot.

All six axes of the ML-360 robot are driven by electromechanical servos to provide accuracy and repeatability. Rotation at the base is 90°/second; the shoulder axis lifts at 52 in. (1.3 m)/second; the elbow extends at 56 in. (1.4 m)/second; yaw and pitch moves are 103°/second; and roll rates are 155°/second. And, the ML-360 robot automatically uses the shortest path between programmed points.

Full-feature CNC, the Dynapath System 5AR CNC, has been specifically tailored for robot applications by Bendix Industrial Controls Division. It provides simultaneous control of all six axes, operator friendly programming, customer programmable "macro cycles," full editing, and diagnostics.

Specifications

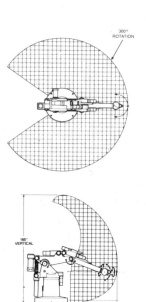

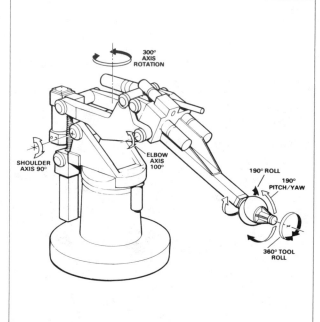

Robot
Type:
6 Electric Servo-Driven Axes

Load Capacity:
150 lbs. (67.5 kg) 18" (46 cm) from wrist center
Reach:
Vertical 165" (419 cm)
Horizontal 98" (249 cm)
Rotation 300 degrees

Speed:
Rotation 90 degrees/sec.
Shoulder Lift (X axis) 52"/sec. (132 cm/sec)
Elbow Extension (Y axis) 56"/sec. (142 cm/sec)
Maximum velocity at wrist center: 100"/sec. (254 cm/sec)
Yaw and Pitch (U, V, W axis) 103 degrees/sec.
Tool Nose Roll (W,V axis) 155 degrees/sec.
Positioning Accuracy: ±.020" (±0.5 mm)
Repeatability: ±.005" (± 0.13 mm)
Weight: 6,000 lbs. (2700 kg)

Controller - Dynapath® System 5AR

Derivative of Bendix Dynapath® System 5A CNC

Memory Size: 64K

Programming Capacity:
30,000 characters (minimum 900 points) expandable to 120,000 characters

Battery Support:
72 hours normal (Lighting circuit bypass available)
Power consumption: 1Kw

Special features:
• Simultaneous coordinated motion of all six axes — software controlled
• Software controlled acceleration/deceleration
• Branching capability
Programming:
• Detachable teach pendant
• Combination edit/teach mode
• CRT display for edit and diagnostics

Programmable interface

• Any combination of up to 96 DC or 64 AC inputs.
• 72 DC outputs
• 40 AC outputs of 3 amps
• 8 time delays
• 24 VDC power for operation of input sensors available

Note:
For display purposes, the machines shown here have been photographed and depicted without protective guards in place

Bendix Robotics Div. (AA-160 Robot).

This industrial robot system has a spherical work envelope to provide a "bend over backwards" capability. Units can be closely spaced on a line without sacrificing the ability to service a parallel line or reach off-line parts. The AA-160 robot is a six-axis, all-electric polar coordinate unit providing six degrees of freedom and a 45-pound (20-kg) load carrying capacity.

All six axes of the robot are driven by dc servo motors. The system utilizes all six axes simultaneously; the Dynapath System 5AR CNC automatically traverses the tool nose through the shortest path between programmed points. The AA-160 robot rotates at its base at 170°/second; its "bend over backwards" shoulder tilt covers 170°/second; the arm extends at 32 in. (81 cm)/second; and yaw and pitch moves at the wrist are at 200°/second. Roll rates at the tool point are 600°/second.

The Dynapath System 5AR is a derivation of the System 5 CNC incorporating modifications for advanced robotics applications. Memory size is 64K with a programming capacity of 30,000 characters (900 steps minimum) expandable to 120,000 characters. Integral programmable interfaces, customer-programmable macro cycles, combination edit–teach modes, and software-controlled acceleration and deceleration provide ease of operation and robot/machine dependability.

Specifications

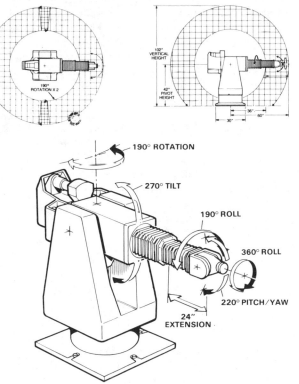

Robot

Type:
6 Electric Servo-Driven Axes

Load Capacity:
45 lb. (20 kg) 12" (30 cm) from wrist
center

Reach:
Vertical 102" (259 cm)
Horizontal 60" (152 cm)
Rotation 190 degrees × 2

Speed:
Rotation 170 degrees/sec.
Vertical axis 170 degrees/sec.
Extension axis 32"/sec. (81 cm/sec)
Maximum velocity at wrist center 255"/sec.
(648 cm/sec)
Barrel roll 200 degrees/sec.
Yaw/pitch 200 degrees/sec.
Tool point roll 600 degrees/sec.
Positioning Accuracy: ±.004" (±0.1 mm)
Repeatability: ±.002" (± 0.05 mm)
Mounting Position Universal
Weight: 3,000 lbs. (1350 kg)

Controller - Dynapath® System 5AR

Type:
Derivative of Bendix Dynapath®
System 5A CNC

Memory Size 64K

Programming Capacity:
30,000 characters (minimum 900 points)
expandable to 120,000 characters

Battery Support:
72 hours normal (Lighting circuit bypass
available)
Power consumption 1Kw

Special features:
• Simultaneous coordinated motion of all
  six axes—software controlled
• Software controlled
  acceleration/deceleration
• Branching capability
Programming:
• Detachable teach pendant
• Combination edit/teach mode
• CRT display for edit and diagnostics

Programmable interface

• Any combination of up to 96 DC or
  64 AC inputs.
• 72 DC outputs
• 40 AC outputs of 3 amps
• 8 time delays
• 24 VDC power for operation of input
  sensors available

Note:
For display purposes, the machines shown here have been
photographed and depicted without protective guards in place

Cincinnati Milacron (T³ Robot).

The T³ Robot is a simply built six-axis computer-controlled industrial robot. The jointed-arm construction provides the flexibility needed to perform in difficult to reach places. The unit has sealed-for-life lubrication and rotary joints with large antifriction bearings. Each of the six axes of the robot is direct-driven by its own electrohydraulic servo system. The robot is capable of the high torque, speed, and flexibility needed to handle payloads anywhere within an area of up to 1000 ft³ (28 m³). Each axis has its own position feedback device, consisting of a resolver and tachometer, to ensure accurate arm repeatability. The Milacron Acramatic robot computer control provides variable six-axis positioning and controlled-path (straight-line) motion between programmed points. Tell the robot where you want it to go, and it automatically figures out the shortest way to get there at the velocity selected. The robot is taught by using a hand-held teach pendant to lead it through the required moves. The operator has available three different spatially coordinated motion systems or paths along which he or she can move the arm from point to point while teaching. These are: (a) cylindrically coordinated motion, which moves the arm at a fixed radius around the vertical axis of the robot and radially in-or-out from that axis; (b) rectilinearly coordinated motion, which moves the arm along X, Y, and/or Z coordinate lines; (c) hand coordinated motion, which moves the arm through as many as all six of the robot's available axes (X, Y, Z, roll, pitch, and yaw) simultaneously. Stop points and functions are entered into the control memory with the push of a button. Various optional sequencing abilities permit the T³ to make decisions to add, change, or delete specified parts of its normal sequences.

Many types of sequences can be performed on the T³. Three typical types of sequencing that the T³ can perform are termed "conditional," "relocatable," and "utility." These sequences are effective because the CRC knows precisely the position of the robot's tool center point at all times. The T³ goes into a "conditional" routine in response to one or more external signals received from peripheral equipment. It employs its "relocatable" sequencing capability when software in the CRC is used to remember repetitive actions which were taught as a subroutine just once and then called up for instant use as needed at new positions in space, much like a canned cycle on a machine tool. A cathode ray tube is included on the computer control for display of pertinent data to the operator. Editing capability, through an alphanumeric keyboard on the control console, allows the operator to add, delete, or alter this information in the program, without actually moving the robot arm as would be done during initial teaching. Some of the uses are loading and unloading machine tools, forging presses, and injection molding machines; arc welding aluminum electronic housings and steel back hoe buckets; spot welding car bodies as they move past on conveyors; drilling airplane parts and putting vent holes in sand molds; moving materials to and from conveyors and storage areas; packaging and palletizing; inspecting, sorting, and assembling.

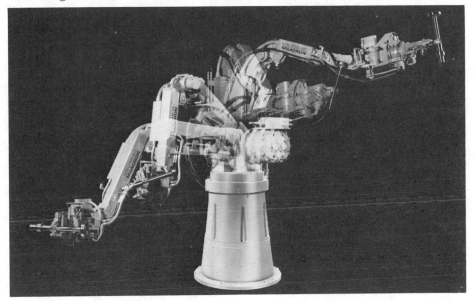

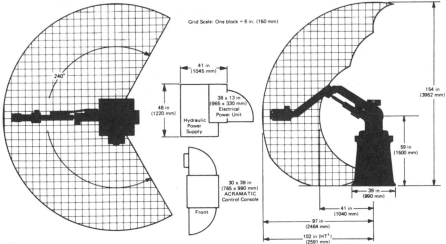

Grid Scale: One block = 6 in. (150 mm)

240°

41 in
(1045 mm)

48 in
(1220 mm)

38 x 13 in
(965 x 330 mm)
Electrical
Power Unit

Hydraulic
Power
Supply

30 x 39 in
(765 x 990 mm)
ACRAMATIC
Control Console

Front

154 in
(3962 mm)

59 in
(1500 mm)

39 in
(990 mm)

41 in
(1040 mm)

97 in
(2464 mm)

102 in (HT³)
(2591 mm)

NOTE: Standard interconnection
between units 20 ft. (6 m) radius
from base of arm.

Basic range and floor space drawings.

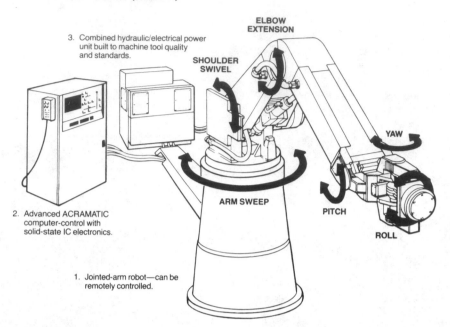

3. Combined hydraulic/electrical power
   unit built to machine tool quality
   and standards.

ELBOW
EXTENSION

SHOULDER
SWIVEL

YAW

ARM SWEEP

PITCH

ROLL

2. Advanced ACRAMATIC
   computer-control with
   solid-state IC electronics.

1. Jointed-arm robot—can be
   remotely controlled.

Specifications

Load Capacity

Load 10 in. (254 mm) from tool mounting
plate   T³ 100 lb (45 kg)[1]
Load 10 in. (254 mm) from tool mounting
plate   HT³ 225 lb (102 kg)[1]

Number of Axes, Control Type

Number of servoed axes (hydraulically
powered)   6
Control type   Controlled path at tool
center point

Positioning Repeatability

Repeatability to any programmed
point   ±0.050 in (±1.27 mm)[2]

Jointed-Arm Motions, Range, Velocity

Maximum horizontal sweep   240°
Maximum horizontal reach to tool
mounting plate   T³ 97 in. (2464 mm)
Maximum horizontal reach to tool
mounting plate   HT³ 102 in.
(2591 mm)
Minimum to maximum vertical reach   0
to 154 in. (0 to 3911 mm)

Maximum working volume from 9 ft²
floor area   1000 ft³ (28.32 m³)
Maximum velocity of tool center point
(TCP)   T³ 50 ips (1270 mmps)
Maximum velocity of tool center point
(TCP)   HT³ 35 ips (890 mmps)
Pitch   180°
Yaw   180°
Roll   270°

Memory Capacity

Number of points which may be
stored   400[3]

Floor Space and Approximate Net Weight

Robot   9 ft² (0.8 m²); 5000 lb (2267 kg)
Hydraulic power supply   17 ft² (1.5 m²);
1200 lb (544 kg)
Electric power unit   3.4 ft² (0.3 m²);
700 lb (317 kg)
ACRAMATIC robot control console   8.3
ft² (0.8 m²); 800 lb (365 kg)

Power Requirements	Environmental Temperature
460 volts, 3 phase, 60 HZ[4]	40 to 120°F (5 to 50°C)[1]

[1]Consult factory for special applications. [2]With the T[3] only, optional positioning repeatability of ±0.025 in. (±0.64 mm) is available. [3]Additional memory available. [4]50 Hz available.

Cincinnati Milacron (T[3] Arc Welding System)

A flexible robot arc welding system consisting of a high repeatability T[3] computer-controlled robot, a programmable weld positioner (PWP), a wire feed unit, a weld power supply, and special arc welding software. All the components of this arc welding system are integrated into a single working unit through the robot control. The T[3] robot accurately controls the position, orientation, and velocity of the weld gun. As the control center, it communicates with all the peripheral equipment in the cell — turning on the welding gun, the cooling water, the shielding gas, the power to the weld controller and other equipment. The robot then waits for inputs from the peripheral equipment indicating that everything is ready prior to starting the welding cycle.

The robot has been modified for welding speed with smaller servo valves on the positioning axes. This modification results in both smooth low-speed performance and improved positioning repeatability required for arc welding. In addition to this hardware change, a special software package is provided to simplify the programming task and expand the capabilities of the robot in arc welding applications.

Cincinnati Milacron (Weld Positioner).

To achieve the optimum results in an automated robot welding cell, each weld seam must be positioned in the best possible attitude. Typically, weld positioners are controlled by cam-driven limit switches. The number of limit switches determines the number of unique positions of the weld positioner. For complicated assemblies, the available number of limit switches may not suffice to ensure the seam is in the best attitude. The problems involved in setting the limit switches and their relatively poor repeatibility presents a high possibility of positioning error. Through the T[3] robot arc welding system a programmable weld positioner (PWP) has been developed that is easy to teach and control accurately through the robot control. The cam-driven limit switches on each axis are replaced with resolvers that are interfaced to the robot control. Axis positions are measured by the resolvers. The motor controls are interfaced to the robot input and output contacts. The operator drives the positioner to the desired configuration using the PWP function in the robot control, causing the positioner's axis values to be stored in the robot memory. When the PWP function is executed, the robot retrieves the stored values from memory and compares them with the positioner's current position. If the values differ, the positioner is commanded to move in the proper direction until the values coincide. The typical repeatability on each controlled axis is ±0.045° of the programmed position.

Comau Company (Polar 6000 Welding Robot).

The six-axis polar configuration gives the robot an ability to maneuver even in limited spaces. The 145-kVA power rating current transformer for spot welding is mounted directly on the robot arm, which also carries the entire pick-up hand adjustment and closing system. This eliminates the need for connecting cables between the guns and separate power units. The drive package is completely hydraulic and the power unit, in the horizontal version, is located in the base. The unit is self-contained. The machine is equipped with a

Comau Polar 6000 arc welding robot.

multimicroprocessor capable of performing both continuous and point-to-point control of the gun path, and the machine may be programmed in terms of robot axes, Cartesian coordinates, or Cartesian coordinates referred to the robot wrist attachment surface. The measurement system is absolute, using resolvers. The machine has a 16-program automatic selection capability and a memory extension capability of from 360 to 2000 program steps. The programming is performed on a self-learning console using a programming gun, while a portable video unit may be used for recording, editing, and changing programs via keyboard; displaying axis position and location values; and displaying troubleshooting messages. The Polar 6000 robot may also be mounted vertically on a bridge-type frame.

Comau Company (COSIL).

A simulation language for production systems devised by Comau for the study of complex production systems prior to their manufacture. COSIL makes it possible to identify subsystems and define them in terms of the proposed objective, as well as to set up data-generation banks and subsequently unite the various subsystems in a complete system. Its operational features are the following: simplified definition of models, the possibility of quick analysis of large numbers of cases, the automatic generation of basic statistical data, and an ability to analyze specific portions of the model.

Control Automation, Inc. (CA-R1000 Sembler).

This robot is comprised of a family of automation modules — a single or multiarmed, high-precision assembly robot system and a scene analysis vision system (CA-V1000 Vision System). Up to three arms can be used on a single robot system for assembly purposes. In addition, each system includes a system controller, touch control pendant, and a keyboard.

This robot system uses the concept of distributed processing and hierarchical control. The vision system has two levels of control. The vision processor itself (V-1000) performs data gathering, image analysis, part identification, and orientation. The V-1000 is driven by an external computer, usually the system controller, SC-1000, but it may be any external computer desired.

The V-1000 performs parts recognition and location, inspection, and measurement on nonoverlapping objects using the Stanford Research Institute "SRI Algorithm." Communication between the V-1000 and the user is through an RS-232C (or optional RS-422) standard serial line for compatability with most computers. The SC-1000 is programmed in Hewlett Packard industrial BASIC as standard but other languages such as FORTRAN may be used.

Photograph of the CA-R1000 Sembler.

Control Automation, Inc. — Robot System*

System Descriptions:

Single arm robot
Control Automation system controller
Touch control teach pendant
Plug-in keyboard

Key Features

All electric
All digital
Plug compatible (via STD RS 232C)
Speaks in English (HP BASIC)
Full mathematic capability standard
Can add up to two additional arms
Can be mounted on floor, wall, or ceiling
Adaptive control system (modify motion on the fly)
Can program time or speed of task
User friendly (ease of teaching, programming, use)

Key Specifications
General

Configuration   four-axis Cartesian coordinate
Joint ranges X=40 in./1.02 m
(56 in./1.4 m for single arm)
    Y=20 in./0.5 m
    Z=20 in./0.5 m
    θ=designed to handle continuous spin
**Accuracy (planer)   ±0.001 in. (0.025 mm)
**Repeatability   ±0.002 in. (0.05 mm)
Minimum programmable movement   0.001 in. (0.26 mm)
Load capacity   10 lb (4.5 kg)
Max tip velocity   30 in./s (0.8 m/s)
Robot wt (approx)   900 lb (400 kg)

Work envelope   40 in. (56 in. for single arm) × 20 in. × 20 in. (1.0 × 0.5 × 0.5 m)
Floor space requirements   19.5 ft² (3 × 6.5 ft), 1.8 m² (0.9 × 2.0 m)
**W/Full Load

Drive/Control/ I/O /Feedback

Digital encoders, optical & linear
Brushless electric dc servo
System controller — Hewlett Packard 85 based
32 I/O TTL (STD)
32 I/O (16 I/O TTL level, 16 I/O ac/dc) (optional)

Teaching Method/Language

Menu driven
Touch control treach pendant/keyboard
Industrial HP BASIC

Safety Protection

Software limits   all joints
Electromechanical   limit switches all joints
Mechanical   hardware limit on joints X, Y, Z

Power Requirements

110–130 Vac, 60 Hz, 1500 W max

Environmental Operating Range

10–40°C (50–104°F)
    0-80% relative humidity (noncondensing)
Shielded against industrial line fluctuations and human electrostatic discharge

*Specifications subject to change without notice.

Control Automation, Inc. — Vision System*

System Description

Vision processor
Control Automation system controller
Plug-in keyboard
GE TN 2200 camera with lens

Key Features

Key word programming,
Plug compatible (via STD RS 232C)
Works in English (HP BASIC)
Full math capability standard

Can be used as measurement tool
Can recognize up to 50 different objects
  simultaneously
Protects up to 10 objects in nonvolatile
  memory
Can handle up to four cameras
User friendly (menu driven teaching
  system)
Can recognize parts placed upside down
Can be mounted on robot arm

Key Specifications
General

Communication   via RS 232C
  (R 422 optional)
Controller/processor
weight   20 lb (9 kg)
Controller/processor
Dimensions   5.25 × 19.0 × 21.0 in.
  (0.1 × 0.5 × 0.5 m)
Accuracy   1% of field view
Camera type   GE TN 2200
Camera resolution   128 × 128 pixels

Recognition speed   up to 120
  parts/minute
Lighting   requires contrast (part
  vs background)

Control

Vision processor   Intel 86 based
System controller   Hewlett Packard
  85 based

Teaching Method

Menu-driven CRT/keyboard

Power Requirements

110–130 Vac, 60 Hz, 60 W max

Environmental Operating Range

0–50°C (32–120°F)
0–90% max relative humidity
  (noncondensing)
Shielded against industrial line voltage
  fluctuations and electrostatic
  discharge

*Specifications subject to change without notice.

Copperweld Robotics (AP-10).

A pneumatically powered, microprocessor-controlled industrial robot. It is used for a variety of tasks requiring parts handling, parts feeding, and parts mating. It is programmed through a hand-held master teach control. The AP-10 consists of the robot itself, an electronic controller, and a teach control programming device. The robot is protected by a Fiberglass enclosure.

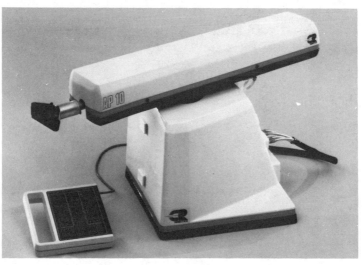

The AP-10 from Copperweld Robotics.

AP-10 Specifications

- **AXIS OF MOTION**
  HORIZONTAL STROKE.............0-12 inches (two adjustable fixed stops)
  VERTICAL LIFT.....................0-2 inches (two adjustable fixed stops)
  ROTATION (arm about vertical
      centerline of rotation) ... 0-200° (two adjustable fixed stops)
  ARM TURNOVER ....0-270° (two adjustable fixed stops)
  DOUBLE ACTION GRIPPER ....Open-Close (fingers optional)
- **AXIS DRIVE** - Pneumatic @ 80 p.s.i.
  HORIZONTAL ....Air Cylinder
  VERTICAL.......................P-3 Polygon lift piston (minimizes piston rotation)
  ROTATION.......................Rack & Pinion via Air Cylinder
  ARM TURNOVER ....Rotary Actuator
  GRIPPER........................Cylinder Actuated Draw Bar
- **SYSTEM REPEATABLE PLACEMENT ACCURACY** - ±0.003
- **SYSTEM SPEED** - 12-18 inches per second linear depending upon load
  - 80-90° per second radial depending upon load
- **LOAD CAPACITY (End-of-arm)** - Up to 5 pounds including gripper/tooling
- **AXIS MOTION DETECTORS** - Vacuum Switches - standard
  - Electrical Limits - optional

- **UTILITY REQUIREMENTS** - Shop air @ 80 p.s.i. - robot
  - 115 VAC, 60 HZ, 2 amps - control
- **OPERATING TEMP.** - 32°F to 120°F
- **CONTROL** - Electronic, Microprocessor Based
  MEMORY CAPACITY................Up to 250 steps
  MEMORY TYPE ....Non volatile EAROM
  PROGRAM CAPACITY ....Multiple
  PROGRAM METHOD ....Push button via portable teach pendant
  INPUTS/OUTPUTS ....Eight (8) each rated at 115 VAC, 60 HZ, 3 amps
  TIME DELAYS....................Selectable in tenths of a second
      increments from 0.1 to 99.9 seconds

OPTIONS: Special Tooling - Design & Build
  Vacuum Cup Gripper
  Single Action Gripper
  Parallel Action Gripper
  Overgrip Sensing
  Electrical Limit Switches for each Axis

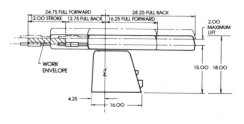

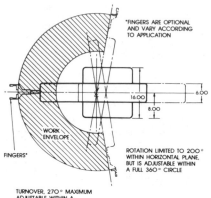

FINGERS ARE OPTIONAL
AND VARY ACCORDING
TO APPLICATION

WORK
ENVELOPE

ROTATION LIMITED TO 200°
WITHIN HORIZONTAL PLANE,
BUT IS ADJUSTABLE WITHIN
A FULL 360° CIRCLE

FINGERS*

TURNOVER, 270° MAXIMUM
ADJUSTABLE WITHIN A
FULL 360° CIRCLE

Copperweld Robotics (AP-50).

A pneumatically powered, microprocessor-controlled industrial robot. It can be used for a variety of tasks requiring parts handling, parts feeding, and parts mating. It is easily programmed through a hand-held master teach control. The AP-50 consists of the robot itself, all electronic controller, and a teach control programming device. The robot and the controller are protected by a Fiberglass enclosure.

AP-50 Specifications

- **AXIS OF MOTION**
  HORIZONTAL STROKE.............0-18 inches (two adjustable fixed stops)
  VERTICAL LIFT.....................0-5 inches (two adjustable fixed stops)
  ROTATION (arm about vertical
      centerline of rotation) ... 0-200° (two adjustable fixed stops)
  ARM TURNOVER ....0-270° (two adjustable fixed stops)
  DOUBLE ACTION GRIPPER ....Open-Close (fingers optional)
- **AXIS DRIVE** - Pneumatic @ 80 p.s.i.
  HORIZONTAL .....Air Cylinder
  VERTICAL.......................P-3 Polygon lift piston (minimizes piston rotation)
  ROTATION ....Rack & Pinion via Air Cylinder
  ARM TURNOVER . Rotary Actuator
  GRIPPER ....Cylinder Actuated Draw Bar
- **SYSTEM REPEATABLE PLACEMENT ACCURACY** - ±0.010
- **SYSTEM SPEED** - 12-18 inches per second linear depending upon load
  - 80-90° per second radial depending upon load
- **LOAD CAPACITY (End-of-arm)** - Up to 30 pounds including gripper/tooling
- **AXIS MOTION DETECTORS** - Vacuum Switches - standard
  Electrical Limits - optional

- **UTILITY REQUIREMENTS** - Shop air @ 80 p.s.i. - robot
  115 VAC, 60 HZ, 2 amps - control
- **OPERATING TEMP.** - 32°F to 120°F
- **CONTROL** - Electronic, Microprocessor Based
  MEMORY CAPACITY.. Up to 250 steps
  MEMORY TAPE ....Non volatile EAROM
  PROGRAM CAPACITY..Multiple
  PROGRAM METHOD...Push button via portable teach pendant
  INPUTS/OUTPUTS .....Eight (8) each rated at 115 VAC, 60 HZ, 3 amperes
  TIME DELAYS.........Selectable in tenths of a second
      increments from 0.1 to 99.9 seconds

OPTIONS: Special Tooling - Design & Build
  Vacuum Cup Gripper
  Single Action Gripper
  Parallel Action Gripper
  Overgrip Sensing
  Electrical Limit Switches for each Axis

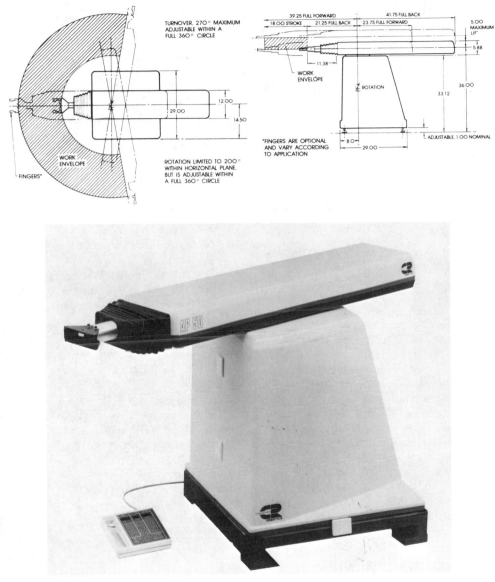

TURNOVER, 270° MAXIMUM
ADJUSTABLE WITHIN A
FULL 360° CIRCLE

WORK
ENVELOPE

FINGERS*

12.00

29.00

14.50

WORK
ENVELOPE

ROTATION LIMITED TO 200°
WITHIN HORIZONTAL PLANE,
BUT IS ADJUSTABLE WITHIN
A FULL 360° CIRCLE

39.25 FULL FORWARD   41.75 FULL BACK
18.00 STROKE   21.25 FULL BACK   23.75 FULL FORWARD

11.38

WORK
ENVELOPE

Z ROTATION

5.00
MAXIMUM
LIFT

5.88

36.00

33.12

*FINGERS ARE OPTIONAL
AND VARY ACCORDING
TO APPLICATION

8.0

29.00

ADJUSTABLE, 1.00 NOMINAL

The AP-50 from Copperweld Robotics.

Copperweld Robotics (Opto-Sense).

A computer-controlled vision system, which can be used alone or interfaced with a robot, is used in such industrial applications as measuring automobile frames on a moving assembly line, looking for missing parts in metal subassemblies, detecting missing objects in packages prior to sealing, and inspecting complex stampings for presence and location of holes and other details in subassemblies. When used with a robot or robotic system, Opto-Sense cameras provide the robot with visual feedback capabilities. The robot then acts according to the input received from the controller. The system incorporates solid-state video cameras, which can measure with repeatable accuracy within thousandths of an inch. The vision system consists of a solid-state video camera mounted in a cast aluminum protective housing, a NEMA 12 control cabinet, and interconnect cables. The camera enclosure can be mounted up to 50 ft (15 m) from the controls. All camera functions, inputs, outputs, and decisions are made within the enclosure. The camera used is a solid-state imager made by General Electric. The controls consist of interface cards that receive camera signals and perform counting functions and also input–output cards that send and receive information to and from other devices. The "brain" of the control system is a Digital Equipment Corp. Mini-Computer (LSI 11/2). Computer communicates with the Opto-Sense electronics through a standard DEC parallel card.

Opto-Sense® Specifications

Electrical

Input power 115 Vac, 60 Hz, 20 A Max including air conditioner

Computer type Digital Equipment Corp. LSI-11/2

Input/output 16 solid-state programmable input/output modules for ac or dc (specify). Expandable to 32 modules. 1 serial line (RS232G compatible) for communication between a terminal or another computer. 2 optional counters or displays available

Memory type EPROM (nonvolatile) for main program. EPROM (nonvolatile) for window information

Memory capacity 20K words - standard. Expandable to 28K words

Camera Type GE TN2500 Solid State Matrix Array 244 × 248 elements

Inspection rate variable depending upon information required to be processed. Each window will require 50 milliseconds.

Window criteria up to 255 windows per controller. Independent upon the number of cameras or parts involved.

Part Selection up to 255 parts optionally available. Selection is through a selector switch.

Mechanical

Camera housing 8 in. H × 8 in. W × 15 in. long (20 × 20 × 38 cm).

Control cabinet with integral air conditioner 30 in. H × 33 in. W × 20 in. deep (76 × 84 × 51 cm).

System weight 200 lb/90 kg

Ambient operating temperature 10°C–65°C (50°F–149°F)

Cybotech Inc. (G80).

The G80 is a precision industrial robot designed for applications with tool and part loads of up to 175 lb (80 kg). The gantry configuration is suited for applications where overhead mounting is advantageous such as cutting with a torch, plasma arc, or water jet. It is designed for maximum productivity. With a 175-lb (80-kg) load, travel time between two points 16 in. (400 mm) apart is less than 0.4 seconds and repeatability is better than ±0.008 in. (±0.2 mm). Multiple G80 robots can be suspended from the same gantry and are appropriate for assembly-line applications where similar or identical operations are required on both sides of a work piece. Primary applications include resistance welding, arc welding, cutting operations with various tools, and heavy handling and loading tasks.

ENGINEERING DATA

Axis or Degree of Freedom	Translation (T) Rotation (R)	Maximum Velocity	Load Capacity
1(x)[1]	2000 − 5000 mm (78.8 − 197.0 in.)	1 m/sec (3.3 ft/sec)	80 kg (175 lb)
2 (y)	1500−3000 mm (59.0−118.1 in.)	1 m/sec (3.3 ft/sec)	80 kg (175 lb)
3 (z)	1000 mm (39.4 in.)	0.5 m/sec (1.65 ft/sec)	80 kg (175 lb)
4	335°	3.0 rad/sec	80.1 slug-ft[2(2)]
5	210°	3.0 rad/sec	61.8 slug-ft[2(3)]
6	344°	3.0 rad/sec	61.8 slug-ft[2(3)]

[1] **Units with special translational ranges can also be provided.**
[2] **46.7 slugs at 1.31 ft from the rotating axis.**
[3] **46.7 slugs at 1.15 ft from the rotating axis.**

Drive System

Hydraulic motors and gear reducers

Accuracy

(with 80 kg load at maximum speed)
Position: ± 0.5 mm (±0.020 in.)
Repeatability: ± 0.2 mm (± 0.008 in.)

Control System

The RC5 provides a maximum of control options and versatility. It is specifically designed to make training, operation, maintenance, and troubleshooting easy and understandable. It also provides several safety features.

Power Requirements

20 kVA, 440 V, three phase (x2 for double G80)
(total for hydraulic unit and controls)

Cooling Water

11 gpm (x2 for double G80) maximum

Weight

4200 − 12,000 kg (9000 − 26,000 lb)
(depending on gantry dimensions and single or double configuration)

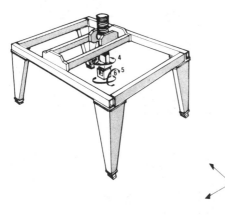

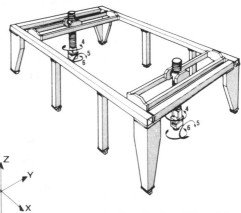

The G80 robot from Cybotech Inc.

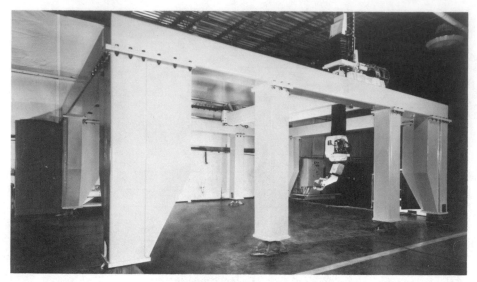

The G80 from Cybotech Inc.

Cybotech Inc. (H8).

The H8 is a high-speed, precision electric robot with a telescopic, horizontal configuration. It is designed to perform light handling, assembly, and inspection tasks. It is capable of working with tool and work loads of up to 17 lb (8 kg), and has repeatability accuracy of ± 0.004 in. (± 0.1 mm).

Primary Dimensions and Work Envelope

All dimensions are stated metric (English).

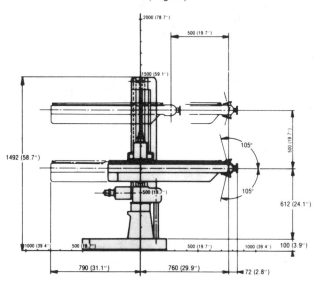

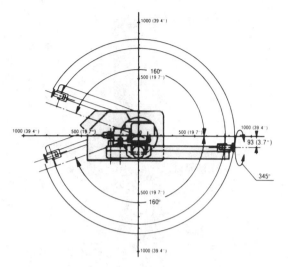

ENGINEERING DATA

Axis or Degree of Freedom	Motion	Speed
1	Rotation ± 160°	2 rad/sec
2	Vertical translation 500 mm (20 in.)	1 m/sec (16.4 ft/sec)
3	Horizontal translation 500 mm (20 in.)	1 m/sec (16.4 ft/sec)
4	Rotation ± 105°	1.5 rad/sec
5	Rotation 345°	1.5 rad/sec

Drive System
Electric motors
Accuracy [with 8 kg (17.6 lb) load at maximum speed]
Position: ± 0.5 mm (0.020 in.)
Repeatability: ± 0.1 mm (0.004 in.)

Control System
The RC5 control provides a maximum of control options and versatility. It is specifically designed to make training, operation, maintenance, and troubleshooting easy and understandable. It also provides several safety features.

Weight
100 kg (220 lb)

The H8 robot
from Cybotech Inc.

Cybotech Inc. (H80).

The H80 is designed for applications with tool and part loads of up to 175 lb (80 kg). Its mechanical configuration makes it suited for assembly-line applications requiring work on large parts, such as spot welding of automobile or truck bodies. The H80 is designed for maximum productivity. With an 175 lb (80 kg) load travel time between two points 16 in. (400 mm) apart is less than 0.4 seconds, and repeatability is better than 0.008 in. (± 0.2 mm). Primary applications include resistance welding, arc welding, cutting operations with various tools, and heavy handling and loading tasks.

ENGINEERING DATA

Axis or Degree of Freedom	Translation (T) or Rotation (R)	Maximum Velocity	Load Capacity
1	R ± 135°	1.0 rad/sec	80 kg (175 lb)
2	T 1600 mm[1] (63 in.)	660 mm/sec (2.2 ft/sec)	80 kg (175 lb)
3	R ± 135°	1.0 rad/sec	80 kg (175 lb)
4	R 335°	3.0 rad/sec	80.1 slug-ft^{2}[2]
5	R 210°	3.0 rad/sec	61.8 slug-ft^{2}[3]
6	R 344°	3.0 rad/sec	61.8 slug-ft^{2}[3]

[1] Units with 2000 mm translation can also be provided
[2] 46 7 slugs at 1 31 ft from the rotating axis
[3] 46 7 slugs at 1 15 ft from the rotating axis

Drive System

Hydraulic motors and gear reducers

Accuracy

[with 80 kg (176 lb) load at maximum speed]:
Position: ± 0.5 mm (0.020 in.)
Repeatability: ± 0.2 mm (0.008 in.)

Control System

The RC5 provides a maximum of control options and versatility. It is specifically designed to make training, operation, maintenance, and troubleshooting easy and understandable. It also provides several safety features.

Power Requirements

20 kVA, 440 V, three phase (total for hydraulic power supply and control system)

Cooling Water

11 gpm maximum

Weight

1850 kg (4100 lb)

The H80 robot from Cybotech Inc.

Cybotech Inc. (P15).

The P15 is a hydraulically powered, seven-axis robot specifically designed for complex industrial coating application tools weighing up to 33 lb (15 kg). The large work envelope and the seventh degree of freedom give the P15 the capability of performing tasks such as painting the interiors of automobiles on continuous conveyors. Primary uses include the application of primer, paint, adhesives, mastics, and enamel; sandblasting; and metallizing.

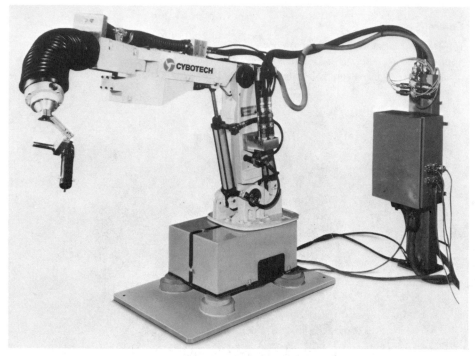

The P15 robot from Cybotech Inc.

ENGINEERING DATA

Axis or Degree of Freedom	Motion	Amplitude
1	Base rotation	± 115°
2	Vertical arm rotation	± 40°
3	Horizontal arm rotation	−35° +55°
4	Forearm rotation	± 105°
5 & 6	Trunk rotations	± 90°
7	Tool rotation	± 175°

Drive System

Direct hydraulic cylinders, hydraulic motors and gear reducers

Maximum Velocity

[with 15 kg (33 lb) load]: 2m/sec (6.6 ft/sec)

Accuracy

[with 15 kg (33 lb) load at maximum speed]:

Position: ± 1 cm (±0.40 in.)

Repeatability: ± 5 mm (±0.020 in.)

Control System

The RC5 provides a maximum of control options and versatility. It is specifically designed to make training, operation, maintenance and troubleshooting easy and understandable. It also provides several safety features.

Training of the P15 is done with a lightweight training mechanism that geometrically duplicates the P15. The standard program capacity is 8 minutes, however, at the user's option, this can be extended to 16 hours.

Power Requirements

20 kVA, 440 V, three phase (total for hydraulic unit and controls)

Cooling Water:

11 gpm maximum

Weight:

750 kg (1600 lb)

Cybotech Inc. (V80).

The V80 is a precision industrial robot designed for applications with tool and part loads of up to 175 lb (80 kg). Its mechanical configuration makes it suitable for applications where horizontal obstacles must be avoided or access to the work is best from the top. Among the best applications of the V80 are parts handling, loading, and palletization tasks. Primary applications for the V80 include resistance welding, arc welding, cutting operations with various tools, and heavy handling and loading tasks.

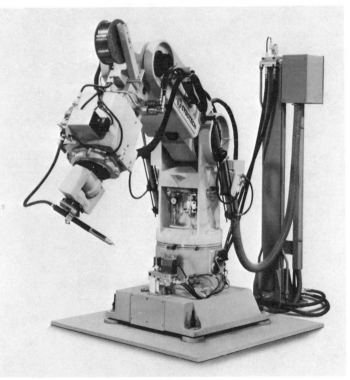

The V80 robot from Cybotech Inc.

Devilbiss Co. (Trallfa robot).

An automatic spray-painting robot designed specifically for spray finishing, this unit consists of three elements: the manipulator, the control center, and the hydraulic power unit. The manipulator is the working end; the arm and wrist actions provide six axes of motion, including wrist rotation. Two types of control center are available. The simplest is a single cassette tapereader (SCT). The SCT memory is designed for use when identical parts are to be sprayed or when production consists of batch quantities of several different parts. Each tape cassette holds one program with a length up to 85 seconds. The second module is the Computer Robot Control or CRC System. The CRC combines a microcomputer with a dual floppy disk memory system and an LED display. The CRC System allows 64 programs to be stored in the disk memory for recall in 0.5 second, making it ideal for painting parts loaded randomly on a conveyor. The hydraulic power unit contains the fluid reservoir, gear pump, and a 5.5 horsepower motor. Fluid level and temperature sensors are continuously monitored in the control center to provide a fail-safe system. In programming the operator attaches a teaching handle and function control box to the manipulator arm. A disk is loaded in the memory unit and the console switch is set for programming. A limit switch or photocell is used to sense the presence of a part. When the signal is received, indicating the part is in position, the operator begins to spray the part. The movements of the Trallfa manipulator can be synchronized with the conveyor by use of a pulse generator to compensate for speed changes. The Trallfa control can be programmed to make automatic color changes. Programs on the CRC floppy disk can be internally duplicated to provide additional copies for production and backup. The CRC module provides both continuous-path and point-to-point programming capability. PROM memory can be added to the CRC for extending memory capability for such purposes as program linking and automatic part identification.

Primary Dimensions and Work Envelope

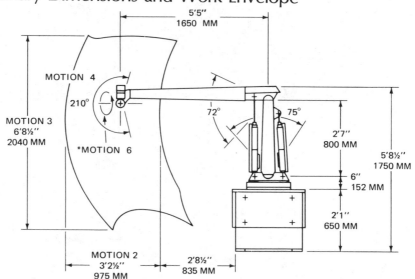

*OPTIONAL 6TH MOTION: 210° SPRAY FAN ROTATION.

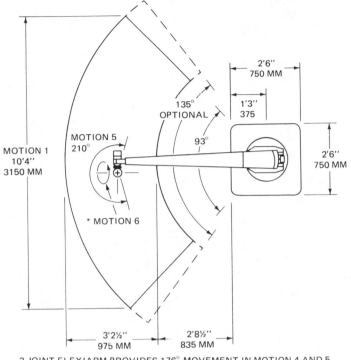

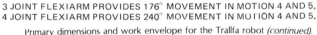

3 JOINT FLEXIARM PROVIDES 176° MOVEMENT IN MOTION 4 AND 5.
4 JOINT FLEXIARM PROVIDES 240° MOVEMENT IN MOTION 4 AND 5.

Primary dimensions and work envelope for the Trallfa robot *(continued)*.

ESAB (A 30 system).

A customized robot welding package, including a constant-voltage, rectifier-type, solid-state power supply; a wire feed; a welding gun with welding conduit assembly; a cooling unit; and a welding programmer. The rectifier-type power supply units used with the system have operating characteristics tailor-made for robot welding. When the heavy-duty MEC 44 wire feed unit is used, it is pivoted on the power supply with a counterbalanced boom that lifts the welding conduit off the floor to provide free movement of the welding gun. The MEC 44 feeder has creep-start, for softer striking of the arc when using heavy-guage wire, and four-wheel wire drive from two motors connected in series. The PAG 16 programmer communicates with the robot's main computer. Five seperate welding programs can be selected, which the robot can use automatically. Welding guns provided with A 30 systems are designed by ESAB to match wire sizes and service system each system requires. The extra-heavy-duty A 30 EHD is used for heavier welding, requiring currents up to 630 A. It incorporates the constant-voltage, solid-state LAH 630 rectifier, as well as the PAG 16 programming unit to tie it in with the robot computer control board. The heavy-duty A 30 HD unit is used in medium guage welding, in the 500-A range. The LAH 500 constant-voltage power supply is solid state and electrically controlled by the PAG 16 control unit. The MEC 44 Optimatic wire feed is electronically controlled. The special light-duty A 30 SLD is a special system intended primarily to meet the needs of the automotive industry or for other applications of thin-guage welding at currents up to 250

A. Powering this system is the solid-state LAH 250 constant-voltage rectifier. The MEC 30 Optimatic wire feed can be mounted directly on the robot to move with it so that lateral forces due to feed conduits are eliminated.

Technical Data

The Robot

ASEA IRb6
Weight — 275 lb (125 kg)
Powered motions — 5
Motion power — DC motors
Wrist drive — patented,
   no-backlash linkage
Position sensors — resolvers on motor
   shafts
Repetitive accuracy — ± 0.008 in.
   (0.2 mm)
Mounting — any position to fit application

Welding Power Supplies

ESAB LAH 630 — 630A/39V
   LAH (A30 EHD System)
ESAB LAH 500 — 500A/39V
   LAH (A 30 HD System)
ESAB LAH 250 — 250A/39V
   LAH (A30 SLD System)

Open circuit voltages — 15-51 V
Constant voltage, thyrister controlled
   rectifier type
Mains voltage variation ± 10% without
   welding current change
All functions controlled by computer

Wire Feeders

ESAB MEC 44 Optimatic (A 30 EHD,
   A 30 HD Systems)
   Wire diameter — 0.035 to 0.095 in.
   (0.8 to 2.4 mm)
   Feed speed — 5 to 6 ft/min
   (1.5 to 1.8 m/min)
   Drive — dual reversible motors, 4-wheel
ESAB MEC 30 Optimatic (A 30 SLD
   System)
   Wire diameter — 0.024 to 0.063 in.
   (0.6 to 1.6 mm)
   Feed speed — 0.060 to 0.095 in./min
   (1.5 to 1.8 m/min)
   Drive — single motor, 2 wheel

Program Selector

ESAB PAG 16
   Computer controlled during welding
      process
   Number of welding programs — 5
   Safety features — emergency stop,
      automatic check of shielding gas
      and current at each welding
      start

Welding Guns

ESAB PKD 630M (A 30 EHD System)
   Cooled by — water
   Nozzle cleaning — automatic
ESAB PSB 400V-M (A 30 HD System)
   Cooled by — water
   Nozzle cleaning — automatic
ESAB PSD 250M (A 30 SLD System)
   Cooled by — air
   Nozzle cleaning — automatic

Pulsing Unit

ESAB PAA6 — Optional on all systems

   Pulses current or voltage separately or
   synchronously

Control System

Computer with both PROM and ROM
   program storage, 14 programmable
   outputs, 16 programmable inputs
Welding gun movements programmed
   for both point to point and linear
   control
Complete programs can be revised or
   erased irrespective of
   sequence
Computer storage capacity, four
   complete programs
Programs not in use can be preserved on
   cassette tape
Removable programming unit may be
   hand-held when programming

Memory positions — 500 (increased to
15,000 with ''mass memory'' option)

Handling Units

MHS150
Handling stations — 2
Rotational speed, welding — 0.3 to
12.6 rpm
Tilting time, 0° to 90° — 4 sec

Station shift time, to turn 180° — 6 sec
MHS500
Handling stations — 2
Rotational speed, welding — 0.07 to
2.8 rpm
Tilting time, 0° to 90° — 5 sec
Station shift time — 2 to 3 sec
Other ESAB handling units are available
for special applications.

ESAB (MHS 500).

Designed to operate as an integrated handling module within the A 30A robot welding system to increase the accessibility and reach of the arm. The MHS 500 is primarily intended to handle workpieces that together with the related fixture weigh more than 330 lb (150 kg) and less than 880 lb (400 kg). The unit consists of two positions mounted on a base frame at right angles to the IRb6. The movement pattern of each positioner is programmed individually together with the welding robot from a separate control board. The positioner carries a round worktable that rotates at constant speed between 1 and 12 selected positions and can also tilt from the horizontal position to 90°. The worktable has guide and fastening holes for the attachment of the fixture and the workpiece. In operation the robot swings alternately between the two positioners as welding is completed on the workpiece and the next has been mounted on the worktable ready for welding. Utilization of the robot swiveling action when changing stations gives a very fast switch-over of between 2 and 3 seconds.

Technical data

Max load, workpiece incl. fixture   500 kg
(1100 lb)
Rotational speed, circular
welding   0.07-2.8 rpm
Torque during rotation   30 kpm
Max tilting moment 0-90°, 6 bar   135
kpm
Max center of gravity distance from

upper edge of table, workpiece/
fixture weight 500 kg   130 mm
Switching time   2-3 sec
Tilting time   0-90°   5 sec
90- 0°   11 sec
Number of positions   12
Tilting angles   0°, 30°, 45°, 60°, and 90°
Overall weight   475 kg (1045 lb)

ESAB (MHS Travel Carriage Assembly).

The purpose of the track is to increase the working range of the IRb-6 robot while maintaining the dual station concept. Any length of track can be supplied. However, there are two standard lengths, 20 ft (6 m) and 8 ft (2.5 m), which correspond to travel distances of 15.5 ft (4.7 m) and 3.6 ft (1.1 m). Holders of V-block type are attached to the rack to position and lock the carriage, providing a minimum interspace of 20 in. (500 mm). The carriage is powered by an A6-VEC electric motor operating through gear wheels and the rack. The motor is mounted on the carriage and is pneumatically disconnected in locking positions. The positioning unit consists of a movable idler roller controlled by a pneumatic cylinder. The robot is attached to a pair of base rails on the carriage. All control signals and position feedback are monitored by the robot's control cabinet. All motions are consequently controlled by the robot's reference signals. The welding equipment is also mounted on the carriage. Robot and welding cables are suspended on cable supports behind the track.

Technical data

Mains connection   200 V; 220 V; 380 V;
  400 V; 440 V; 480 V; 500 V; 550 V.
Operating voltage   110 V/50 Hz;
  130 V/60 Hz.
Power consumption   1.5 kVA.
Standard length of track   6.0 m and
  2.5 m
Travel distance   4.7 m and 1.1 m
Transport time   0.5 m–4 s, 1.0 m–6 s

Stop positions   Optional (minimum
  interspace 500 mm)
Position accuracy   ± 0.05 mm
Carriage weight   300 kg
Track weight   90 kg/m
Travel motor   A6-VEC
Output speed   2.7–108 rpm
Output torque   16 Nm
Transport speed   14 m/min (230 mm/s)

ESAB (MHS Twin Rotary Handling Unit).

Each unit can rotate about two axes. It can rotate the workpiece about its own longitudinal axis in the horizontal plane. In addition, the entire unit can rotate about its vertical axis through the slewing base. The workpiece is secured in a jig between the headstock and the tailstock. The length of the handling unit can, within reasonable limits, be adjusted to the customer's requirements. The rotary motion is effected by electric motors, type A6-VEC. The axes have similar, independent driving units. Only the transmission varies. The speed of rotation is variable. Since the robot's control cabinet monitors all positioning, the entire working cycle is stored in the robot's memory. A sequence control is used while a program is operating. All preprogrammed positions are interlocked with the microcomputer for operational safety. Eight different positions (8 × 45°) can be attained on each axis. Programming of the various positions is performed with sensors and cams. The positions are exact and independent of the direction of rotation. The turning motors are pneumatically disconnected when locked in position. The maximum static load for each table is 880 lb (400 kg), including the workpiece, jigs, etc.

TECHNICAL DATA

Mains connection:	200 V; 220 V; 380 V; 400 V; 440 V; 480 V; 500 V; 550 V.		
Operating voltage:	110 V/50 Hz; 130 V/60 Hz.		
Power consumption:	3 kVA.		
	Horizontal turning unit	Slewing base turning unit	Complete station
Maximum load	5000 N	5000 N	4000 N
Bending moment	1000 N	1000 N	
Torque	125 Nm	250 Nm	
Inertia	25 kgm^2	(170 kgm^2)	80 kgm^2
Maximum speed of rotation	5.5 rpm	2.75 rpm	
Minimum speed of rotation	0.14 rpm	0.07 rpm	
Locking positions	8	8	
Indexing time, 45°	5s	5s	
90°	6s	6s	
180°	8s	14s	
360°	13s	23s	
Total gear ratio	1456:1	2912:1	
Weight	100 kg	100 kg	290 kg

Expert Automation, Inc. (KUKA IR 601/60).

This robot can easily carry out complicated motion sequences because its six axes enable it to copy all human arm and hand movements with precision. In addition to this, the three basic axes have such a wide span that the working zone of the robot wrist is unusually large (working zone: machine = 5:1), despite its extremely small machine volume. Moreover, its positioning repeat accuracy for workpieces is ±0.05 in. (±1.2 mm). Its wrist not only has a powerful grip but its three axes with their full 360° swivel capacity provide it with optimum mobility.

The boom is of light-weight construction in order to maintain rigidity of the machine during acceleration and deceleration of the boom. The three electric motors required for driving the wrist axes are positioned near the machine's center of gravity; this contributes to stability.

The motor power is transmitted via toothed belts and shafts at high rpm to the wrist axes, where it is transformed into low speeds and high torques by means of space-saving harmonic drive gears – this means even more rigidity. This type of power transmission also reduces play to a minimum which is important for the repeat accuracy.

The Sinumerik S 7 microprocessor control is programmed through the teach method, and a position control system for all motors enables "guided" movement. This system controls and regulates (no overshooting) the traveled path continuously until the end position is reached. Path control is possible through appropriate software modification. The interface for periphery and external controls is designed according to IEC Standard 550, thus enabling communication with other systems.

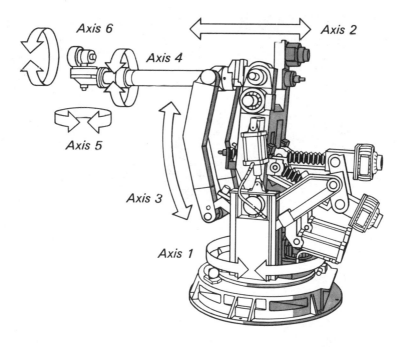

The KUKA IR 601/60.

KUKA Floor-Mounted Robot Type IR 601/60

General View with Working Zone

Reference point for working zone

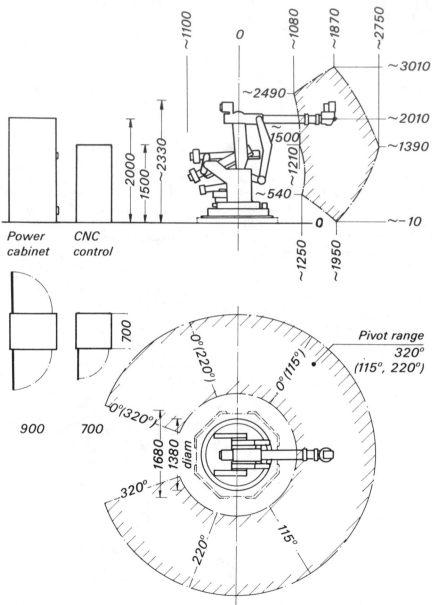

Power cabinet

CNC control

Pivot range
320°
(115°, 220°)

900   700

Dimensions in mm

Technical Data

Data for the 6 axes

	Zone	Speed
Basic axes		
Axis 1	320° (220°, 115°)	76°/s
Axis 2	1.5 m (4.9 ft)	1.2 m/s (47 ips)
Axis 3	2.5 m (8.2 ft)	1.2 m/s (47 ips)
Wrist axes		
Axis 4	360°	120°/s
Axis 5	360°	120°/s
Axis 6	360°	120°/s

Max. load capacity
60 daN (132 lb) at full speed
100 daN (220 lb) at reduced speed

Repeat accuracy ± 1.2 mm (0.047 in)

Dimensions (LxWxH) and weights
Robot
3000 x 1380 x 2100 mm, 2000 daN
(118 x 54 x 82 in, 4400 lb)
CNC control cabinet
700 x 700 x 1500 mm, 200 daN
(27 x 27 x 59 in, 440 lb)
Power cabinet
900 x 700 x 2000 mm , 800 daN
(35 x 27 x 79 in, 1760 lb)

Drive system
Electro-mechanical, thyristor
controlled DC motors

Noise level ≦ 80 dB (A)

Power supply
CNC control
220 V a. c. single phase
(+10 to −15 %); 50/60 Hz

Power cabinet
380 . . . 550 V a. c. three phase, PE,
if available 220 V a. c. single phase
(+10 to −15 %); 50 Hz (60 Hz)
Power consumption 21 kVA at 70 %
duty cycle. Fuses: 3 x 40 A
Robot: Air supply 8 bar (116 psi)

Memory capacity
1000 program steps, extension to
2000 program steps possible

Linkages 26 inputs, 32 outputs

Expert Automation, Inc. (KUKA IR 200).

These robots are primarily designed for spot-welding operation in which rocker-guns or welding cylinders are used against backing electrodes. This series of portal robots can place welds even where conventional, welding-gun-equipped robots cannot be used, for instance, in cases where the weld spots are located within large-surface workpieces or where access is difficult.

In order to ensure that the welds are faultless, the electrode tip can be pressed against the backing electrode with a welding force of up to 500 daN. The mechanical rigidity required for this is provided by an unconventional joint design for axes 2 and 3, in which both cranks can rotate around the same axis independently in both directions. Two additional links support the boom, which is carried in the central joint. The optional rotary or translatory versions of axis 1 result in the working envelopes illustrated. Axes 2 and 3 can pivot the boom and/or make it move in translatory fashion. Axes 4 and 5 are located centrally and provide circular movements.

KUKA Portal Robots Series IR 200

Kinematic features of the axes

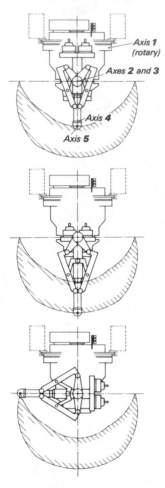

Axis **1** (rotary)

Axes **2** and **3**

Axis **4**

Axis **5**

Motor-driven trolley for the translational axis

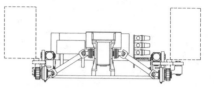

"Axis 6 on the boom" (can be used as an electrode holder, for instance)

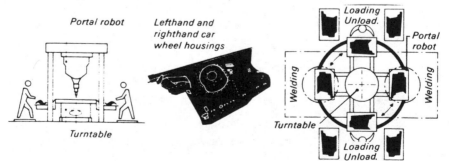

Portal robot

Turntable

Lefthand and righthand car wheel housings

Loading Unload.

Portal robot

Welding

Welding

Turntable

Loading Unload.

General View with Working Zone

Dimensions in mm

Type IR 250/500.2

Type IR 250/500.4

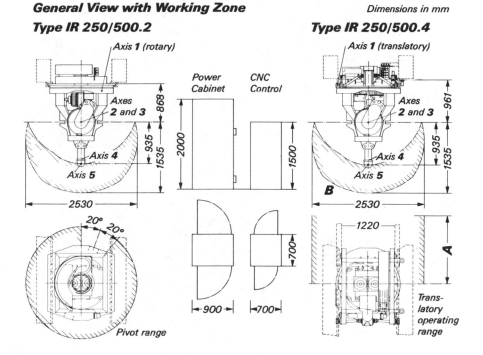

Type legend for KUKA Industrial Robots IR 200

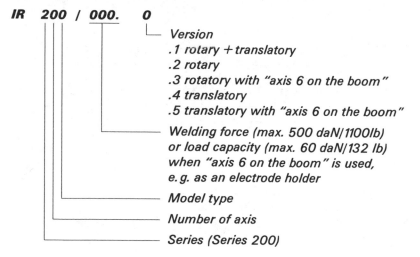

IR   200 / 000.   0

└─ *Version*
.1 rotary + translatory
.2 rotary
.3 rotatory with "axis 6 on the boom"
.4 translatory
.5 translatory with "axis 6 on the boom"

── *Welding force (max. 500 daN/1100lb)*
or load capacity (max. 60 daN/132 lb)
when "axis 6 on the boom" is used,
e.g. as an electrode holder

── *Model type*

── *Number of axis*

── *Series (Series 200)*

Technical Data

Axes data

Axes	Zone	Speed
1 (rotary)	320°	160°/s
1 (translat.)	max. 6 m [**A**]	1.2 m/s
	(max. 19.7 ft)	(47 ips)
2	180°	125°/s
3	180°	125°/s
4	350°	200°/s
5	180°	200°/s

Max. load capacity
500 daN (1,100 lb) welding force
60 daN (132 lb) load

Max. speed
3.4 m/s (134 ips) [curve **B**]

Repeat accuracy
± 1 mm (± 0.04 in)

Drive system
Electro-mechanical, thyristor
controlled DC motors

Noise level
≦80 dB (A)

Power supply
CNC Control
220 V a. c. single phase
(+10 to –15 %); 50/60 Hz
Power cabinet
380 . . . 550 V a. c. three phase, PE,
if available 220 V a. c. single phase
(+10 to –15 %); 50 Hz (60 Hz)
Power consumption 28 kVA at 70 %
duty cycle
Fuses > 440 V : 3 x 50 A
< 440 V : 3 x 63 A
Robot
Air supply 6 bar (87 psi)

Control system
Micro processor control, bit-slice
technology

Memory capacity
1000 program steps, extension to
2000 program steps possible

Linkages
26 inputs, 32 outputs

Fanuc Machinery Ltd. (Robot A-Model 00 Series).
A small robot for assembly, sealing, etc. (three to four axes at a time).

Fanuc Machinery Ltd. (Robot M Series).
Industrial robots providing loading and unloading of workpieces, etc., to a machine tool; they realize machining cells in combination with CNC machine tools. The Fanuc Robot M Series has a variety of functions and simple operations. The M series are the teach-and-repeat-type robots driven by FANUC DC servo motors, and freely taught motion paths. The free motion paths can adapt the robot flexibility to different types of parts or various machining jobs. The FANUC hand series are specially developed for the machining process and are capable of handling a variety of workpieces and of changing tools. The connecting interface between the FANUC Robot M series and the machine tools is standardized, and can easily be connected to NC machine tools already installed.

GMFanuc Robot Series

MODEL	M-00	M-0
Coordinate system	Cylindrical coordinate type	Dual cylindrical coordinate type
Controlled axes (Simultaneously controlled axes)	5 axes (1)	6 axes equivalent (1)
Motion range (Maximum speed)	Mechanical unit X within 150mm (500mm/s) (ON/OFF) A within 60° (90°/s) (ON/OFF) α 4 positions ON/OFF by 90° step (90°/s) Workpiece feeder- Z 300mm (66mm/s) C (within 3.5 s/pallet)	Z 150mm (500mm/s) X 150mm (500mm/s) A 90° (120°/s) C 120° (120°/s) B 180° (120°/s) Wrist B Wrist D α0°/90° or 0°/180° α90° steps (2 positions (4 positions ON/OFF) ON/OFF) (90°/s) (90°/s)
Max. load capacity at wrist	20kg	20kg
Repeatability	±0.3 mm	±0.5 mm
Driving method	DC servo/Pneumatic	DC servo (Wrist B/D: Pneumatic)
Control unit	SYSTEM R-MODEL A	SYSTEM R-MODEL B
Operation method	Teach and repeat	Teach and repeat
Data memory	600 points	300 ~ 1320 points
External auxiliary memory	—	LSI cassette A Bubble cassette B1/B2
Functions		Palletizing Safety interlock Program control Simple & quick instructions Hand & peripheral device control Remote operations Computer control
Hand (Graspable weight)	HAND D6 (5 kg x 2)	HAND D3/D3B/D4/D4B/D5 (5 kg x 2) HAND T0/M0 (10 kg)
Motion of the Robot		

GMFanuc Robot Series

MODEL	M-1	
Coordinate system	Cylindrical coordinate type	Cylindrical coordinate type
Controlled axes (Simultaneously controlled axes)	3 ~ 5 axes (1)	3 ~ 5 axes (5)

Motion range (Maximum speed)	Z 500mm (500mm/s)
	θ 300° (60°/s)
	R 500/800/1100mm (1000mm/s)
	
	Wrist A Wrist B Wrist C
	          α0°/90° α270°
	          or (60°/s)
	          0°/180° βwithin ±5°
	   — (ON/ (ON/
	          OFF) OFF)
	          (60°/s) (30°/s)
		Z 550mm (500mm/s)
		θ 300° (60°/s)
		R 500/800/1100mm (1000mm/s)
		
		Wrist A Wrist B Wrist E Wrist F
		         α0°/90° α300° α300°
		         or (120°/s) (90°/s)
		         0°/180° β190°
		  — (ON/ (60°/s)
		        OFF)
		        (60°/s)

Max. load capacity at wrist	47 kg (3 axes), 31 kg (4/5 axes)	47 kg (3 axes), 31 kg (4 axes) 20 kg (5 axes)
Repeatability	± 1 mm	± 1 mm
Driving method	DC servo (Wrist B/C: Pneumatic)	DC servo (Wrist B: Pneumatic)
Control unit	SYSTEM R-MODEL B	SYSTEM R-MODEL C
Operation method	Teach and repeat	Teach and repeat
Data memory	300 ~ 1320 points	300 ~ 6000 points
External auxiliary memory	LSI cassette A Bubble cassette B1/B2	Bubble cassette B1/B2

Functions	Palletizing Safety interlock
	Program control
	Simple & quick
	  instructions
	
	Hand & peripheral
	  device control
	Remote operations
	Computer control
		Same as M-3

Hand (Graspable weight)	HAND D1/D1B/D2 (10 kg x 2) HAND T0/M0 (10 kg) HAND T1/M1 (20 kg)	HAND D1/D1B/D2 (10 kg x 2) HAND T0/M0 (10 kg) HAND T1/M1 (20 kg)
Motion of the Robot	Z550mm R500, 800 or 1100mm Within ±5° α300° θ300°	

GMFanuc Robot Series

M-3	A-0
Cylindrical coordinate type	Cylindrical coordinate type
5 axes (5)	3~5 axes (5)

Z 1200mm (500mm/s)
θ 300° (60°/s)
R 1200mm (1000mm/s)
α 300° (80°/s)
β 190° (80°/s)
	Z 300mm (600mm/s)
	θ 300° (120°/s)
	R 300mm (1200mm/s)
	
	Wrist A Wrist E Wrist F
	          α300° α300°
	          or (90°/s)
	  — 90° x n β190°
	          (120°/s) (60°/s)

80 kg	10 kg (3 axes), 5 kg (4 axes) 3 kg (5 axes)
± 1 mm	± 0.05 mm
DC servo	DC servo
SYSTEM R-MODEL C	SYSTEM R-MODEL C
Teach and repeat	Teach and repeat
300~6000 points	300~6000 points
Bubble cassette B1/B2	Bubble cassette B1/B2
Linear control Hand direction control Palletizing Program control	Simple & quick instructions Hand & peripheral device control Remote operations Computer conrol
Sensor interface Safety interlock	
HAND W1 (50 kg) HAND W2 (50 kg) HAND W3 (50 kg)	Hand A0 (1 kg) Automatic hand changer

GMFanuc Robot Series

MODEL	A-1	S-1
Coordinate system	Cylindrical coordinate type	Articulated type
Controlled axes (Simultaneously controlled axes)	3~5 axes (5)	5 axes (5)

Motion range (Maximum speed)	Z 500mm (600mm/s)
	θ 300° (120°/s)
	R 500mm (1200mm/s)
	
	Wrist A Wrist E Wrist F
	        α300° α300°
	       or (90°/s)
	 — 90° x n. β190°
	     (120°/s) (60°/s)
		Y 1000/2000mm (500mm/s)
		θ 300° (90°/s)
		   (Select Y or θ)
		W 75° (120°/s)
		U 85° (120°/s)
		β 210° (90°/s)
		α 360° (120°/s)

Max. load capacity at wrist	30 kg (3 axes), 15 kg (4 axes) 9 kg (5 axes)	10 kg
Repeatability	± 0.05 mm	± 0.2 mm
Driving method	DC servo	DC servo
Control unit	SYSTEM R-MODEL C	SYSTEM R-MODEL C
Operation method	Teach and repeat	Teach and repeat
Data memory	300~6000 points	300~6000 points
External auxiliary memory	Bubble cassette B1/B2	Bubble cassette B1/B2
Functions	Linear control Hand direction control Palletizing Program control	Simple & quick instructions Hand & peripheral device control Remote operations Computer conrol
	Sensor interface Safety interlock	
Hand (Graspable weight)	Hand A1 (5 kg) Automatic hand changer	
Motion of the Robot		

GCA Corp. (XR Series 3, 4, 5, and 6 Robots).

This series comprises continuous-path extended-reach robots providing the versatility of multiple robots. Bridge and trolley construction enables an expanded work envelope up to 40 ft × 20 ft (12 m × 6 m). Load capacity is an astonishing 2500 lb (1125 kg); repeatability is ± 0.02 in. (0.5 mm). The XR is ceiling mounted—its pedestal can move from station to station performing different functions at each station, while leaving the floor area open. X and Y motions are performed by bridge and trolley; telescoping tubes provide the vertical motions. Up to three additional axes can be added.

The XR robots are dc servo driven, microprocessor controlled, with 1500 points to enable performance of multiple tasks without reprogramming. Programming methods include on-line teach/playback using remote pendant and off-line manual data input (MDI) with computer prompting for either local or absolute coordinates. The playback function includes combining previously programmed routines to perform a complex task. Optional animation simulator permits a visual check of a program.

The large work envelope, heavy payload, and high repeatability make the XR robots capable of a wide range of activities such as machine loading, deburring, welding, assembly, and materials transfer.

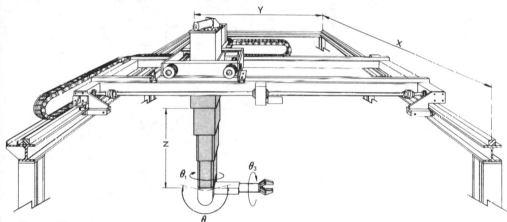

Specifications

MODEL	XR3	XR4	XR5	XR6
Degree of Freedom	3	4	5	6
(Bridge) X	(36 ips) 10 ',20 ',40 '	(36 ips) 10 ',20 ',40 '	(36 ips) 10 ',20 ',40 '	(36 ips) 10 ',20 ',40 '
(Trolley) Y	(36 ips) 10 '-20 '	(36 ips) 10 '-20 '	(36 ips) 10 '-20 ' (2 ' increments)	(36 ips) 10 '-20 '
(Telescoping Tubes) Z	(0-36 ips) 0 "-84 "	(0-36 ips) 0 "-84 "	(0-36 ips) 0 "-84 "	(0-36 ips) 0 "-84 "
(Yaw) θ_1		330 ° (1 rad/sec)	330 ° (1 rad/sec)	330 ° (1 rad/sec)
(Pitch) θ_2 *			210 ° (1 rad/sec)	210 ° (1 rad/sec)
(Roll) θ_3 **				330 ° (1 rad/sec)
Inputs/Outputs		8 each (standard)		
Driving Method	DC Servo	DC Servo	DC Servo	DC Servo
Repeatability	± 0.02 in.	± 0.02 in.	± 0.02 in.	± 0.02 in.
Power Requirements	230/460 V 3 phase, 60 Hz, 30 amp	230/460 V 3 phase, 60 Hz, 30 amp	230/460 V 3 phase, 60 Hz, 30 amp	230/460 V 3 phase, 60 Hz, 30 amp

No. of Tubes	TELESCOPING TUBES		LOAD CAPACITY (lbs.)
	Max. Tube Travel (in.)	Max. Tube Speed (ips)	(less weight of end effector)
4	84	36	350
	84	18	800
3	56	24	700
	56	12	1,350
2	28	12	1,450
	28	6	2,500

*Payload limited by pitch torque of 7000 in. lb.
**Payload limted by roll torque of 500 in. lb.

GCA Corp. (B Series 1440, 2660, and 4700 Robots).

The B Series robots are specifically designed to fulfill the need for reasonably priced, heavy-duty, high-performance robots with large travel areas. Without sacrificing smoothness or accuracy of operation, the B Series can carry up to a 770-lb (347 kg) payload in a work envelope up to 638 ft³ (18 m³) with up to six axes of flexibility. The compact design, requiring minimum floor space, contributes to the speed, smoothness, and high repeatability.

A uniquely engineered combination of dc servo-drive/motor and pneumatic linear actuators provide an automatic counterbalance for heavy loads. This feature achieves nearly constant performance characteristics regardless of load. The combination of speed, payload, compact design, high repeatability, and special counterbalance function makes the B Series suitable for material handling, machine load/unload, and similar heavy-duty applications. The large work envelope and performance capabilities also suit it for large process work such as welding.

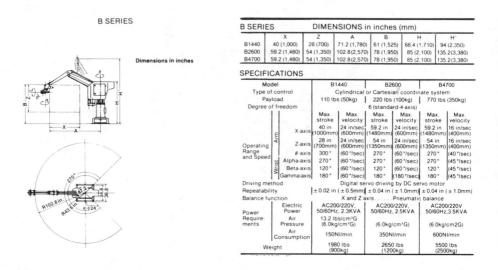

B SERIES

Dimensions in inches

B SERIES	DIMENSIONS in inches (mm)					
	X	Z	A	B	H	H¹
B1440	40 (1,000)	28 (700)	71.2 (1,780)	61 (1,525)	68.4 (1,710)	94 (2,350)
B2600	59.2 (1,480)	54 (1,350)	102.8 (2,570)	78 (1,950)	85 (2,100)	135.2 (3,380)
B4700	59.2 (1,480)	54 (1,350)	102.8 (2,570)	78 (1,950)	85 (2,100)	135.2 (3,380)

SPECIFICATIONS

Model		B1440		B2600		B4700	
Type of control		Cylindrical or Cartesian coordinate system					
Payload		110 lbs (50kg)		220 lbs (100kg)		770 lbs (350kg)	
Degree of freedom		6 (standard-4-axis)					
		Max. stroke	Max. velocity	Max. stroke	Max. velocity	Max. stroke	Max. velocity
Operating Range and Speed	Arm X-axis	40 in (1000mm)	24 in/sec (600mm)	59.2 in (1480mm)	24 in/sec (600mm)	59.2 in (1480mm)	16 in/sec (400mm)
	Z-axis	28 in (700mm)	24 in/sec (600mm)	54 in (1350mm)	24 in/sec (600mm)	54 in (1350mm)	16 in/sec (400mm)
	θ-axis	300°	(60°/sec)	270°	(60°/sec)	270°	(40°/sec)
	Wrist Alpha-axis	270°	(60°/sec)	270°	(60°/sec)	270°	(45°/sec)
	Beta-axis	120°	(60°/sec)	120°	(60°/sec)	120°	(45°/sec)
	Gamma-axis	180°	(60°/sec)	180°	(180°/sec)	180°	(45°/sec)
Driving method		Digital servo driving by DC servo motor					
Repeatability		±0.02 in (±0.5mm)		±0.04 in (±1.0mm)		±0.04 in (±1.0mm)	
Balance function		X and Z axis ...... Pneumatic balance					
Power Require- ments	Electric Power	AC200/220V, 50/60Hz, 2.3KVA		AC200/220V, 50/60Hz, 2.5KVA		AC200/220V 50/60Hz,3.5KVA	
	Air Pressure	13.2 lbs/cm²G (6.0kg/cm²G)		(6.0kg/cm²G)		(6.0kg/cm2G)	
	Air Consumption	150Nl/min		350Nl/min		600Nl/min	
Weight		1980 lbs (900kg)		2650 lbs (1200kg)		5500 lbs (2500kg)	

GCA Corp. (R Series 250 and 350 Robots).

These robots are designed to handle the big, heavy jobs. In a work area up to 12 ft high (3.7 m) and 13 ft (4 m) across, a 1600-lb (720-kg) payload can be maneuvered with accuracy. Rugged body construction resists the torque generated by the heavy tasks.

An ingenious combination of electric servomotor, oil pressure, and stepping motor drives the six axes to provide repeatability of ± 0.10 in. (2.54 mm) despite the heavy loads. Control is microprocessor based, point-to-point with 256 memory steps. Battery backup maintains memory during power failure.

The R Series robot is ideal for palletizing, supplying workpieces to forging equipment, exchanging press dies, and material handling for process functions such as grinding, cutting, or drilling.

R SERIES

Dimensions in inches

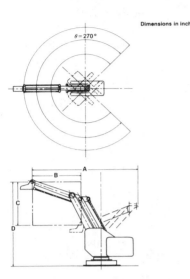

$\theta = 270°$

SPECIFICATIONS

Model	R			
Type of control	Cylindrical coordinates			
Payload	Maximum 1650 lbs (750kg)			
Degree of freedom	6			

			Max. stroke	Max. velocity
	Arm	X-axis (Backwards-forwards) (Separately listed)		16 in/sec (400mm/sec)
		Z-axis (Up-down) (Separately listed)		16 in/sec (400mm/sec)
Operating Range and Speed		θ-axis (Turning)	270°	45°/sec
	Wrist	α-axis (Turning)	180°	40°/sec
		β-axis (Bending)	90°	45°/sec
		γ-axis (Rotation)	180°	45°/sec
	Arm	X-axis	Electricity, oil pressure, stepping motor	
		Z-axis	(digital servo control)	
		Z-axis	Electricity, oil pressure (digital servo control)	
Driving method		θ-axis	Electricity, oil pressure (digital servo control)	
	Wrist	α-axis	Electric servo motor	
		β-axis	Electric servo motor	
		γ-axis	Electric servo motor	
Repeatability	± 0.04 in ～ ± 0.12 in(± 1mm ～ ± 3mm)			
Power Requirements	AC200/220V, 50/60Hz, Main structure AC100/200V, 30VA, Control			

R250 DIMENSIONS in inches (mm)

R250	A	B	C	D	Payload
R250-51	62.8 (1570)	38.4 (960)	55 (1375)	70 (1750)	1100 (500)
R250-71	89.2 (2230)	57.6 (1440)	77 (1925)	98 (2450)	660 (300
R250-91	115.6 (2890)	76.8 (1920)	99 (2475)	126 (3150)	550 (250)

R350

R350	A	B	C	D	Payload
R350-51	89.2 (2230)	54.4 (1360)	68 (1700)	94 (2350)	1650 (750)
R350-71	126.8 (3170)	81.6 (2040)	95.2 (2380)	131.6 (3290)	1100 (500)
R350-91	164.4 (4110)	108.8 (2720)	122.4 (3060)	169.2 (4230)	770 (350)

GCA Corp. (P Series 800 Robot).

The P800 is an accurate, high-speed robot designed for multi-purpose industrial use. With a large work envelope and a 66-lb (30-kg) lifting capacity, it is extraordinarily compact for its reach and payload. It requires minimal floor space; installation among existing equipment is easy. Offered with microprocessor-based control, the P800 can be used for material handling, machine loading and assembly, as well as numerous processes including arc or spot welding, gluing, drilling, etc.

The P800 is available with up to five axes. Control can be either point-to-point or continuous path with simplified programming or edit programming via Manual Data Input (MDI) or teach/playback.

SPECIFICATIONS

Model		P800
Type of control		Articulated
Payload		66 lbs (30kg)
Degree of freedom		5
	X-axis	—
	Z-axis	—
Operating Range and Speed	ϕ-axis	270°(60°/sec)
	ϕ_1-axis	180°(60°/sec)
	ϕ_2-axis	300°(66°/sec)
	Beta-axis	200°(75°/sec)
	Alpha-axis	270°(75°/sec)
Driving method		Digital servo driving by DC servo motor
Repeatability		± 0.02 in (± 0.5mm)
Power Requirements	Electric Power	AC200/220V, 50/60Hz, 2.5KVA
	Air Pressure	—
Weight		400 lbs(180kg)

P800

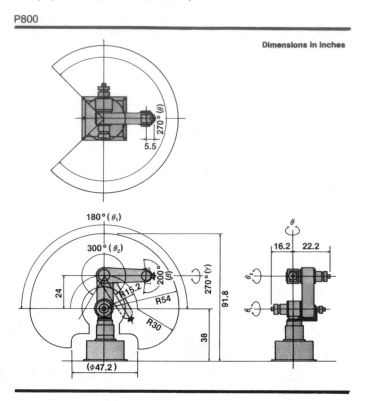

Dimensions in inches

GCA Corp. (P Series 300H, 300V, and 500).

The P500 and P300 robots are accurate, high-speed robots capable of a broad range of precision industrial applications. Microprocessor controlled, with up to 15-lb (6.75-kg) payload, they can be used for assembly, material handling, sorting, and similar tasks, and for processes including arc or spot welding. Space requirement is approximately the same as for a person; installation and relocation among existing equipment is easy. Low cost, combined with increased productivity, results in quick payback. All-electric dc servo drives are used.

The model P300 is available in vertical (P300V) and horizontal (P300H) configurations. The horizontal format is especially well suited for simple assembly as well as packaging and certain processes such as welding. The P300H has up to four axes; all other P Series models have up to five axes. All P Series robots may be configured with either point-to-point or continuous-path control and simplified programming or edit of program in Manual Data Input (MDI) or teach/playback.

P300V   P300H   P500

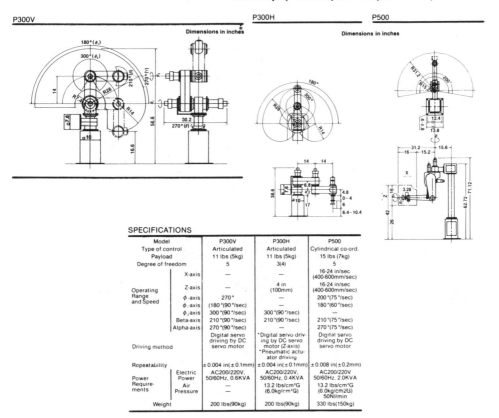

Dimensions in inches

Dimensions in inches

SPECIFICATIONS

Model		P300V	P300H	P500
Type of control		Articulated	Articulated	Cylindrical co-ord.
Payload		11 lbs (5kg)	11 lbs (5kg)	15 lbs (7kg)
Degree of freedom		5	3(4)	5
Operating Range and Speed	X-axis	—	—	16-24 in/sec (400-600mm/sec)
	Z-axis	—	4 in (100mm)	16-24 in/sec (400-600mm/sec)
	ϕ-axis	270°	—	200°(75°/sec)
	ϕ_z-axis	(180°(90°/sec)	—	180°(60°/sec)
	ϕ_j-axis	300°(90°/sec)	300°(90°/sec)	—
	Beta-axis	210°(90°/sec)	210°(90°/sec)	210°(75°/sec)
	Alpha-axis	270°(90°/sec)	—	270°(75°/sec)
Driving method		Digital servo driving by DC servo motor	*Digital servo driving by DC servo motor (Z-axis) *Pneumatic actuator driving	Digital servo driving by DC servo motor
Repeatability		±0.004 in(±0.1mm)	±0.004 in(±0.1mm)	±0.008 in(±0.2mm)
Power Requirements	Electric Power	AC200/220V, 50/60Hz, 0.6KVA	AC200/220V, 50/60Hz, 0.4KVA	AC200/220V 50/60Hz, 2.0KVA
	Air Pressure	—	13.2 lbs/cm²G (6.0kg/cm²G)	13.2 lbs/cm²G (0.0kg/cm2G) 50Nl/min
Weight		200 lbs(90kg)	200 lbs(90kg)	330 lbs(150kg)

GCA Corp. (F Series Special-Purpose Robot).

The F Series robot is a three to five axes robot specially designed for flat range operations. It provides a flexible, easily programmed, medium to high-speed system for plasma or torch cutting, gluing, marking or other flat plane work. Despite its modest space requirement, it has a 3500 in.² (2.3 m²) operating range. Dc servomotor drive provides accuracy and reliability, and the unique pantograph-type mechanism enables a high capacity for accurate repeat functions, especially important for gang cutting of fabrics and materials. Vibrations are eliminated by inertia force.

SPECIFICATIONS

Model		F	
Type of control		Articulated/cartesian	
Payload		22 lbs (10kg)	
Degree of freedom		5(standard 3)	
		Max. stroke	Max. velocity
Operating Range and Speed	Arm X-axis	62.4 in (1560mm)	24 in/sec (600mm/sec)
	Arm Y-axis	58.8 in (1470mm)	24 in/sec (600mm/sec)
	Wrist θ-axis	90°	45°/sec
	Wrist Z-axis	6 in (150mm)	16 in/sec (400mm/sec)
	Beta-axis	120°	60°/sec
Driving method	X, Y, and β-axis	DC servo motor driving	
	θ and Z-axis	Pneumatic actuator hand	
Repeatability		±0.02 in (±0.5mm)	
Driving source	Electric Power	AC200/220V, 50/60Hz, 2.5KVA	
	Air pressure	13.2 lbs/cm²G (6.0kg/cm²G)	
Weight		770 lbs (350kg)	

Accessories and Options:
• Hand (mechanical, vacuum, magnet, etc.)
• Plasma cutting
• Metering and dispensing systems
• Complete systems, including fixturing, conveyors, covers, guards, special tooling and interfacing
Control:
• A250 Point-to-point and continuous path (simultaneous 6-axes)
• A300 Point-to-point and continuous path (simultaneous 6-axes)

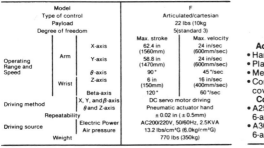

F SERIES

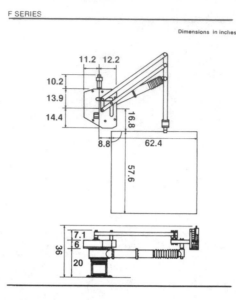

Dimensions in inches

General Electric Co. (Model A12 Robot).

This model is known as the Allegro programmable assembly robot. It offers advanced solutions to productivity/quality control problems. The Allegro is a versatile, high-performance assembly robot that performs many different tasks with a high degree of precision, repeatability, and speed, ensuring maximum output. Sensor capabilities allow the programmer to include testing and reselection of parts and operations during the assembly process, thus ensuring consistent quality.

An interactive, high-level language developed for assembly applications makes programming and reprogramming particularly easy.

Standard Specifications Model A12

WORKING SPACE

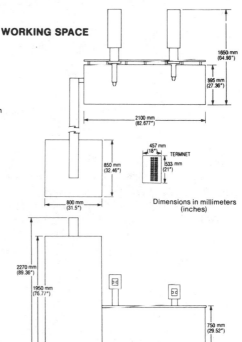

1650 mm (64.96")
595 mm (27.36")
2100 mm (82.677")
457 mm (18")
TERMNET
850 mm (32.46")
533 mm (21")
800 mm (31.5")
2270 mm (89.36")
1950 mm (76.77")
750 mm (29.52")

Dimensions in millimeters (inches)

• ARMS

— One to four arms
— Three to five degrees of freedom per arm
— Arms supported by rollers on the x axis slideway
— More than one arm can be applied to the same bench and more than one x axis slideway may be utilized

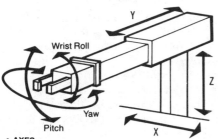

Y
Wrist Roll
Z
Yaw
Pitch
X

• AXES

— Three standard linear movements (x, y, z axes)
— Two of three optional rotations
    Roll
    Pitch
    Yaw
— Axes powered by d.c. servomotors
— Displacements continuously measured by high resolution optical transducer
— Rack and pinion gearing with reduction unit
— Y and z axes columns are guided by zero clearance rollers on hardened tracks
— Adjustable pneumatic counterbalance system on z axis offsets weight of the arm assembly, tooling, and part

• MECHANICAL

— Useful strokes:	x axis up to 1300 mm (51.18 in.) y axis up to 310 mm (12.20 in.) z axis up to 265 mm (10.43 in.) roll/yaw 360° pitch 196°
— Resolution:	x, y, z axes 0.020 mm average roll/pitch/yaw 0.02° average
— Accuracy-Positioning:	± 0.16 mm (0.0063 in.)/axis (full strokes)
— Repeatability:	x, y, z axes ± .025 mm (0.001 in.) roll/pitch/yaw ± 0.025°
— Maximum speed:	x, y, z axes 40 m/min. (131.23 ft./min) roll/pitch/yaw 2.3 rad/sec.
— Maximum acceleration:	x axis 2.5 m/sec.² (8.2025 ft./sec.²) y and z axes 3.5 m/sec.² (11.4853 ft./sec.²) roll/pitch/yaw 18 rad/sec.²
— Design payload:	from 1.5 kg (3.3 lbs.) to 6.5 kg (14 lbs.) depending on weight of rotational accessories, grippers and parts
— Power requirement	380/440/500 3-phase, 3.5 kw 50/60 Hz

• CONTROL SYSTEM

— Multiprocessor system with distributed functions:
  • central processing unit DEC LSI 11/2 (general supervision)
  • microprocessor INTEL 8080 (axis motion control)
— Mass memory device
  • floppy disc (optional)
  • magnetic cassette
— Optional peripherals:
  • keyboard printer — Terminet 2030
  • portable teach box
— Point-to-point control of linear and rotary movements
— Control of arm speed along entire work path
— Axes simultaneously powered and controlled: up to 12
— Up to 16 analog sensor inputs
— Off-part part programming through interactive high level PASCAL-type language: HELP
— Complete operation of self teach capability via terminal and teach box for definition and storage of cycle points
— Multi task operating system allowing parallel independent execution of different processes and coordination of different arms
— Input/output control of application devices for part feeding and orientation, and of tools and instruments, as part of the whole assembly system
— Start, halt, stop of machine and cycle, and local intervention enabled by control panel
— Part-program executed from random access memory
— Data processing and monitoring of production data on printer terminal
— Storage of debugged application programs by filing in mass memory
— Access to stored application programs for direct modifications

General Electric Co. (Model AW7 Robot).

This is basically an arc welding robot. It has a miniature noncontact sensor serving as the robot's guide for accurate welding along the weld line or a self-correcting track. The path of the torch tip will not be adversely affected by surface irregularities caused by spatter that develops in carbon dioxide welding or holes less than 0.39 in. (10 mm) in diameter. The sensor is effective with a wide range of metals including stainless steel, aluminum, and other nonferrous metals.

The sensor on the AW7 detects deviations caused by shearing and tack welding and by the effects of thermal strain and setting deviations and activates the robot to make the necessary tracking corrections.

Programming the robot requires only two points for straight welding, only five points for welding a corner including straight parts. Partial corrections are made by manually setting the step number and programming new data. Additional points are added by reprogramming new data without destroying the original instructions. The programming data can be stored on cassette tapes. Once taught, the robot will automatically weld as many identically shaped workpieces as required with precision. It will check both ends of welding lines and corners and automatically correct for deviations. In horizontal fillet welding, the robot can perform welding of the corners continuously, without cutting the arc while it computes its own track. The robot can perform track welding of curves where the sensor can be used, specifically curves with a radius of more than 12 in. (300 mm).

Standard Specifications
Model AW7

● ROBOT MAIN BODY

Motion	Traverse (X)	1,500 mm (59″)
	Out-in (Y)	1,000 mm (39″)
	Up-down (Z)	1,100 mm (43″)
	Swing (SW)	±100°
	Wrist Bend (BD)	−5° - +50° (measured from right below the hand)
	Sensor withdrawal	50 mm (2″)
Speed	Welding (at torch tip)	150-990 mm/min (6″-39″/min)
	Quick feed	6,000 mm/min (240″/min)
Positioning repeatability		±1.0 mm (±0.04″)
Hydraulic power source		Operating pressure 70 kg/cm² (995 psi), air-cooled
Pneumatic power source		4 kg/cm² (57 psi), or more
Weight		1,300 kg (2,866 lbs.)

● POSITIONER

Motion function	Revolution	−200° - +200°
	Tilt	−200° - +200°
Speed		18°/min-114°/min
	Quick Feed	660°/min
Maximum weight of work		600 kg (1,323 lbs.) (including jigs)
Maximum permissible unbalanced load		20 kg/m (13.4 ft. lbs.)
Weight		1,000 kg (2,205 lbs.)

MODEL AW7A

● ROBOT MAIN BODY

Motion	Traverse (X)	1,500 mm (59″)
	Out-in (Y)	800 mm (32″)
	Up-down (Z)	500 mm (20″)
	Swing (SW)	±100°
	Wrist Bend (BD)	−5° - +50° (measured from right below the hand)
	Sensor withdrawal	50 mm (2″)
Speed	Welding (at torch tip)	150-990 mm/min (6″-39″/min)
	Quick feed	6,000 mm/min (240″/min)
Positioning repeatability		±1.0 mm (±0.04″)
Hydraulic power source		Operating pressure 70 kg/cm² (995 psi), air-cooled
Pneumatic power source		4 kg/cm² (57 psi), or more
Weight		1,100 kg (2,425 lbs.)

● POSITIONER

Motion function	Revolution	−200° - +200°
	Tilt	−200° - +200°
Speed		18°/min-114°/min
	Quick Feed	660°/min
Maximum weight of work		600 kg (1,323 lbs.) (including jigs)
Maximum permissible unbalanced load		20 kg/m (13.4 ft. lbs.)
Weight		1,000 kg (2,205 lbs.)

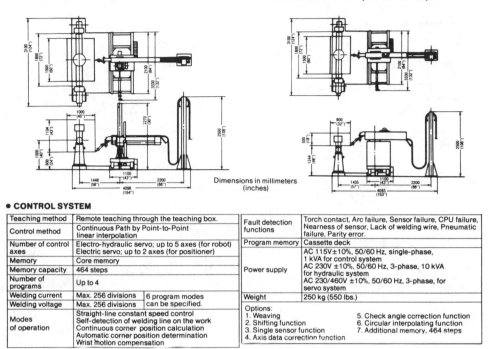

Dimensions in millimeters
(inches)

● **CONTROL SYSTEM**

Teaching method	Remote teaching through the teaching box.
Control method	Continuous Path by Point-to-Point linear interpolation
Number of control axes	Electro-hydraulic servo; up to 5 axes (for robot) Electric servo; up to 2 axes (for positioner)
Memory	Core memory
Memory capacity	464 steps
Number of programs	Up to 4
Welding current	Max. 256 divisions
Welding voltage	Max. 256 divisions
Modes of operation	Straight-line constant speed control Self-detection of welding line on the work Continous corner position calculation Automatic corner position determination Wrist motion compensation

(Welding current / Welding voltage: 6 program modes can be specified.)

Fault detection functions	Torch contact, Arc failure, Sensor failure, CPU failure, Nearness of sensor, Lack of welding wire, Pneumatic failure, Parity error.
Program memory	Cassette deck
Power supply	AC 115V±10%, 50/60 Hz, single-phase, 1 kVA for control system AC 230V ±10%, 50/60 Hz, 3-phase, 10 kVA for hydraulic system AC 230/460V ±10%, 50/60 Hz, 3-phase, for servo system
Weight	250 kg (550 lbs.)

Options:
1. Weaving
2. Shifting function
3. Single sensor function
4. Axis data correction function
5. Check angle correction function
6. Circular interpolating function
7. Additional memory, 464 steps

General Electric Co. (Model GP 66).

This is a general-purpose robot designed as a modular unit system allowing a selection of one to three axes. The three-pivot wrist design allows movements that minimize working space. The use of grippers, spot welding pincers, or similar tools gives capability for a wide variety of production operations and products.

The GP 66 features dc servomotor axis drives, an absolute optical encoder position control system, and programming by teach box and push-button. Remote program storage on magnetic tape is optional.

Standard Specifications
Model GP 66

ROBOT MAIN BODY

Axes		Operating area	Operating speed
Rotation	Axis I	320°	80°/sec.
Vertical swivel	Axis II	65°	30°/sec.
Linear	Axis III	700 mm (27.6 in)	450 mm/sec. (17.7 in/sec.)
Wrist rotation	Axis IV	350°	120°/sec.
Wrist swivel	Axis V	350°	180°/sec.
Wrist turnover	Axis VI	350°	180°/sec.
Transversal location unit	Axis VII (optional)	600 - 2400 mm (23.6 - 94.5 in)	450 mm/sec. (17.7 in/sec.)
Power requirement	230/460 V, 60 Hz, 12 kW, 3 phase		
Average power consumption	2 kW		
No. of standard axes	6, Axis VII optional		

Positioning repeatability	± 1 mm (0.039 in)
Mounting position	any
Weight	robot: 875 kg (1925 lbs) approx.
Load capacity at gripper-flange	30 kg (66 lbs)
Operating area	4 m (157.4 in)
Space requirement	bed plate size, robot 1 x 1 m (39 x 39 in)
Gripper actuating	pneumatic, pressure 5 bar (73 psi) 12 bar (175 psi) max.
Ambient temperature	50°C (122°F)

CONTROL SYSTEM

Teaching Method	Remote teaching through teaching box
Memory	RAM with battery backup
Memory Capacity	290 points at 6-axis
Control Method	Design Principle: modular elements • microprocessor (PTP) for program logic, path control, parameter storage for coordination and all additional auxiliary functions • 15 input and 15 output ports with connectors • plug-in capacity for 7 servo amps for 7 independent axes • motor contactor section and main circuit breakers for power supply
Number of programs	15
Power supply	230/460 V, 60 Hz, 12 kW, 3 phase
Weight cabinet	470 kg (1,035 lbs)
Size cabinet	0.6 x 1 m (23.6 x 39.3")
Ambient temperature	35°C (95°F)
Umbilical cord	up to 25 m (81') approx.
Optional equipment • overload cutout on gripper-flange • unit for lateral shifting of robot as additional axis • pneumatic rotating unit for gripper • pneumatic swiveling unit for gripper • memory expansion to 4370 teach points in increments of 340 teach points for 6 axis unit	

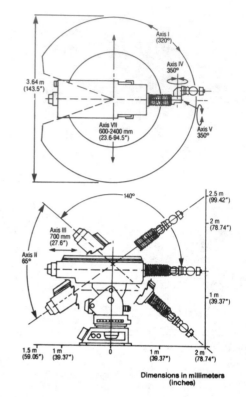

Dimensions in millimeters (inches)

General Electric Co. (Model GP 132).

This articulated-arm, general-purpose robot is designed for heavy-duty operations with a flexible arm with an extensive reach. It can be mounted in any position on floor, wall, or ceiling, maximizing space utilization. Based on proven technology, the all-electric-drive GP 132 provides easy programming via teach box techniques. This design is for heavy-duty material-handling operations, loading, unloading and spotwelding applications. Loads of up to 132 lb (60 kg) can be handled.

The GP 132 features dc servomotor axis drives, an absolute optical encoder position control system, and programming by teach box and push-button. Remote program storage on magnetic tape is optional equipment.

Standard Specifications
Model GP 132

ROBOT MAIN BODY

Axes		Operating area	Operating speed
Rotation	Axis I	300°	59°/sec.
Vertical swivel	Axis II	110°	50°/sec.
Linear arm	Axis III	120°	87°/sec.
Wrist rotation	Axis IV	345°	144°/sec.
Wrist swivel	Axis V	210°	142°/sec.

Wrist turn	Axis VI	540°	140°/sec.
Transversal location unit	Axis VII (optional)	600 - 4,200 mm (23.6 - 165.35")	.5 m/sec. (19.7"/sec.)
Power requirement	230/460 V, 60 Hz, 17 kW, 3 phase		
Average power consumption	2.9 kW		
No. of standard axes	6, Axis VII optional		
Positioning repeatability	± 0.75 mm (.030")		
Mounting position	any (axis I restricted 160° rotation when used in other than standing position)		
Weight	robot: 1000 kg (2,205 lbs)		
Load capacity at gripper-flange	60 kg (132 lbs)		
Operating area	min: 2 m (78.74") diameter max: 4.4 m (173.22") diameter		
Space Requirement	bed plate: 0.9 x 1.2 m (35.4 x 47.2")		
Gripper actuating	pneumatic, pressure 6 bar (87 psi) max.		
Ambient temperature	50°C (122°F)		

CONTROL SYSTEM

Teaching Method	Remote teaching through teaching box
Memory	RAM with battery backup
Memory Capacity	290 points at 6-axis PTP
Control Method	Design Principle: modular elements • microprocessor for program logic, path control, parameter storage for coordination and all additional auxiliary functions • 15 input and 15 output ports with connectors • plug-in capacity for 7 servo amps for 7 independent axes • motor contactor section and main circuit breakers for power supply
Number of programs	15
Power supply	230/460 V, 60 Hz, 17 kW, 3 phase
Weight cabinet	470 kg (1,035 lbs)
Size cabinet	0.6 x 1 m (23.6 x 39.3")
Ambient temperature	35°C (95°F)
Umbilical cord	up to 25 m (81') approx.

Optional equipment
• overload cutout on gripper-flange
• unit for lateral shifting of robot as additional axis
• pneumatic rotating unit for gripper
• pneumatic swiveling unit for gripper
• memory expansion to 4370 teach points in increments of 340 teach points for 6 axis unit
• 29 cm (11.4") arm extension

WORKING SPACE

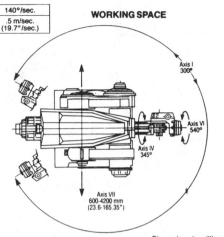

Axis I 300°
Axis VI 540°
Axis IV 345°
Axis VII 600-4200 mm (23.6-165.35")

Dimensions in millimeters (inches)

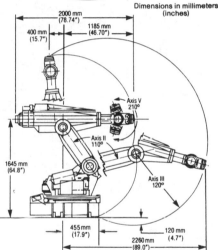

2000 mm (78.74")
400 mm (15.7")
1185 mm (46.70")
Axis V 210°
Axis II 110°
1645 mm (64.8")
Axis III 120°
455 mm (17.9")
120 mm (4.7")
2260 mm (89.0")

General Electric Co. (Model MH33).

This is a linear-type material-handling robot designed for high-speed parts transfer between production line work stations. By means of the fast-moving linear arm, 47.2 in/sec (1.2 m/sec), relatively long distances can be covered in a short time. The gripper attachment can be mounted at one end or both ends, and can be given rotary action or vertical swivel action. By combining these alternatives the work speed can be increased and the robot adapted to the application.

The MH33 features dc servomotor axis drives, an absolute optical encoder position control system, and programming by teach box or push-button. Remote program storage on magnetic tape is optional.

Standard Specifications
Model MH 33

ROBOT MAIN BODY

Axes		Operating area	Operating speed
Rotation	Axis I	320°	160°/sec.
Vertical swivel	Axis II	20°	30°/sec.
Stroke (linear)	Axis III	1800 mm (70.8 in)	1200 mm (47.2 in/sec.)
Transversal location unit	Axis VII (optional)	600 - 2400 mm (23.6 - 94.5 in)	450 mm/sec. (17.7 in/sec.)
Power requirement	230/460 V, 60 Hz, 9 kW, 3 phase		
Average power consumption	1.7 kW		
No. of standard axes	3, Axis VII optional		
Positioning repeatability	± 2.5 mm (0.1 in)		
Mounting position	any		
Weight	robot: 730 kg (1606 lbs) approx.		
Load capacity at gripper-flange	15 kg (33 lbs)		
Operating area	5 m (197 in) diameter		
Space requirement	bed plate size, robot 1 x 1 m (39 x 39 in)		
Gripper actuating	pneumatic, pressure 5 bar (73 psi), 12 bar (175 psi) max.		
Ambient Temperature	50°C (122°F)		

CONTROL SYSTEM

Teaching Method	Remote teaching through teaching box
Memory	RAM with battery backup
Memory Capacity	435 points at 4-axis PTP
Control Method	Design principle: modular elements
	• microprocessor (PTP) for program logic, path control, parameter storage for coordination and all additional auxiliary functions • 15 input and 15 output ports with connectors • plug-in capacity for 7 servo amps for 7 independent axes • motor contactor section and main circuit breakers for power supply
Number of programs	15
Power supply	230/460 V, 60 Hz, 3 phase
Weight cabinet	470 kg (1,035 lbs)
Size cabinet	0.6 x 1 m (23.6 x 39.3")
Ambient temperature	35°C (95°F)
Umbilical cord	up to 25 m (81') approx.
Optional equipment • overload cutout on gripper flange • unit for lateral shifting of robot as additional axis • pneumatic rotating unit for gripper • pneumatic swiveling unit for gripper • memory expansion to 6555 teach points in increments of 510 teach points for 4 axis unit	

WORKING SPACE

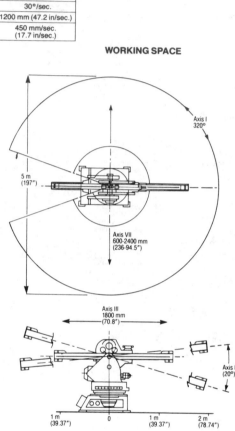

Dimensions in millimeters
(inches)

General Electric Co. (Model P5 Robot).

This model is known as the process robot. It is an electrically driven basic machine able to perform functions required for production over a wide variety of applications. Its performance is a result of advanced mechanical and microprocessor technology combined with flexible software. The typical applications are welding, deburring, sealing, polishing, grinding, and other continuous-path processes.

The robot unit weighs only 500 lb (230 kg). The parallelogram linkage keeps the position of the wrist constant at all times ensuring easy operation. Multijoint action is taught by identifying start and end points. A built-in microprocessor accurately controls each motion, and a control panel displays errors made by the equipment. Taught points can be easily modified or new points added without cancelling the stored data.

The standard robot accommodates up to nine programs. A change in program to be executed is accomplished immediately upon receipt of the appropriate signal. Standard memory capacity is sufficient to teach up to 448 points. Extra capacity is available as an option. The robot operates on Cartesian coordinates as well as joint angle coordinates.

Standard Specifications
Model P5

• ROBOT MAIN BODY

Motion	Arm	Turn	±150°
		Upper arm	+50°, −45°
		Fore arm	+25°, −45°
	Wrist	Bend	+85°, −95°
		Twist	±185°
Speed	Arm		Max. 1,000 mm/sec (39.4 in/sec)
	Wrist	Bend	120°/sec
		Twist	180°/sec
Weight capacity			Max. 10kg (22 lbs) (including grippers)
Repeatability			±0.2 mm (±.008″)
Weight			230 kg (500 lbs.)

Welding speed	120-1,980mm/min (4.7-78.0 in/min), 99 divisions, 9 settings/program, can be designated
Quick speed	10-990 mm/sec (0.4-39.0 in/sec), 99 divisions, 6 settings/program can be designated

• CONTROL SYSTEMS

Teaching method	Remote teaching using the teaching box
Control method	Continuous Path by Point-to-Point linear interpolation
Number of control axes	5 axes
Memory	Core memory
Memory capacity	448 steps
Number of programs	9
Kinds of operation	Straight-line constant speed control, converting operation of multi-joint coordinates into cartesian coordinates
External input/ output points	13 inputs, 15 outputs
Timer	0.1-9.9 sec, 99 div., 7 settings/program
Fault detection function	Overrun Overload Sensor failure CPU failure
Power supply	230/460 VAC ± 15% 60 Hz, 3∅, 4 KVA

• CONTROL SYSTEM FOR WELDING

Welding current	99 divisions	15 settings/program can be designated
Welding voltage	99 divisions	

Arc failure Torch contact Welding current detection	

Options: 1. Memory storage system (cassette deck)
2. Additional memory 512 steps
3. Circular interpolation
4. Path selection — 7 inputs + 2 outputs

WORKING SPACE

4 holes of 18mm dia. (0.7″ dia.)

Rotation ±150°

826 (33″)

400 (15.7″)

500 (20″)

140 (5.5″)

1257r (49″r)

1257 (49″)

301 (12″)

200 (8″)

800 (31″)

100 (4″)

+85°

−95°

Forearm +25° −45°

Upperarm +50° −45°

597 (24″)

600 (24″)

Twist ±185°

1588 (63″)

650 (26″)

683 (27″)

470 (18″)

Dimensions in millimeters (inches)

General Electric Co. (Model P6 Robot).

This is an articulated arm process robot equipped with a maximum of six axes. It is a high-performance, high-precision unit specially developed for stacking, palletizing, and other material-handling processes.

The P6 features dc servomotor axis drives, an absolute optical encoder position control system, and programming by teach box and push-button. Remote program storage on magnetic tape is optional.

Standard Specifications
Model P6

ROBOT MAIN BODY

Axes		Operating area	Operating speed
Rotation	Axis I	320°	80°/sec.
Vertical swivel	Axis II	65°	30°/sec.
Vertical bend	Axis III	100°	50°/sec.
Wrist swivel	Axis IV	270°	120°/sec.
Wrist rotation	Axis V	350°	120°/sec.
Transversal location unit	Axis VII	600 - 2400 (23.6 - 94.5 in)	450 mm/sec. (17.7 in/sec.)
Power requirement	230/460 V, 60 Hz, 8 kW, 3 phase		
Average power consumption	1.6 kW		
No. of standard axes	5, Axis VII optional		
Positioning repeatability	± 1 mm (0.039 in)		
Mounting position	any		
Weight	robot: 760 kg (1675 lbs) approx.		
Load capacity at gripper-flange	15 kg (33 lbs)		
Operating area	4.2 m (165.3 in) diameter		
Space requirement	bed plate size, robot 1 m x 1 m (39 x 39 in)		
Gripper actuating	pneumatic, pressure 5 bar, (73 psi), 12 bar (175) psi) max.		
Ambient temperature	50°C (122°F)		

CONTROL SYSTEM

Teaching Method	Remote teaching through teaching box
Memory	RAM with battery backup
Memory Capacity	350 points at 5-axis PTP
Control Method	Design principle: modular elements • microprocessor (PTP) for program logic, path control, parameter storage for coordination and all additional auxiliary functions • 15 input and 15 output ports with connectors • plug-in capacity for 7 servo amps for 7 independent axes • motor contactor section and main circuit breakers for power supply
Number of programs	15
Power supply	230/460 V, 60 Hz, 8 kW, 3 phase
Weight cabinet	470 kg (1,035 lbs)
Size cabinet	0.6 x 1 m (23.6 x 39.3")
Ambient temperature	35°C (95°F)
Umbilical cord	up to 25 m (81') approx.

Optional equipment
• overload cutout on gripper-flange
• unit for lateral shifting of robot as additional axis
• pneumatic rotating unit for gripper
• pneumatic swiveling unit for gripper
• memory expansion to 5270 teach points in increments of 410 teach points for 5 axis unit.

WORKING SPACE

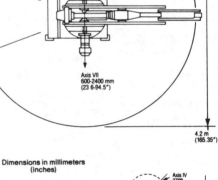

Axis VII
600-2400 mm
(23 6-94.5")

1 m
(39.37")

4.2 m
(165.35")

Dimensions in millimeters
(inches)

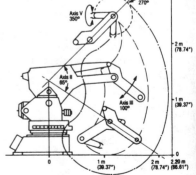

Axis IV
270°

Axis V
350°

Axis II
65°

Axis III
100°

2 m
(78.74")

1 m
(39.37")

0

0   1 m   2 m   2.20 m
   (39.37")   (78.74") (86.61")

General Electric Co. (Model S6 Robot).

This is a high-performance spraying robot system that combines the ability of a skilled worker with the accuracy, durability, and repeatability of a machine. The robot's six axes are powered by a hydraulic power supply in order to allow for a smooth, rapid performance of the spraying system. The robot's coordinated operation provides flexible movement of the spray gun to produce the desired pattern on the object being sprayed.

Movement of the robot is controlled and taught by the hand-held teach box. Up to 15 different programs can be stored at one time in the controller, with either manual or automatic program selection available. Once a program has been taught, points can be easily edited, added, or deleted to improve the spraying process. The robot can easily be instructed to spray parts with difficult access such as automobile roofs and trunks.

Spraying can be performed while the object is at rest and then synchronized with a conveyor, to allow for assembly-line production. The spraying speed can be modified while synchronized with the conveyor to ensure even coating. The robot's controller contains the microprocessor system that controls the robot's arm as it moves through its taught points in space. System parameters such as robot speed and program selection can be changed from the portable control box while the robot is in operation.

Alternate spraying devices can easily be connected to the robot. The robot can be used for diverse coating applications, such as paint, anticorrosive oil, and sealing chemicals. The robot requires a small floor space. Its base diameter is 16 in. (400 mm). The arm of the robot will not project backwards, so that the robot can easily be installed in a small booth.

Standard Specifications
Model S6

WORKING SPACE

VERTICAL TYPE

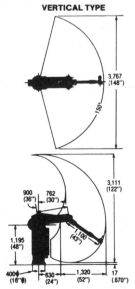

● ROBOT MAIN BODY

		Vertical Type	Horizontal Type
Motion	Turning of arm	150°	110°
	Up-down of arm	3,111 mm (122")	1,320 mm (52")
	Out-in of arm	1,320 mm (52")	3,111 mm (122")
	Swing of wrist	250°	250°
	Bend of wrist	250°	250°
	Twist of wrist	250°	250°
Speed		Max. 1,750 mm/sec (69 in/sec) Painting 1,000 mm/sec (39"/sec)	
Weight		500 kg (1,100 lbs.)	

● HYDRAULIC POWER SOURCE

Operating pressure	90 kg/cm², (1280 psi)
Capacity of tank	100 liters (26 gal)
Cooling system	Air-cooled
Electric power	AC 230/460V ± 10%, 3-phase, 50/60 Hz, 10 kVA
Weight	300 kg (661 lbs.)

Option: Water-cooled system

• CONTROL SYSTEM

Teaching method	Remote teaching through the teaching box
Control method	Continuous Path by Point-to-Point linear interpolation
Memory	Core memory
Number of programs	15
Modes of operation	Converting operation of multi-joint coordinates into cartesian coordinates Wrist correction operation Linear-speed control operation Conveyor synchronizing operation
Fault detection function	Sensor failure CPU failure Hydraulic power source failure Painting machine failure Conveyor failure
External input/output points	7 inputs, 7 outputs
Electric power source	AC 115V ±10%, 50/60 Hz, 1 kVA
Weight	150 kg (330 lbs.)

Options: 1. Memory storage system (cassette deck)
2. Additional memory 512 steps (maximum 3)

HORIZONTAL TYPE

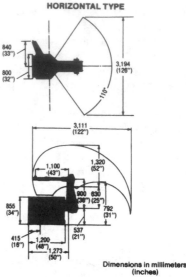

Dimensions in millimeters (inches)

General Electric Co. (Model SW 220 Robot).

This spot welding robot is a tubular unit with lateral travel of 78.74 in. (2000 mm) and gripper-flange load capacity of 220 lb (100 kg). It is for heavy-duty applications such as spot welding operations with extremely large pincers and materials handling.

The SW 220 features dc servomotor drive, an absolute optical encoder position control system, and programming by teach box and push-button. Remote program storage on magnetic tape is optional.

Standard Specifications
Model SW 220

ROBOT MAIN BODY

Axes		Operating area	Operating speed
Vertical swivel	Axis II	40°	6°/sec.
Stroke	Axis III	100 mm (39.37 in)	250 mm (9.84 in)/sec.
Wrist rotation	Axis IV	340°	90°/sec.
Wrist swivel	Axis V	80°	80°/sec.
Transversal location unit	Axis VII	2000 mm (78.74 in)	250 mm (9.84 in)/sec.
Power requirement	230/460 V, 60 Hz, 15 kW, 3 phase		
Average power consumption	2.2 kW		
No. of standard axes	5,		
Positioning repeatability	± 2.5 mm (0.098 in)		
Mounting position	floor		
Weight	robot: 3800 kg (8360 lbs) approx.		
Load capacity at gripper-flange	100 kg (220 lbs)		
Operating area	1 x 2 m (39 x 78 in)		
Space requirement	bed plate size, robot 2 m x 4 m (79 x 157 in)		
Gripper actuating	pneumatic, pressure 5 bar, (73 psi), 12 bar (175 psi) max.		
Ambient temperature	50°C (122°F)		

WORKING SPACE

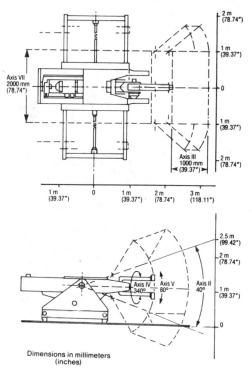

Dimensions in millimeters
(inches)

CONTROL SYSTEM

Teaching Method	Remote teaching through teaching box
Memory	RAM with battery backup
Memory Capacity	350 points at 5-axis PTP
Control Method	Design principle: modular elements
	• microprocessor for program logic, path control, parameter storage for coordination and all auxiliary functions • 15 input and 15 output ports with connectors • plug-in capacity for 7 servo amps for 7 independent axes • motor contactor section and main circuit breakers for power supply
Number of programs	15
Power supply	230/460 V, 60 Hz, 15 kW, 3 phase
Weight cabinet	470 kg (1,035 lbs)
Size cabinet	0.6 x 1 m (23.6 x 39.3")
Ambient temperature	35°C (95°F)
Umbilical cord	up to 25 m (81') approx.
Optional equipment • overload cutout on gripper-flange • pneumatic rotating unit for gripper • pneumatic swiveling unit for gripper • memory expansion to 5270 teach points in increments of 410 teach points for 5 axis unit	

General Numeric (GN0 Robot).

Robot designed for machine mounting. It can be externally mounted on a machine tool frame or integrated into transfer or assembly lines. It is capable of handling weights of up to 22 lb (10 kg). It can be adapted for use with a wide variety of electric and air-powered tools for assembly operations. It is also designed to use the same computer numerical control that operates the machine tool. The GN0 control is a six-axis, point-to-point, microprocessor control with "teach-in/playback" capability. One axis can be moved at a time, with the exception that the *a* (wrist rotation) axis can be moved simultaneously with any other axis. The GN0 robot has a choice of two wrist rotation mechanisms (*a* axis), operated by air pressure. The Model B is a two-position wrist that can be adjusted mechanically to stop hand rotation at 0° and 90° or 0° and 180°. It can accommodate five GN robot hands. Model D is a four-position wrist with stops at −90°, 90°, 0°, and 180°. Both wrists rotate at a maximum speed of 90°/sec. Five grippers can be specified: Model T, a three-finger design for lathe workpieces; Models D3 (two finger) and D4 (two-finger), double gripper (loading gripper and unloading gripper) hands for simultaneously handling two lathe workpieces weighing up to 11 lb (5 kg) each; Model D5 is adapted for shift-type workpieces weight up to 11 lb (5 kg) each; Model M with three-finger gripper for milling and drilling machine workpieces weighing up to 22 lb (10 kg) and a rotation mechanism permitting workpiece indexing on milling machines. The two- and three-finger centripetal grip linkages are designed so that the gripping center is constant, regardless of workpiece diameter and minor misalignment.

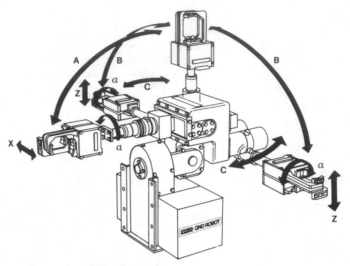

The GN0 robot from General Numeric.

General Numeric (GN1).

Designed for handling workpieces or assembly tools weighing up to 44 lb (20 kg). It can provide workpiece transfer, tool changing, and chip removal services for either one or two machine tools to greatly expedite floor-to-floor time. It is also used by metalworking, appliance, and electronic manufacturers in a variety of assembly applications. The GN1 has five controlled axes: the Z axis, vertical motion; the O axis, rotation in the horizontal plane; the R axis, in-and-out motion of the arm; the a axis, wrist rotation; and the β axis, wrist bending. Other controlled functions include: hand rotation, opening and closing of fingers of hand, and activation of air nozzle on the wrist to blow away chips. The robot can be furnished with either a separate or integrated-type control. The program memory in the control has a capacity of 300 points. For external program storage, an LSI cartridge with a capacity of a maximum of 100 points is available. There are three wrists available for the GN1 robot: Model A, used as a fixed fitting between the arm and the hand, with no rotation or bending capability; Model B, with a wrist rotation (a axis) mechanism, providing a choice of two sets of stop positions, either 0°/90° or 0°/180°, and a wrist bending mechanism (β axis), adjustable mechanically within the range of $-3.5°$ to 3.5°; and Model C, having a wrist rotation mechanism that can be programmed in steps of approximately 1.15° to stop anywhere in a 270° arc between $-90°$ and 180°, plus a wrist bending mechanism with selectable stop positions. There is a choice of four hands: the Model T hand for lathe applications, capable of handling workpieces weighing up to 44 lb (20 kg); the Model M hand for milling machines and machining centers; plus the Model D1 side-by-side double hand and the Model D2 back-to-back double hand, for handling two workpieces simultaneously, weighing up to 22 lb (10 kg) each.

General Numeric (GN3).

A heavy-duty industrial robot designed to lift workpieces weighing up to 110 lb (50 kg) that is ideal for use in loading and unloading workpieces on large lathes and milling machines, machining centers, vertical boring machines, grinding machines, transfer lines, etc. It has five controlled axes: the Z axis, vertical motion; the O axis, horizontal rotation; the R axis, in-and-out motion of the arm; the a axis, wrist rotation; and the β axis, wrist bending. Control is provided by a General Numeric five axis point-to-point microprocessor control with teach-in/playback capability and program memory with up to 6000-point capacity. The wrist is part of the robot arm. It is designed to rotate 300° around the a axis, from −105° to 195° at a speed of 80°/sec. The wrist also bends along the β axis through a 190° arc, from −95° to 95°. The robot is programmed either by teaching (lead through) or by external data inputs, including: (1) LSE cartridge memory capacity of 300 points and (2) bubble-memory cartridge (2700 point capacity). An optional CRT display for the control facilitates program editing and troubleshooting. There is a choice of three types of hands. The Model W1 hand has a centripetal gripper with a four-finger mechanism and standard claws. The Model W2 is a double gripper hand designed to load/unload shaft-type lathe workpieces with diameters from 3.2 to 5.5 in. (8 to 14 cm). The Model W3 is a "forklift" type hand for lifting heavy workpieces and palletized parts. All three hands have a rated capacity of 110 lb (50 kg).

General Numeric GN3 robot specifications

Items		Specifications
No. of CNC machine tools to be controlled		One or two
Controlled axes		Z, θ, R, a, β axes
Motion range (Max rotation speed)	Z axis: up/down	47.2 in. (20 ips)
	θ axis: rotation	300° (60°/sec)
	R axis: in/out	47.2 in. (40 ips)
	a axis: wrist rotation	300° (80°/sec)
	β axis: wrist bending	190° (80°/sec)
Max load capacity at wrist		176 lb
Applicable hand unit (Max load capacity of workpiece)		Model W1, W2 and W3 (110 lb)
Driving method		Z, θ, R, a, β axes: dc servomotors Hand: pneumatic control
Motion control		Point-to-point, 5 axes at a time
Repeatability		±0.039 in.
Teaching method		Playback system with program memory Program memory capacity: up to 6000 points
Auxiliary data memory (for external program storage)		LSI cartridge: 300 points capacity Bubble-memory cartridge: 2700 points capacity
Character display		Optional
Operations		Jog Feed, Step Feed, Automatic Operation, Single Block, Feed Hold, Emergency Stop, Feed Rate Override, Zero Return
Machine interface		Open/close of splash guard, tailstock, chuck jaws, etc. Control of chip disposal, workpiece feeder, etc.
Teaching operations (1)		Branch, Variables, Subprogram, Palletizing, External Data Input, External Data Output, Dwell, etc.
Teaching operations (2)		Palletizing C and D
Power source		AC200/220/230/380/415V $^{+10\%}_{-15\%}$ 50/60 Hz ±1 Hz, 3ϕ, 15 kva
Weight		Approx. 3740 lb

Hitachi America Ltd. (Hitachi Spray-Painting Robot).

This robot is a high-performance machine that combines the ability of a skilled worker with the accuracy and durability of a machine. The robot is instructed with a teaching box (portable type). The information on one point covers gun position, gun posture, painting start and stop, painting speed, and various operational signals. Once the robot is given the necessary information, a microcomputer automatically controls painting from one point to another. Parts that are difficult to access, such as automobile roofs and trunks, can be done easily.

Even if the robot is instructed while the workpiece is still, it will, automatically, paint on the moving workpiece as commanded by conveyor signals in pace with conveyor speed. Up to four programs can be memorized by the robot, and programs can be changed instantly. If a different product comes on the same line, the program for it will be selected instantly. Painting speed between instructed points can be corrected with a speed dial. Only two points are needed to cover a long straight surface, and up to 464 points can be used. In case extra capacity is needed, an additional memory can be installed.

The robot proper, which is designed for installation in a paint booth, is of intrinsically safe explosion-proof construction. Any painting machine in use can easily be connected to the robot. The robot can also be used for other than painting, such as spraying anticorrosive oil and sealing chemicals.

Standard Specifications

• Robot main body

		Type	Vertical type	Horizontal type
Robot main body	Moving function	Arm Rotation	150°	110°
		Arm Up-down	3,128 mm	3,128 mm
		Moving Out-in	1,320 mm	1,320 mm
		Wrist Swing	250°	250°
		Wrist Bend	250°	250°
		Wrist Twist	250°	250°
	Speed		Max. 1,750 mm/sec	
	Weight		500 kg	500 kg
Hydraulic power source	Operating pressure		90 kg/cm², 25 ℓ/min	
	Capacity of tank		60 ℓ	
	Cooling system		Water-cooled	
	Electric power		AC 200 V ±10%, 3-phase, 50/60 Hz, 10 kVA	
	Weight		300 kg	

• Control system

Teaching method	Remote teaching through the teaching box
Control method	CP cortrol on linear interpolation calculation by Point-to-Point teaching
Memory	Core memory
Number of programs	Up to 4
Kinds of operation	Converting operation of multi-joint coordi-nates into cartesian coordinates, Wrist correction operation, Linear-speed control operation, Conveyor synchronizing operation
Fault detection function	Sensor failure CPU failure Hydraulic power source failure Painting machine failure Conveyor failure
External Synchronizing signal	7 inputs, 7 outputs
Electric power source	AC 100V ±10%, 50/60 Hz, 1 kVA
Weight	150 kg

Working Space

• Vertical type

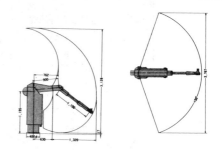

• Horizontal type

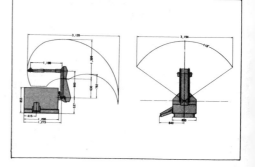

Hitachi America Ltd. ("Mr. AROS").

This is an arc welding robot with a miniature noncontact sensor that serves as the robot's eye for accurate welding along a welding line. This "eye" will not be adversely affected by surface irregularities of the work caused by spatter that develops in carbon dioxide gas welding on holes of less than 0.4 in. (10 mm) in diameter. The sensor is effective with a wide range of metals, including stainless steel, aluminum, and other nonferrous metals.

The noncontact-type sensor detects cutting deviations (caused by shearing and tack welding), effects of thermal strain, and setting deviations, and activates the robot to make the necessary tracking corrections in welding according to preprogrammed instructions. You can teach the robot to check such points at both ends of the welding line and corners in advance to serve as references for making adjustments for tracking work precision deviations. The ability to correct its own track permits the robot to perform automatic welding on as many identically shaped workpieces as necessary. Teaching data can be stored in cassette tapes.

The robot requires only two points for straight welding, or only five points for welding a corner including straight parts. In case additional points are needed, the points can be added. In welding any structure there are always several corners that must be welded. In horizontal fillet welding, the robot can perform welding at the corners continuously without cutting the arc while it computes its own track. Motion in two degrees of freedom with servo drive permits the robot to weld almost every workpiece.

Standard Specifications

● "Mr. AROS"-SP

Robot main body	Stroke	Traverse (X)		1,500 mm
		Out-in (Y)		1,000 mm
		Up-down (Z)		1,100 mm
		Wrist	Swing (SW)	±100°
			Bend (BD)	−5° - 50° (measured from right below the hand)
			Sensor withdrawal	50 mm
	Speed	Welding (at torch tip)		150 - 990 mm/min
		Quick feed		6,000 mm/min
	Positioning repeatability			±1.0 mm
	Hydraulic power source			Operating pressure 70 kg/cm², air-cooled
	Pneumatic power source			4 kg/cm² or more
	Weight			1,300 kg
Positioner	Moving function	Revolution		−200° - +200°
		Tilt		−200° - +200°
	Speed	Revolution/tilt		24°/min - 480°/min
	Maximum weight of work			600 kg (including jigs)
	Maximum permissible unbalanced load			20 kg·m
	Weight			1,000 kg

Option: 1. Weaving of wrist bend axis
2. Wrist bend: −45° - 45°

● "Mr. AROS"-JP

Robot main body	Stroke	Traverse (X)		1,500 mm
		Out-in (Y)		800 mm
		Up-down (Z)		500 mm
		Wrist	Swing (SW)	±100°
			Bend (BD)	−5° - 50° (measured from the right below the hand)
			Sensor withdrawal	50 mm
	Speed	Welding (at torch tip)		150 - 990 mm/min.
		Quick feed		6,000 mm/min
	Positioning repeatability			±1.0 mm
	Hydraulic power source			Operating pressure 70 kg/cm², air-cooled
	Pneumatic power source			4 kg/cm² or more
	Weight			1,100 kg
Positioner	Moving function	Revolution		−200° - +200°
		Tilt		−200° - +200°
	Speed	Revolution/tilt		24°/min - 480°/min
	Maximum weight of work			600 kg (including jigs)
	Maximum permissible unbalanced load			20 kg·m
	Weight			1,000 kg

Option: 1. Weaving of wrist bend axis
2. Wrist bend: −45° - 45°

● CONTROL SYSTEM

Teaching method	Remote teaching through the teaching box.
Control method	CP control on linear interpolation calculation by point-to-point teaching.
Number of control axes	Electro-hydraulic servo; up to 5 axes (for robot) Electric servo; up to 2 axes (for positioner)
Memory	Core memory
Memory capacity	464 steps
Number of programs	Up to 4
Welding current	Max. 256 divisions
Welding voltage	Max. 256 divisions

(Welding current / Welding voltage: 6 kinds/program can be specified.)

Kinds of operation	Straight-line constant speed control
	Self-detection of welding line on the work
	Continuous corner position calculation
	Automatic corner position determination
	Wrist motion compensation

Fault detection functions	Torch contact, Arc failure, Sensor failure, CPU failure, Nearness of sensor, Lack of welding wire, Pneumatic failure, Parity error.
Program memory	Cassette deck
Power supply	AC 100V ±10%, 50/60 Hz, single-phase, 1 kVA for control system
	AC 200V ±10%, 50/60 Hz, 3-phase, 10 kVA for hydraulic system
	AC 200/220V ±10%, 50/60 Hz, 3-phase, for servo system
Weight	250 kg

Options: 1. Weaving of wrist bend axis   2. Shifting function
3. Single sensor function   4. Axis data correction function
5. Check angle correction function
6. Arc line interpolating function
7. Additional memory, 464 steps

Working Space

Dimensions in millimeters

- Mr. AROS''-SP

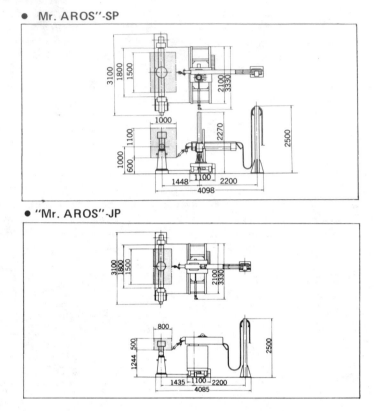

- "Mr. AROS"-JP

Hitachi America Ltd. (Process Robot).

This multipurpose robot can be used for welding, deburring, machine service, assembly, etc., by attaching the optional facilities designed for each application. The totally rotational driving system features a parallelogram linkage to keep the posture of the robot wrist constant at all times.

The built-in microcomputer accurately controls each action. For example, although the robot has multijoint action, teaching can be made by converting into the Cartesian coordinates. Without cancelling the stored data, teach points can be modified and replaced by new points. The standard robot accommodates up to four different programs, which can be selected instantaneously when necessary. In case of a straight line, even with relatively long distances, the robot will work accurately with only two end points having been taught. Up to 448 points are available and, in case extra capacity is needed, an additional memory can be installed. Upon detection of any abnormality, the robot will automatically stop and indicate error on the control panel.

Standard Specifications

● Robot main body

Moving function	Arm	Rotation	±150°
		Upper arm	+50°, −45°
		Fore arm	+25°, −45°
	Wrist	Bend	±90°
		Twist	±185°
Speed	Arm		Max. 1,000 mm/sec
	Wrist	Bend	120°/sec
		Twist	180°/sec
Weight capacity			Max. 10 kg (including grips)
Repeatability			±0.2 mm
Weight			200 kg

● For welding

Welding	120 - 1980 mm/min, 94 divisions, 9 kinds/program, can be specified.
Quick feed	10 - 990 mm/sec, 6 kinds/program

● Control system

Teaching method	Remote teaching through the teaching box
Control method	CP control on linear interpolation calculation by point-to-point teaching
Number of control axes	5 axes to control electric servo systems at one time
Memory	Core memory
Memory capacity	448 steps
Number of programs	Up to 4
Kinds of operation	Straight-line constant speed control, Converting operation of multi-joint coordinates into cartesian coordinates.
External synchronizing signal	13 inputs, 15 outputs
Timer	0.1 - 9.9 sec, 99 steps
Fault detection function	Overrun Overload Sensor failure CPU failure
Power supply	AC 100V ±10%, 50/60Hz, single-phase, 1kVA for control system AC 200/220V ±10%, 50/60Hz, 3-phase, 3kVA for servo system

● For welding

Welding current	99 divisions	15 kinds/program
Welding voltage	99 divisions	can be specified.
Arc detection		
Torch contact		
Arc cut off detection		

Option: 1. Memory storage system (interface, cassette deck)
2. Additional memory 512 steps

Working Space
Dimensions in millimeters

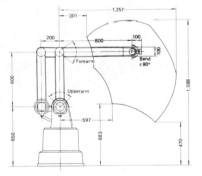

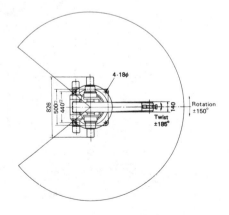

International Business Machines Corp. (IBM 7535 Manufacturing System).

This robot has been designed for light assembly work as well as other tasks that require speed and high repeatability. It is an electric-drive, microprocessor-controlled robotic system for automatic assembly; feed and insertion of odd-shaped parts; multiple-point drilling, tapping, and chamfering; multiple-point soldering and screw tightening; assembling and inspecting many parts in a process; packing products into cases in rows — or taking products out of cases; loading and unloading of parts on automated production lines.

The IBM 7535 Manufacturing System consists of a jointed-arm structure and a control unit with easy-to-use operating panel. A separate programming unit is available for application development.

This jointed-arm structure provides a selective compliance design to compensate for lateral offsetting. The structure has compliance along the horizontal direction and limited compliance in the vertical direction for inserting component parts and other light assembly tasks.

The structure is the basis for a flexible, four-axis robotic system which has a jointed arm. The system rotates the first and second joints of the arm, using two individual dc servomotors, about the θ_1 and θ_2 axes, respectively, to establish the positions in the horizontal plane; it swivels the tool by a stepping motor about the roll-axis; and it moves the tool vertically by an air cylinder about the Z axis.

IBM 7535 Manufacturing System.

The control unit drives the robotic system. This unit comes with an easy-to-use operating panel that can be conveniently placed near the operator.

The memory of the control unit can store from one to five multipoint application programs in a total of 6000 bytes of memory. Each application program can be selected simply by using a switch on the control panel.

The programming unit is designed to support multiple IBM 7535 systems. The unit is used to develop or update application programs — and can be disconnected for use on other IBM 7535 Manufacturing Systems. The programming unit uses a special robotics programming language, AML/E.

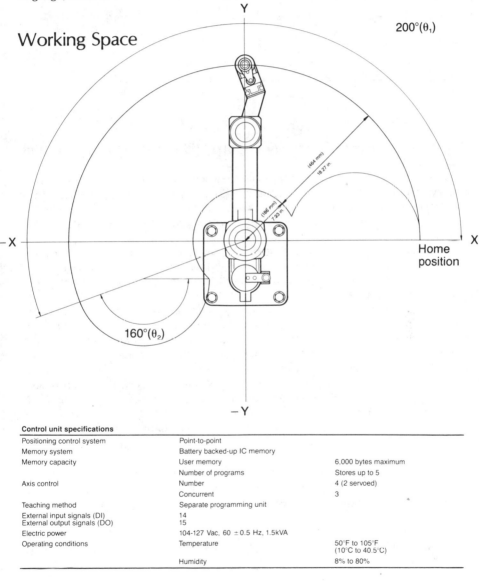

Working Space

$200°(\theta_1)$

$160°(\theta_2)$

Home position

Control unit specifications

Positioning control system	Point-to-point	
Memory system	Battery backed-up IC memory	
Memory capacity	User memory	6,000 bytes maximum
	Number of programs	Stores up to 5
Axis control	Number	4 (2 servoed)
	Concurrent	3
Teaching method	Separate programming unit	
External input signals (DI)	14	
External output signals (DO)	15	
Electric power	104-127 Vac, 60 ± 0.5 Hz, 1.5kVA	
Operating conditions	Temperature	50°F to 105°F (10°C to 40.5°C)
	Humidity	8% to 80%

Manipulator performance specifications

Coordinate system		Cartesian coordinate system			
Degrees of freedom		4			
Maximum payload (includes end of arm tooling)		13.2 lb (6 kg)			
Repeatability		± 0.002 in. (± 0.05 mm)			

Axis movement	Range	Max. load	Speed in./sec (mm/sec) Low	Med.	High
θ_1 axis (Arm swivel)	0-200°	2.2 lb (1 kg)	23 in./sec (600 mm/sec)	43 in./sec (1100 mm/sec)	57 in./sec (1450 mm/sec)
		13.2 lb (6 kg)	23 in./sec (600 mm/sec)	43 in./sec (1100 mm/sec)	—
θ_2 axis (Arm swivel)	0-160'	2.2 lb (1 kg)	15 in./sec (400 mm/sec)	31 in./sec (800 mm/sec)	39 in./sec (1000 mm/sec)
		13.2 lb (6 kg)	15 in./sec (400 mm/sec)	31 in./sec (800 mm/sec)	—
Roll-axis	± 180	13.2 lb (6 kg) Centered on Z-axis	—	—	—
Z-axis (Up/down)	3 in. (75 m	13.2 lb (6 kg)	—	—	—
Weight		132 lb (60 kg)			
Operating Conditions		Temperature	50°F to 105°F (10°C to 40.5°C)		
		Humidity	8% to 80%		

Specifications are subject to change.

International Business Machines Corp. (IBM RS 1 Manufacturing System).

This system provides a programmable, multifunctional manipulator designed for light assembly, fabrication, testing, and materials handling. It is suited for applications where speed, repeatability and product quality are important factors. Tactile and optical sensing features in combination with computer control make the IBM RS 1 robot a very flexible and adaptable system for manufacturing.

A typical IBM RS 1 Manufacturing System consists of a manipulator; a manufacturing language (AML), which is designed specifically for IBM robotic systems; a system controller with keyboard/display station and matrix printer; a programmable teach pendant; and a hydraulic power supply.

The manipulator uses a rectangular frame to support an arm with wrist and a two-finger gripper. The arm and wrist comprise six degrees of freedom or joint motions. There are three linear motions corresponding to the X, Y, and Z movements of the arm; three rotary motions corresponding to roll, pitch, and yaw of the wrist; plus the controlled gripping/releasing motion of the gripper fingers.

The gripper opens and closes to grasp an object between its fingers. The fingers remain essentially parallel so that various objects can be grasped squarely and firmly. The work envelope of the manipulator's rectangular frame is approximately 18 in. (457 mm) wide, X axis; 58 in. (1473 mm) long, Y axis; and 17 in. (431 mm) high, Z axis. Motion of the joints is powered hydraulically and directed by the system controller through a servo feedback control loop.

Adaptability to the application environment is accomplished through the use of sensors. Strain gauges located in the gripper provide force-sensing capabilities at the tip, side, and pinch surfaces of each finger. A photoelectric cell can also be used to detect the presence of objects between the fingers.

In addition, the system has provisions for digital input/digital output points to assist in integrating the IBM RS 1 Manufacturing System with most automated manufacturing processes.

Manipulator features

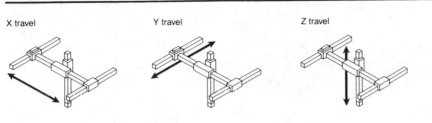

X travel   Y travel   Z travel

Axis	Travel	Top speed
X	18 in. (457 mm)	40 in./sec (1,016 mm/sec)
Y	58 in. (1,473 mm)	40 in./sec (1,016 mm/sec)
Z	17 in. (431 mm)	40 in./sec (1,016 mm/sec)

Manipulator features

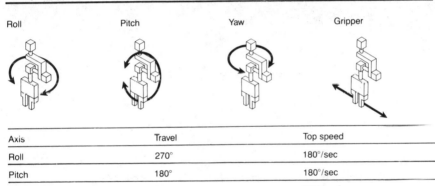

Roll   Pitch   Yaw   Gripper

Axis	Travel	Top speed
Roll	270°	180°/sec
Pitch	180°	180°/sec
Yaw	270°	180°/sec
Gripper	0-3.25 in. (82 mm)	5 in./sec (127 mm/sec)

Specifications

Item	Specifications	
Precision of positional repeatability measured at the gripper	X ± 0.008 in. (± 0.20 mm) [1] Y ± 0.007 in. (± 0.17 mm) [1] Z ± 0.006 in. (± 0.15 mm)	
Maximum payload Ambient temperature range Ambient humidity range	5.0 lb (2.26 kg) in addition to gripper 50°F to 105°F (10°C to 40.5°C) 8% to 80%	
Weight	Manipulator Controller Hydraulic power supply	2000 lb (907.2 kg) 554 lb (251.2 kg) 400 lb (181.4 kg)

[1] Pitch motor perpendicular to X-axis.

Specifications are subject to change.

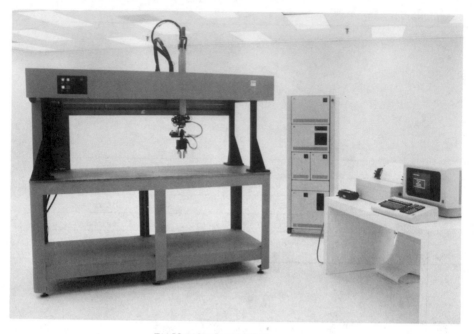

IBM RS 1 Manufacturing System.

International Robomation/Intelligence (M-50 Robot).

This is a self-contained lightweight five-axis unit that employs air motors for its motive force used in conjunction with chain drives to obtain its operating strength and speed. It has been designed and constructed in modules. High-strength aluminum alloy structures are used to provide the required tensile strength. Four functional modules (torso, shoulder, elbow, and wrist) contain the air motors, valve assemblies, encoders, brakes, sprocket assemblies, chains, wiring, and plumbing for the associated axis. The majority of the parts and components are interchangeable among these modules. An equipment module containing the pneumatic pressure control assembly and the pneumatic connection is located adjacent to the spindle box assembly. The spindle box assembly supports the spindle shaft and ties the torso, shoulder, and equipment modules together.

Six separate molded fiberglass skin panels completely enclose the IRI M-50 Robot. The panels are in mating halves; one pair for the torso/shoulder modules, and one each for the elbow and wrist modules.

The IRI M-50 is controlled by a hierarchy of microcomputers with the Motorola 68000 16/32-bit processor as the manager. Each axis has its own control computer and an additional CPU furnishes safety control. The robot may be programmed on-line in IRI's Robot Command Language. Each axis is equipped with an optical encoder to produce a position feedback to its processor which controls the air motor.

Robot arm

Axis   Five axes standard
Clearance Required   Sphere, 80-in.
   (203-cm) radius
Weight   400 lb (180 kg) (without
   optional base)
Drive   Digital air servomotor
Maximum Load   50 lb (22.5 kg) including
   gripper
Reach   Minimum 20 in./maximum 80 in.
Repeatability   ±0.040 inches (± 1 mm)

Motion range and maximum speed

Torso   360° continuous 60° per second
Shoulder   180° ± 90° 30° per second
Elbow   230° + 90° − 140° 60°
   per second
Wrist - pitch   240° ± 120° 120°
   per second
Wrist - roll   360° continuous 120°
   per second

Control

Microcomputer (Torso mounted)
   Motorola 68000 w/ 32 KB Memory,
   five independent axes, computer-
   controlled. Dedicated safety
   computer.

Input/output ports

8 input/8 output (optional 16/16)

Communications

Two independent RS232C connections

Programming

Language   Robot Command Language
   (RCL)
Modes   On line; teach–playback

Environment

Ambient temperature   40°C (104°F) Max.
Relative humidity   90% max -
   non-condensing

Power Inputs

Electrical   115 Vac, 50–60 Hz, 5 A
Air   80–120 psi, 1 in. supply line

Options

Base   48 in. (122 cm) high, 24 X 24 in.
   (61 X 61 cm) base
Universal gripper   Two finger compliant
   hand
Memory   Expandable up to 128 KB
Input/output devices   Move pendant
   System terminal (hard copy or CRT)
   Load terminal (floppy or cassette)
   Utility I/O Module Installation Kit

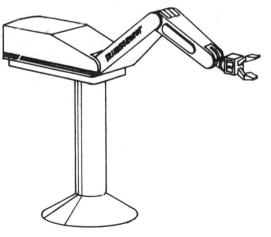

IRI M-50 Robot.

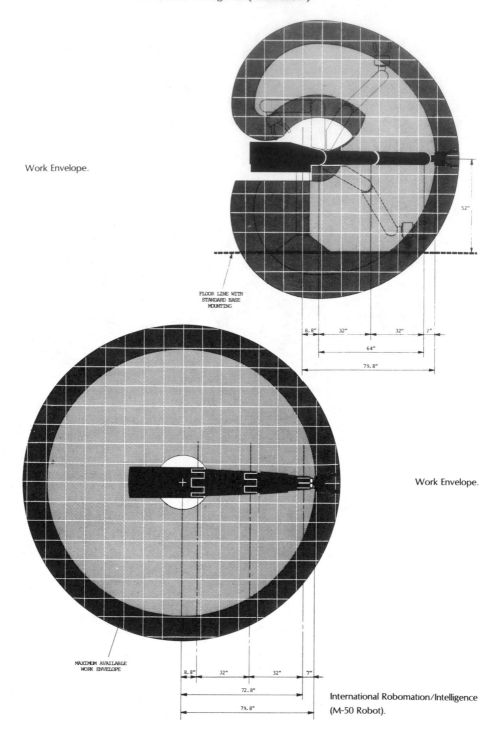

Work Envelope.

FLOOR LINE WITH
STANDARD BASE
MOUNTING

52"

8.8" 32" 32" 7"

64"

79.8"

MAXIMUM AVAILABLE
WORK ENVELOPE

8.8" 32" 32" 7"

72.8"

79.8"

Work Envelope.

International Robomation/Intelligence
(M-50 Robot).

Mobot Corp. (Mobot).

This system is a kind of erector set providing an inventory of straight-line and rotary motion components, each available in a wide variety of sizes, distances of travel, position control options, and power options. It is possible to assemble a Mobot that provides precisely the motions required for a particular task (and no more) with components of the appropriate size and type for that task. Mobots can be understood and maintained by ordinary factory maintenance men and manufacturing engineers after a day of training. Mobots use linear Vectrons (straight-line-motion components) to provide straight-line motions and rotary Vectrons (rotary-motion components) to provide rotary motions. Nonsynchronized servos are needed. Because each Mobot is configured (configuration programmed) to provide the needed motions of the needed kinds precisely where they are needed, a two- or three-motion Mobot typically does the job of a five- or six-motion anthropomorphic robot. Mobot components are made in a large variety of sizes of linear Vectrons, each made in many lengths; there are five sizes of rotary Vectrons; there are many sizes of columns, couplings, brackets, and other structural members; there are three power options with several suboptions; and there are four position control options. Mobots may be built on columns with most of their mechanism located in "free space" in the air overlying the customer's equipment. Specific transfer patterns performed by Mobots are as follows: (a) Transfer from a first fixed position to a second position, for example, loading a workpiece into a machine and/or removing a workpiece from a machine. (b) Transfer to several positions, one after another, for example, unloading a die casting machine, placing the workpiece into a test station, then into a cooling station, and finally into a trim die. (c) Double transfer, for example, transfer of a finished workpiece out of a fabricating machine, followed by transfer of a new workpiece into the fabricating machine. (d) Multiple transfer, for example, moving several workpieces in succession through several positions. (e) Selecting or sorting, for example, transfer from or to different fixed positions in response to external commands. (f) Dealing, for example, a fixed program sorting, like dealing cards, to place parts in rows or to work like an egg-crate-type magazine. (g) Destacking, for example, removing parts one at a time from the top of a vertical stack or the end of a horizontal row. (h) Stacking, for example, adding parts one at a time to the top of a vertical stack or the end of a horizontal row. (i) Conveyor synchronizing, for example, loading or unloading a moving conveyor. (j) NC contouring, for example, moving a workpiece, which may be a tool such as a welding electrode, along a smooth, continuously curved path. (k) NC positioning, for example, placing a workpiece in any position as commanded electrically (point-to-point numerical control). (l) Long distance transfer, for example, moving a workpiece up to 85 ft (26 m) or more with a repeatable accuracy of a small fraction of an inch. (m) Assembling, for example, a number of robots arranged around a conveyor to assemble a product in a sequence of operations.

Nordson Corp. (Nordson Robot System).

Designed for a wide variety of paint finishing applications and to be used with air, airless, powder, and electrostatic spray equipment on workpieces of various sizes and shapes and at varying conveyor line speeds. The six-axis movement of the robot produces exact duplication of the motions of a skilled painter and provides accurate repeatable performances. Basic elements in the system include an electronic solid-state control unit, a hydraulic power pack, a manipulator arm, and a lightweight programming arm. The manipulator arm is a hydraulically powered unit consisting of rugged frame supports and components mounted on a swivel base assembly. The manipulator arm contains high torque rotary actuators, servo valves, oil filters, and control elements. The internal components are totally enclosed so that they are not affected by contamination. The rotary actuators are of a self-lubricating design, eliminating general maintenance. Directing and monitoring the ''arm'' is the electronic control unit, which houses the microprocessor and solid-state memory, which control all the robot system functions. These include a self-diagnostic ''troubleshooting'' circuit, which locates and identifies problems, and a logic circuit, which has the ability to handle up to four auxiliary command functions. The microprocessor and the solid-state memory system compose the main circuit board module that controls all robot system functions, providing programming time of up to 15 minutes. Work instructions for the manipulator arm are accomplished by using the programming arm to transfer the actual work pattern into the memory. The basic memory system is capable of recognizing 31 different parts, arranged in any sequence.

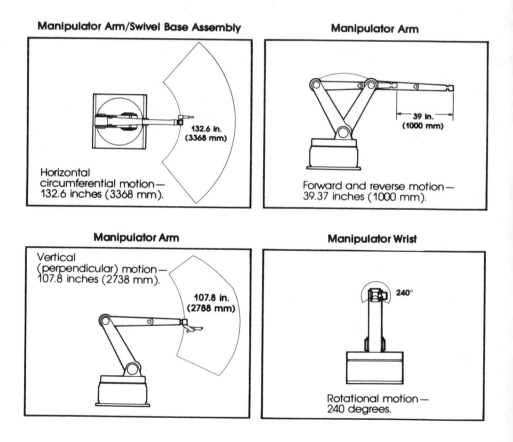

Manipulator Arm/Swivel Base Assembly

132.6 in.
(3368 mm)

Horizontal circumferential motion—
132.6 inches (3368 mm).

Manipulator Arm

39 in.
(1000 mm)

Forward and reverse motion—
39.37 inches (1000 mm).

Manipulator Arm

Vertical (perpendicular) motion—
107.8 inches (2738 mm).

107.8 in.
(2788 mm)

Manipulator Wrist

240°

Rotational motion—
240 degrees.

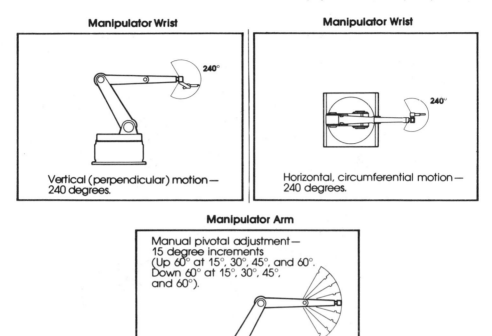

Manipulator Wrist

Vertical (perpendicular) motion — 240 degrees.

Manipulator Wrist

Horizontal, circumferential motion — 240 degrees.

Manipulator Arm

Manual pivotal adjustment — 15 degree increments (Up 60° at 15°, 30°, 45°, and 60°. Down 60° at 15°, 30°, 45°, and 60°).

The six axis movement, illustrated above, is an important feature of the Nordson Robot. It means that the manipulator arm has complete flexibility in the most diversified applications. The Nordson Robot can duplicate and maintain the movements of the most skilled painter.

Specifications

	U.S.A.	Metric			
Manipulator			Depth	33 in.	838 mm
Dimensions			Weight	350 lbs.	159 kg
(Base)	38.6 in. dia.	980 mm dia.	**Hydraulic**		
Weight	1300 lbs.	590 kg	**Power Pack**		
Speed of			Height	78 in.	1981 mm
movement	82 in./sec.	2 m/sec.	Width	28 in.	711 mm
Electronic			Depth	43 in.	1092 mm
Control			Weight	1380 lbs.	625 kg
Height	76.5 in.	1943 mm	Electrical	460V, 60 Hz, 3 Phase	
Width	22 in.	559 mm	Power	10 HP, 6 kW	

Prab Robots, Inc. (Prab).

All Prab robots have three similar main components: a mechanical arm, a hydraulic power supply, and a choice of electronic controllers, including an LSI/11/2 microcomputer. The robots can be mounted in one place or on a traverse base that lets them move between work stations or follow production lines and conveyors. They can also be mounted overhead as either stationary or traversing units. Moving in/out, up/down, and parallel to a moving line lets the Prab reach all points within a cube. This makes it ideal for straight-line loading and unloading of parts plus palletizing, stacking, or tracking a moving conveyor. Up to three servo-controlled end-of-arm motions are added as required for each application. A compact, heavy-duty, two-axis servo wrist develops rotating axis torque of 11,000

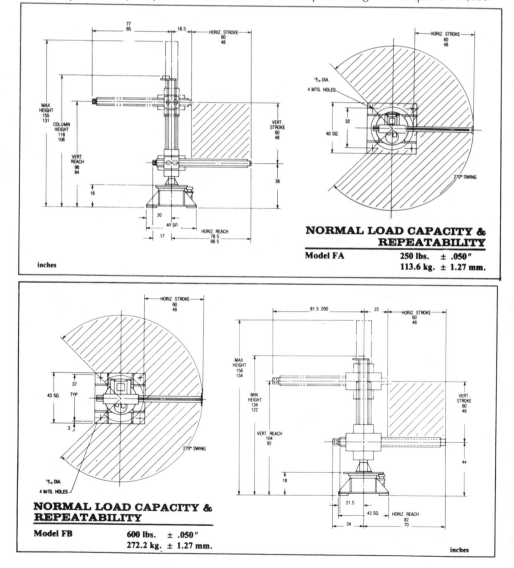

NORMAL LOAD CAPACITY & REPEATABILITY

Model FA	250 lbs.	± .050"
	113.6 kg.	± 1.27 mm.

inches

NORMAL LOAD CAPACITY & REPEATABILITY

Model FB	600 lbs.	± .050"
	272.2 kg.	± 1.27 mm.

inches

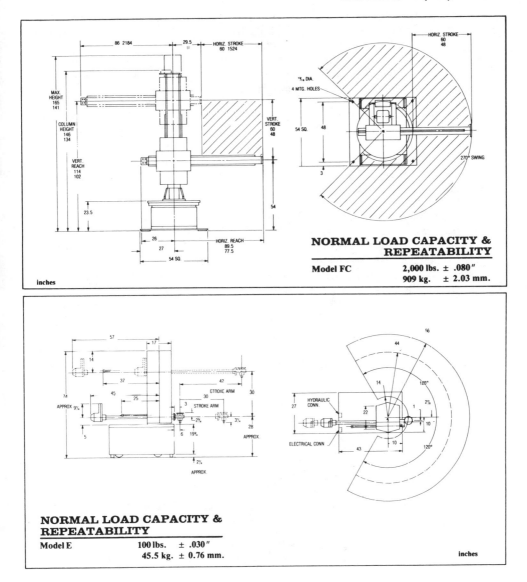

NORMAL LOAD CAPACITY & REPEATABILITY

| Model FC | 2,000 lbs. ± .080″ |
| | 909 kg. ± 2.03 mm. |

inches

NORMAL LOAD CAPACITY & REPEATABILITY

| Model E | 100 lbs. ± .030″ |
| | 45.5 kg. ± 0.76 mm. |

inches

in.-pounds and sweep/bend axis torque of 3500 in.-pounds. The Prab models are Model E, FA, FB, and FC. Models FB and FC provide extension in size, reach, and weight-handling capacity of Models E and FA. Model FC is capable of handling payloads up to 2000 lb (900 kg). A servo-feedback device on each axis is mounted directly in line with the robot's movements. The large robots also feature the ability to be mounted as stationary units, on a traverse base or overhead to provide a wide range of functions in whatever space available. Some of the applications are machine loading/unloading, investment casting, spot welding, forging, stacking/destacking, palletizing, material handling. The basic Prab robot uses a drum memory control system that is programmed by inserting tabs into the drum to control the sequence of motions. Three memory sizes are available offering 24, 30, and 60 steps, which ensure ample range for the great majority of applications such as die casting, injection molding, forging, parts transfer, and machine loading/unloading. A solid-state controller is available, which can be programmed by "walking" the Prab robot through the desired sequence. The unit offers up to 100-step programs with branching and looping capability as well as insert, delete, and diagnostic functions. The Prab Model 600 Control utilizes an LSI/11/2 microcomputer to simultaneously control up to seven servo-axes of motion. The 600 Controller features 64 programs as standard and offers enough memory to store over 4000 points, plus various functions, instructions, time delays, branches, subroutines, and programmable velocities along with 16 acceleration and 16 deceleration instructions programmable on each move.

Schrader Bellows Division (MotionMate).

This five-axis, pneumatically powered industrial robot has a maximum payload of 5 lb (2.25 kg), can operate at speeds up to 24 ips, and has a repeatability of ± 0.005 in. (0.13 mm). It is for light assembly applications, for loading and unloading machines, and for parts transfer from machine to machine. Axes of movement include base rotate to 180°, lift to 3 in. (7.6 cm), extend to 12 in. (30.5 cm), wrist of 90° or 180°, and grasp.

Offering programming and operating ease, MotionMate features a microprocessor controller that operates the robot from memory and interfaces with other equipment associated with the overall automated function. Programming is done on a hand-held teach module that uses graphic symbols for robot commands and requires no special skills of the operator. MotionMate can be supplied with all five axes of motion or as modules for applications that require fewer axes.

MotionMate's Five Axes of Movement

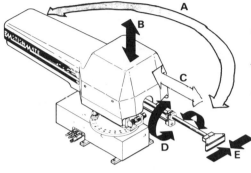

MotionMate offers five axes of movement, or "degrees of freedom." They are as follows:

A — Base Rotate with a motion range of 180° which is adjustable in increments of 15°
B — Lift of 3"
C — Extend to 12"
D — Wrist Rotate 90° or 180°
E — Grasp

System speed	12" to 24" per second linear depending upon load 180° per second base rotate depending upon load
Operating temperature	+20°F to +140°F
CONTROL	Electronic, micro processor with remote portable teaching module
Memory capacity	Up to 300 steps
Program method	Push button via portable teach module
Maximum time interval between steps	10.79 minutes
Auxiliary equipment inputs/outputs	6 outputs and 8 inputs each rated at 115V/60Hz. Other voltages available.
OPTIONS	Linear gripper Wrist Kit Pivot type gripper Extend lift kit 6" Vacuum gripper with pump Extend lift kit 8" Base Rotate — 115V/60Hz Extend reach kit 18" Base Rotate — 220V/50Hz Counter adapter kit, manual reset, 4-digit, 115V/60Hz

Robot Dimensions

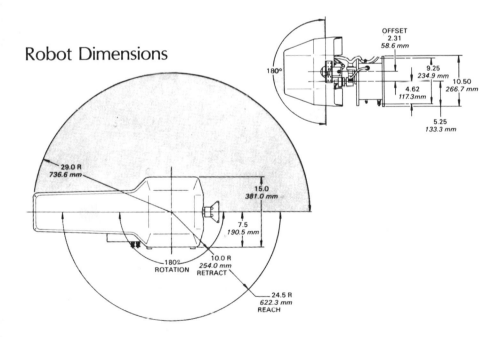

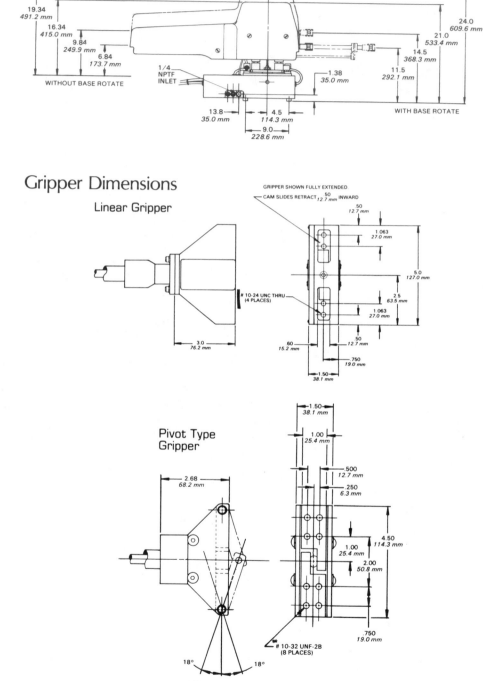

WITHOUT BASE ROTATE

WITH BASE ROTATE

1/4 NPTF INLET

Gripper Dimensions

Linear Gripper

GRIPPER SHOWN FULLY EXTENDED.
CAM SLIDES RETRACT 50 12.7 mm INWARD

10-24 UNC THRU (4 PLACES)

Pivot Type Gripper

10-32 UNF-2B (8 PLACES)

MAX. ACTUATOR ARC

Thermwood Machinery Co. (Cartesian 5).

A one-station system for automated plastic trimming. Provides flexibility needed for most multiple plastic trimming operations with large stationary table size [up to 5 ft × 10 ft (1.5 × 3 m)] and one-station five-axis capability. The specially designed "wrist–arm" is equipped with a high-speed spindle. Complex angled routing and boring operations are performed automatically. The unit also controls external events such as vacuum or clamping holddown systems. Programming can be done from a sample part. Using a calculator-type hand-held programmer, the machine is moved through the motions desired. The program is stored in solid-state memory. Steps can be added, deleted, or changed without rewriting the entire programs, and programs can be retained on cassettes for future use.

	Model Number		
	35P	48P	510P
TABLE SIZE	3 ft × 5 ft	4 ft × 8 ft	5 ft × 10 ft
HEAD TRAVEL:			
Left to right (Axis 1)	60 in.	96 in.	120 in.
Front to rear (Axis 2)	36 in.	48 in.	60 in.
Vertical (Axis 3)	24 in.	24 in.	24 in.
Horizontal rotation (Axis 4)	360°	360°	360°
Vertical rotation (Axis 5)	240°	240°	240°
OVERALL DIMENSIONS:			
Length	108 in.	144 in.	168 in.
Width	88 in.	102 in.	114 in.
Height	135 in.	135 in.	135 in.
FEED RATES:			
Left to right (Axis 1)	0-300 in./min		
Front to rear (Axis 2)	0-300 in./min		
Vertical (Axis 3)	0-300 in./min		
Horizontal rotation (Axis 4)	36°/sec		
Vertical rotation (Axis 5)	36°/sec		
POWER REQUIREMENTS	460 V		30 A
AIR REQUIREMENTS	90 psi		
HIGH SPEED MOTOR	High frequency router; 3 HP, 18,000 rpm, ⅜ in. Collet		

Thermwood Machinery Co. (Series Three).

A general-purpose material-handling robot (five-axis, jointed-arm, servo-controlled, point-to-point) featuring a new language called LEVEL II. The language allows a wide range of control options and decision-tree operating modes. Up to 32 inputs can be scanned to provide on-line branching to appropriate subroutines in the main program when the input information falls into predefined patterns. Loads up to 50 lb (22.5 kg) can be moved in a space 10 ft (3.1 m) in diameter. In addition to the five axes of movement supplied as standard, a sixth servo valve is included that can be used to drive an optional sixth axis, nominally the "hand" mounted on the end of the arm. The hydraulic drive system provides a 280° rotary base sweep, a 100° radial shoulder sweep, a 280° vertical elbow sweep, and 210° wrist pitch. Wrist roll is up to 360°. Speed is 45°/second. Working load limit is calculated by subtracting the weight of the hand from 50 lb (22.5 kg). Repeatability is within ± 0.060 in. (1.5 mm). The control system is a closed-loop servo analog feedback microprocessor-based solid-state system. There are 32 inputs and 32 outputs. Memory size is 200 points, expandable as needed, and provides for random program selection, editing, and programmable velocities.

Thermwood Machinery Co. (Series Six).

The Series Six industrial robot is a servo-controlled six-axis continuous-path robot designed primarily for spray painting. The Series Six offers a large, flexible working envelope, which can be tailored to special needs utilizing a fixed pivot point in the center of the upper arm. The solid-state computer control system can store up to eight programs. With the disk memory option it can be increased to thousands of programs and 60 hours of total programming time. An editing system allows corrections to a program, either motion or gun triggering, without removing the machine from production. The unit is programmed using the lead-through teach method. An editing system allows the program motions to be modified one axis at a time until the exact, desired result is achieved. The jointed-arm design allows a flexible operating envelope, and a manually adjusted pivot on the upper arm increases its flexibility. The omnidirectional wrist allows a very close coupled 180° pivot in all directions around the center of the wrist. A full 48 in. (1.22 m) horizontal stroke is standard. In operation the spray painting robot has the capability of both point-to-point and continuous-path-type programming within the same program. Using point-to-point each point's position and the time necessary to get to the point during the programming are recorded. During playback the point-to-point program will operate at the same speed at which it was input. Eight individual outputs at TTL levels are standard, one of which is required for gun triggering in spray coating applications. This means that seven other auxiliary devices such as fixtures, conveyors, etc., can be operated by the robot control system. The additional outputs are programmed one at a time using the edit box while the machine is executing a program. The microcomputer-based control system of the Series Six robot is equipped with dual RS232C access parts allowing for easy interface with various high-level systems and for incorporation into a large automated system operated by a central processing computer.

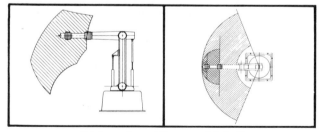

Work envelope of Thermwood Series Six.

Thermwood Series Six Continuous-Path Robot Specifications

Model
Series Six, Model E

Number of axes
6 (additional axes optional)

Configuration
Jointed Arm

Mounting position
Floor/Ceiling

Coordinate system
Jointed Arm

Drive system
Intrinsically safe, hydraulic/mechanical

Load capacity
18 lb (8 kg) — full speed

Horizontal stroke/speed
48 in. (122 cm)
30 in./sec (76 cm/sec)

Vertical stroke/speed
84 in. (213 cm)
30 in./sec (76 cm/sec)

Rotary stroke/speed
135°
60°/sec

Wrist roll/travel speed
270°
150°/sec

Wrist movement
180° cone

Repeatability
± 0.125 in. (± 3.2 mm)

Control system
Closed loop servo
Analog feedback
Microcomputer-based solid state

Memory tape
Semiconductor/disk memory option

Memory size
5 minutes continuous path (expandable)
Point to point dependent on program

Number of programs
8

Random selection
Yes

Operating modes
Point to point
Continuous path

Programming
Lead through teach

Editing
Yes

Programmable velocity
Yes

Outputs
8 outputs

Interface hardware
Terminal strip for external wiring
RS232C selectable baud rate
asynchronous RS232C synchronous

Ambient conditions
40–120° F (4–49° C)
5 – 90% humidity

Power required
10 kW

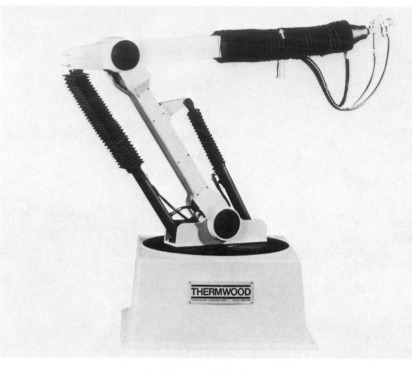

The Thermwood Series Six robot.

Thermwood Machinery Co. (Series Seven).

The Series Seven is a lead-through-teach material-handling robot designed for simple material-handling applications. It has a 25-lb (11.25-kg) load capacity, and a flexible working envelope with small floor space requirement.

Series Seven
Continuous-Path Pick-and-Place
Robot Specifications

Model
Series Seven

Number of axes
Six

Configuration
Jointed arm

Coordinate system
Jointed arm

Drive system
Hydraulic

Load capacity
25 lb (11.25 kg)

Horizontal stroke
39 in. (99 cm)

Vertical stroke
76 in. (193 cm)

Base rotary sweep
280°

Wrist roll
300°

Wrist pitch
180°

Repeatability
± 0.060 in. (1.5 mm)

Control system
Closed loop servo
Analog feedback
Microcomputer-based solid state

Memory tape
Semiconductor

Memory size
5 minutes continuous path (expandable)
Point to point depending on program

Number of programs
Eight

Random selection
Yes

Operating modes
Continuous path
Point to point

Programming
Lead through teach

Editing
Yes

Programmable velocity
Yes

Inputs/outputs
8/8

Interface hardware
Terminal strip for external wiring

Mounting position
Floor

Power required
240/480 V, three phase
60 Hz, 10 kW

Cooling system
Water

Ambient conditions
32°–120° F (0–49° C)
5 – 95% humidity

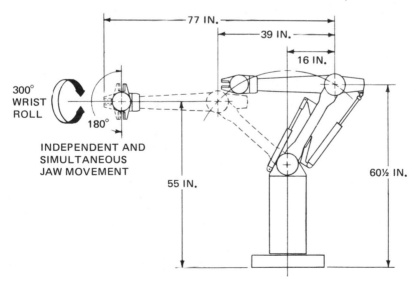

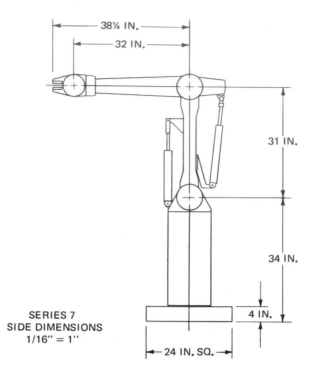

Thermwood Series Seven specifications *(continued).*

Unimation, Inc. (Apprentice Robot).

This welding robot can work with most standard gasless flux core wire and GMAW systems to produce welds on straight or curved surfaces. Difficult vertical weave welding can be performed. Since it takes only seconds to teach, the robot is particularly suited for one-of-a-kind weldments and also for repetitive welding in batch production. The robot is light and can be transported easily to any work site. With its large work envelope the robot can completely weld many components without being repositioned. To use, the robot is placed in position at the weld site and connected to its control unit by a 33-ft (10-m) length of cable. It is totally electrically powered. A teaching head is placed over the torch and rolled along the weld path, causing the robot's memory to record every motion. The robot's control unit is used to set torch speeds, weaving patterns, weave amplitude, and weld sequence. Once set, the information is stored in the solid-state memory. The robot can do 14 stitch welds or any series of welds totaling 27 ft (8.3 m) in length without reteaching.

Specifications

Working envelope
Vertical   35 in. Stroke (45 in. reach)
Depth   64 in.
Width   64 in.
Yaw motion   360°
Wrist motion   165°

General
Weight of robot   125 lbs.
Weight of cabinet   200 lbs.
Weight on torch holder   10 lbs. max.
Cable length   33 ft.
Power   110V., Single phase,
requirements   60 Hz, 1KVA

Performance
Welding distance   up to 27 ft.
Welding speeds   48 in./min. max.
Number of welding speeds   4
Number of preselect welding
  currents   4
Transfer speed   2 in./sec.
Weave channels   2
Weaving frequency   Adjustable
Weaving amplitude   1.2 in. max.
Accuracy   ±.04 in.

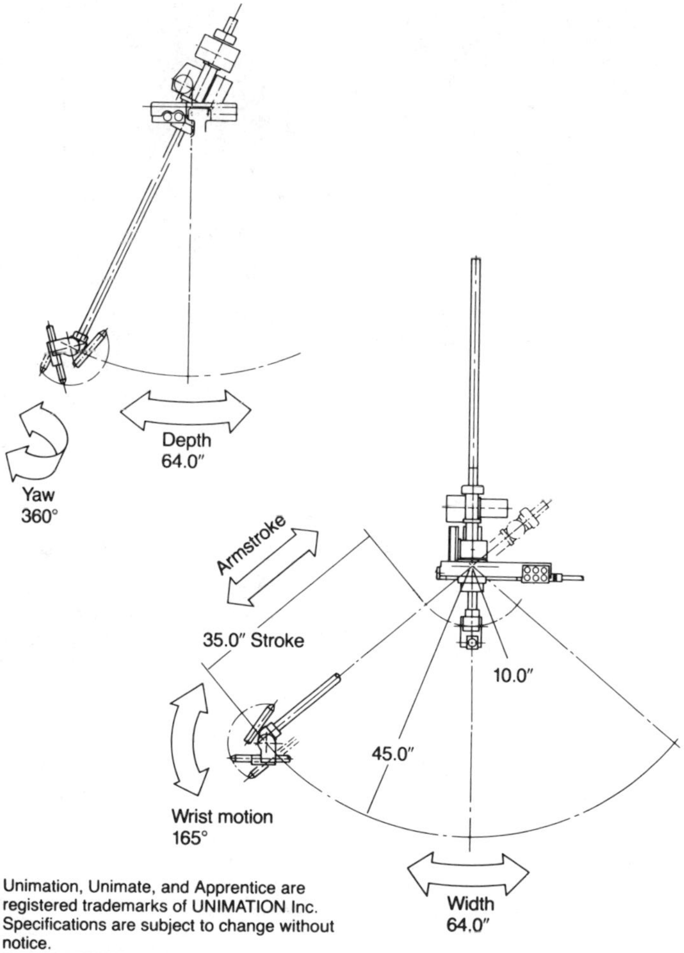

Depth
64.0"

Yaw
360°

Armstroke

35.0" Stroke

Wrist motion
165°

10.0"

45.0"

Width
64.0"

Unimation, Unimate, and Apprentice are
registered trademarks of UNIMATION Inc.
Specifications are subject to change without
notice.

Unimation Inc. (Puma 250 Series).

The most compact Puma robot; it has the greatest speed and repeatability of the Unimation family. Six degrees of freedom combined with the VAL control system make the unit ideal for medium- to high-speed assembly and material-handling applications. Light and compact, the 250 series provides the versatility to be rapidly integrated into changing environments. It is capable of standing on its own or becoming the flexible arm of automated assembly systems. Typical applications are PC board assembly, tester loading, adhesive application, palletizing, component insertion, machine loading, flexible material transfer, and inspection.

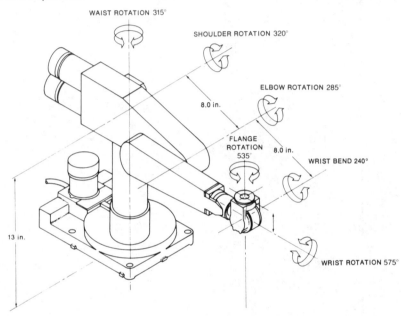

Puma 250.

Specifications

General

Configuration   Six revolute axes
Drive   Electric dc servos
Controller   System Computer (LSI-11)
  Teaching method   By manual control and/or computer terminal
  Program language   VAL®
  Program capacity   8K RAM user memory std (16K RAM max — optional)
  External program storage   Floppy-disk (optional)
Gripper control   Four-way pneumatic solenoid

Power requirement   110–130 Vac, 50–60 Hz, 1500 W
Optional accessories   CRT or TTY terminals, floppy-disk memory storage
I/O module (8 input/8 output signals — isolated ac/dc levels)
Pneumatic gripper w/o fingers [clamping force = 31 lb, finger travel = 0.75 in. (19 mm), flow rate = 1 CFM, air filtered and lubricated]

Performance

Repeatability   ± 0.05 mm (0.002 in.)

Load capacity   2 lb (0.9 kg)

Straight-line velocity/ 1.0 m/s max.

Environmental requirements   10–50° C
    (50–120° F)

80% humidity (noncondensing)

Shielded against industrial line fluctuations
    and human electrostatic discharge

Physical characteristics

Arm weight   15 lb (6.75 kg)

Controller size   0.48 × 0.32 ×
    0.51 m (19 in. rack
    mountable)

Controller weight   80 lb (36 kg)

Controller cable length   4.5 m
    (15 ft) max

Unimation, Inc. (Puma 500 Series).

The 500 series is a five-axis robot with the VAL control system. The arm is sized to human dimensions and designed to duplicate human motions. With its 3.28 ft (1 m) reach and heavier load capacity, this robot is capable of handling most industrial assembly, transfer, or packaging operations. It is easily portable. Typical applications are small part assembly, tester loading, packaging, palletizing, parts transfer, machine tool loading, adhesive application, and inspection.

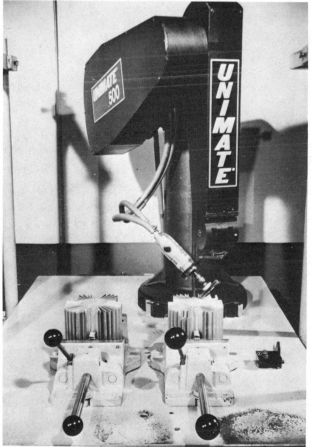

The Puma 500 from Unimation.

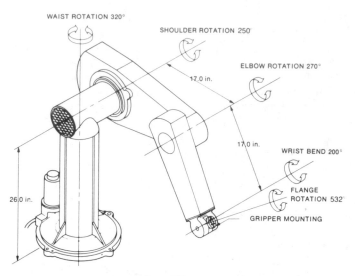

Puma 500

Specifications

General

Configuration   Five revolute axes
Drive   Electric dc servos
Controller   System Computer (LSI-11)
   Teaching method   By manual
      control and/or computer
      terminal
   Program language   VAL®
   Program capacity   8K RAM user
      memory std (16K RAM
      max – optional)
   External program storage   Floppy-
      disk (optional)
Gripper control   Four-way pneumatic
   solenoid
Power requirement   110–130 Vac,
   50–60 Hz, 1500 W
Optional accessories   CRT or TTY
   terminals, floppy-disk memory
   storage
I/O module (8 input/8 output signals –
   isolated ac/dc levels)
Pneumatic gripper w/o fingers [clamping
   force = 31 lb, finger travel =
   0.75 in. (19 mm), flow rate =
   6 CFM, air filtered and lubricated]

Performance

Repeatability   ± 0.1 mm (0.004 in)
Load capacity

At flange rotation,
   5.5 lb (4 in. dia.)

At wrist bend, 5.5 lb at 5 in.
   (5.7 in.-oz-sec^2)

Straight-line velocity   0.5 m/s
   (20 in./s) max.
Environmental requirements   10–50° C
   (50–120° F)
80% humidity (noncondensing)
Shielded against industrial line
   fluctuations and
   human electrostatic discharge

Physical characteristics

Arm weight   120 lb (54 kg)
Controller size   0.48 × 0.32 × 0.51 m (19
in. rack mountable)
Controller weight   80 lb (36 kg)
Controller cable length
   4.5 m (15 ft) max

Unimation, Inc. (Puma 600 Series).

The most dexterous member of the Puma family, the 600 series combines the characteristics of both the 250 and 500 series robots and the VAL control system. Utilizing six degrees of freedom and 3.28 ft (1 m) reach, it has added flexibility to perform complex manipulations within a large working area. This unit has the same working characteristics and dimensions of the 500 series. Applications for this unit are similar to that of the 500 series. Typical applications are small part assembly, tester loading, packaging, palletizing, parts transfer, machine tool loading, adhesive application, and inspection.

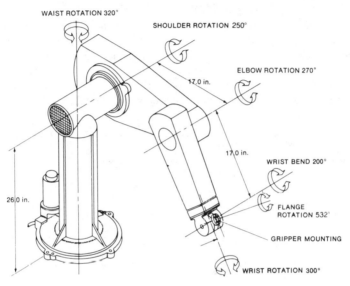

Puma 600

Specifications

General

Configuration   Six revolute axes
Drive   Electric dc servos
Controller   System computer (LSI-11)
    Teaching method   By manual control
        and/or computer terminal
    Program language   VAL®
    Program capacity   8K RAM user
        memory std (16K RAM
        max — optional)
    External program storage   Floppy-disk
        (optional)
Gripper control   Four-way pneumatic
    solenoid
Power requirement   110–130 Vac,
    50–60 Hz, 1500 W

Optional accessories   CRT or TTY
    terminals, floppy disk memory
    storage
I/O module (8 input/8 output signals —
    isolated ac/dc levels)
Pneumatic gripper w/o fingers [clamping
    force = 31 lb, finger travel =
    0.75 in. (19 mm), flow rate =
    6 CFM, air filtered and lubricated]

Performance

Repeatability   ± 0.1 mm (0.004 in.)
Load capacity
At flange rotation, 5.5 lb (4 in. dia.)
    (0.5 in-oz-sec^2)
At wrist bend, 5.5 lb at 5 in.
    (5.7 in.-oz-sec^2)
Straight-line velocity   0.5 m/s

(20 in./s) max.
Environmental requirements   10–50° C
   (50–120° F)
80% humidity (noncondensing)
Shielded against industrial line fluctuations
   and human electrostatic discharge

Physical characteristics
Arm weight   120 lb (54 kg)
Controller size   0.48 × 0.32 × 0.51 m
   (19 in. rack mountable)
Controller weight   80 lb (36 kg)
Controller cable length   4.5 m
   (15 ft) max.

Unimation Inc. (Unimate 2000).

This was the first industrial robot installed in a production operation in 1961. Continual updates and refinements have made it a most versatile manipulator. It is computer controlled, with up to six degrees of motion and lift capacity to 300 lb (135 kg). This model finds application in most material-handling, die casting, investment casting, machine loading, and press transfer operations. The 200F model allows for continuous-path motions for arc welding, sealant placement, and routing applications. The UNIMATE 4000 Series has up to

	1000	2000B	2100B	2000C	2100C	4000B
Mounting Position	Floor	Floor	Floor	Any	Any	Floor
No. of Degrees of Freedom	3 to 5	3 to 6	3 to 6	3 to 6	3 to 6	3 to 6
Positioning Repeatability	0.05 in. (1.27 mm)	0.05 in. (1.27 mm)	0.08 in. (2.03 mm)	0.05 in. (1.27 mm)	0.08 in. (2.03 mm)	0.08 in. (2.03 mm)
Power Requirements	460V,3φ 60Hz,9kVA	460V,3φ 60Hz,11kVA	460V,3φ 60Hz,11kVA	460V,3φ 60Hz,11kVA	460V,3φ 60Hz,11kVA	460V,3φ 60Hz,34kVA
Maximum Lift	50 lb (22.9 kg)	300 lb (136 kg)	300 lb (136 kg)	300 lb (136 kg)	270 lb (123 kg)	450 lb (205 kg)
Standard Wrist Torque						
Bend	500 in.-lb (5.7 kg-m)	1000 in.-lb (11.5 kg-m)	1000 in.-lb (11.5 kg-m)	1000 in.-lb (11.5 kg-m)	1000 in.-lb (11.5 kg-m)	3500 in.-lb (40.3 kg-m)
Yaw	150 in.-lb (1.7 kg-m)	600 in.-lb (6.9 kg-m)	600 in.-lb (6.9 kg-m)	600 in.-lb (6.9 kg-m)	600 in.-lb (6.9 kg-m)	2800 in.-lb (32.2 kg-m)
Swivel	N/A	800 in.-lb (9.2 kg-m)	800 in.-lb (9.2 kg-m)	800 in.-lb (9.2 kg-m)	800 in.-lb (9.2 kg-m)	2300 in.-lb (26.5 kg-m)
Heavy Duty Wrist Torque						
Bend	N/A	2000 in.-lb (23 kg-m)	2000 in.-lb (23 kg-m)	2000 in.-lb (23 kg-m)	2000 in.-lb (23 kg-m)	11000 in.-lb (126.5 kg-m)
Yaw	N/A	1200 in.-lb (13.8 kg-m)	1200 in.-lb (13.8 kg-m)	1200 in.-lb (13.8 kg-m)	1200 in.-lb (13.8 kg-m)	2800 in.-lb (32.2 kg-m)
Swivel	N/A	800 in.-lb (9.2 kg-m)	800 in.-lb (9.2 kg-m)	800 in.-lb (9.2 kg-m)	800 in.-lb (9.2 kg-m)	N/A
Memory Options						
Point to Point	Up to 256 points	Up to 2048 points	Up to 2048 points	Up to 2048 points	Up to 2048 points	Up to 2048 points
Continuous Path	N/A	Up to 500 in. of travel	Up to 500 in. of travel	Up to 500 in. of travel	N/A	N/A
Environment	40°F (5°C) to 120°F (50°C), Humidity 0–90%; all models.					

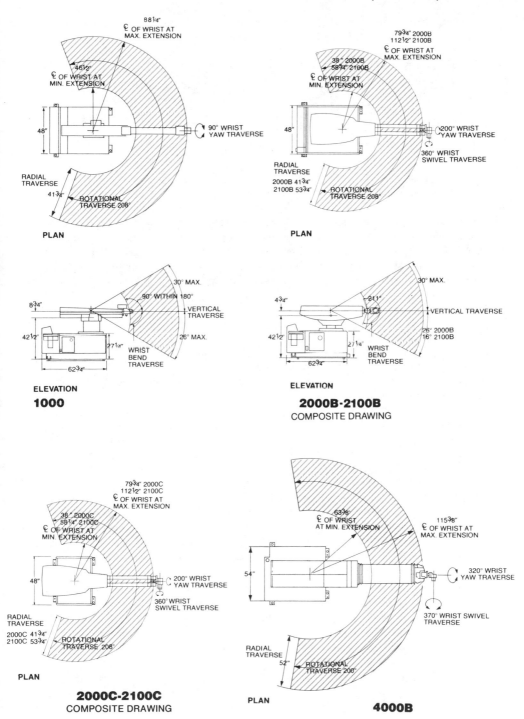

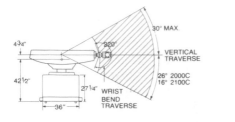

ELEVATION

2000C-2100C
COMPOSITE DRAWING

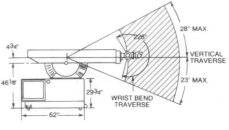

ELEVATION

4000B

six degrees of motion and a lift capacity to 450 lb (203 kg). It is computer controlled. Its larger capacity makes it ideal for heavy jobs such as spot welding, forging, and investment casting. The UNIMATE 1000 Series combines flexibility with economy. With up to five degrees of motion and a 25-lb (11.25-kg) weight capacity, its low cost enables the smaller manufacturers to take advantage of robotic automation.

United States Robots (Maker).

A "smart" assembly robot designed to perform intricate assembly operations, the Maker is a five-jointed computer-controlled arm designed to be used in any repetitive manufacturing operation. The system is composed of two major elements, the arm and the controller. The robot arm has five joints, four rotary and one linear. The linear joint consists of three telescoping members. This design feature allows the robot to reach up to 36 in. (0.9 m) when fully extended, when retracted it measures 16 in. (0.4 m). The arm can reach anywhere within a 76-in.-diameter (1.9 m) sphere, at speeds up to 55 ips. It is capable of lifting up to 5 lb (2.25 kg) with a repeatability of 0.004 in. (0.1 mm). These attributes make it suitable for doing intricate assembly work, machine loading/unloading, and small parts handling. With its standard continuous-path capabilities, the robot can be used for adhesive coating or contour-path applications. Its aluminum construction combines high strength and light weight and permits operation in stringent industrial environments. The controller is microprocessor based. By using a multiprocessing scheme, one microcomputer is dedicated to each of the robot functions. There is one microcomputer for each joint, one for mathematical calculations, and one that coordinates all of the processors and system I/O. All of the processors communicate along a single bus using a shared-memory technique. This scheme allows for virtually unlimited expansion of capabilities by the simple addition of optional modules. (The controller is also able to control other machines or to receive information from other equipment and respond accordingly, either by waiting or by jumping to a subprogram.) The operator teaches the arm by using a hand-held teach pendant, which incorporates a number of different switches and a display panel. The teach pendant also allows the operator to edit programs, such as inserting and deleting points, and single step, backstep, and reset. Also available is the Qwik-Grip pneumatic gripper. This lightweight, double-acting pneumatic hand can be used for almost any application, including those requiring a wide mix of parts.

The Maker from United States Robots.

Model Designation:

The MAKER

Basic design intent:

Assembly operations; other applications may include loading/unloading; complex material handling; contour curve applications such as gluing, painting, and welding with light-weight guns

Approximate size:

Base to shoulder center line: 17 in. (43 cm)

Shoulder center line to wrist pitch axis: 17–37 in. (43–94 cm)

Working spherical volume: 78 in. (198 cm)

(to gripper mounting flange)

Approximate weight:

Five degrees-of-freedom arm: 40 lb (18 kg)

Microcomputer controller: 50 lb (22.5 kg)

Teach pendant: 1 lb (0.45 kg)

Number of axes of motion:

Five degrees-of-freedom: four rotary, one linear

Axis No. 1: Base 355° rotary

Axis No. 2: Shoulder 300° rotary

Axis No. 3: Arm 20 in. (51 cm) linear stroke

Axis No. 4: Wrist pitch 210° rotary

Axis No. 5: Wrist roll 355° rotary

Mode of actuation:

Electric dc servo drives on all five axes. Harmonic drives on all axes except No. 3, which has a ball screw, and No. 4, which has single pass gearing

Type of control:

Computer, using eight microprocessors: one per servo drive, one each for computation, system supervision, and the teach pendant. No programming language required. Teaching is totally accomplished with push buttons on the teach pendant. Memory is CMOS nonvolatile technology. Basic memory is 8K, providing 350 moves. This is expandable up to 32K (1400 moves) in 8K steps

Control flexibility:

Standard software includes four modes of operation: Joint-interpolation, straight line, point-to-point, and continuous path. Standard are 256 robot programs of any desired length, each of which may call any other program at any time. Twenty-four unbuffered input/output lines are standard

Mounting position:

May be mounted in any plane, including floor, ceiling, and wall

Load capacity:

Five pound (2.25 kg) payload (including end effector):
wrist pitch: 50 in.-lb;
wrist roll: 50 in.-lb

Speed of actuation:

Rotary axes: 1.5 rad/second
Linear axis: 55 in./second
(140 cm/second)

Operation volume:

78 in. (198 cm) diameter spheroid

Repeatability:

0.004 in. (0.1 mm)

Power requirement:

105–130 Vac, 47–63 Hz, 1680 VA maximum

United Technologies Corp. (Niko 25, 50, 100, 150, 200, 500, and 600).

This series of robots includes jointed-arm, Cartesian, and cylindrical models in various sizes for welding. Both five- and six-axis models are available with microprocessor control having memory capacity of 400 points in space and extension, up to 1200 points maximum. Programming is by the teach-in operating field method.

Specification Mechanical system	NIKO 25	NIKO 50
■ MECHANICAL STRUCTURE		
degrees of freedom	5 rotational axes	
drive	DC-disc-rotor-motor	
power transmission	harmonic-drive-gear	
■ POWER		
accuracy of repetition max. throat	± 0,25 mm	± 0,25 mm
manipulation weight max. throat	2,5 kg	5 kg
■ OPERATING RANGE		
quasi spherical range	1820 mm	2500 mm
■ ROTATION SPHERE		
axis 1	320°	320°
axis 2	240°	240°
axis 3	250°	290°
axis 4	210°	210°
axis 5	350°	350°

■ MAXIMUM SPEED

axis 1	90^0/ sec.	90^0/ sec.
axis 2	90^0/ sec.	90^0/ sec.
axis 3	110^0/ sec.	110^0/ sec.
axis 4	110^0/ sec.	110^0/ sec.
axis 5	280^0/ sec.	180^0/ sec.

■ MOUNTING AREA $0,23 \ m^2$ $0,30 \ m^2$

■ WEIGHT   130 kg   240 kg

■ LOCATION OF AXES

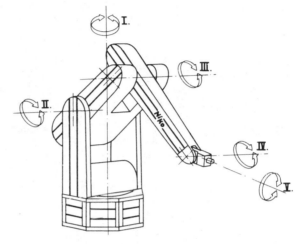

Specification Control System

	NIKO 25	NIKO 50
■ micro-processor-control	5 movement-axes	
■ quasi path control	(max. point to point distance 30 mm)	
■ positioning	incremental – digital	
■ memory capacity	400 points in space	
■ memory extension each	200 points in space	
■ max. memory capacity	1200 points in space	
■ speed	99 programmable areas	
■ storage	in none-volatile memories (EPROM)	
■ extension of input and output each	16	
■ programming	teach-in-method	
■ power supply	380 V; 50 Hz	
■ connected load	2 kw	3 kw
■ ambient temperature	$0-40^0$ C	

- screen indication

  program-flow
  service instruction
  indication of state
  diagnosis of errors
  checking program

- interface V 24

  programming of EPROMs
  print-out of program
  read in of program

- service panel

  control on-off
  selection switch for different modes of
  operation
  indication of state
  key-board for movement-axes and gripper

- teach-in-operating field

  type of service - path measurement -
  typing - step preselection - going to the
  programmed point - cancelling

  step - putting in - cancelling -
  functions - putting in - change

- external inputs and outputs for

  gripper; welding gun; MIG-welding device;
  TIG-welding device; selection of welding
  programs

- dimensions

  control cabinet   800x600x2000
  service panel   290x120x 400
  teach-in-field   230x 80x 280

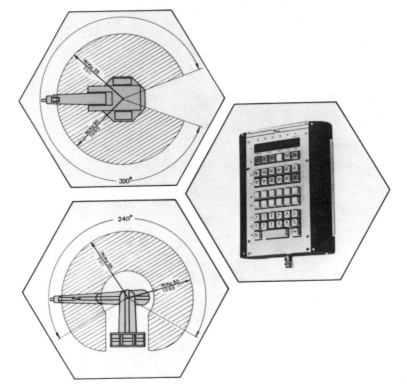

Specification Mechanical system NIKO 150

■ MECHANICAL STRUCTURE

degrees of freedom — 5 rotational axes
drive — DC-disc-rotor-motor
power transmission — harmonic-drive-gear

■ POWER

accuracy of repetition max. throat — ± 0,25 mm
manipulation weight max. throat — 15 kg

■ OPERATING RANGE

spherical — 3150 mm

■ ROTATION SPHERE

axis 1 — 320^0
axis 2 — 240^0
axis 3 — 290^0
axis 4 — 210^0
axis 5 — 350^0

■ MAXIMUM SPEED

axis 1 — 90^0/ sec.
axis 2 — 90^0/ sec.
axis 3 — 110^0/ sec.
axis 4 — 120^0/ sec.
axis 5 — 120^0/ sec.

■ MOUNTING AREA — $0,45 \text{ m}^2$

■ WEIGHT — 550 kg

■ LOCATION OF AXES

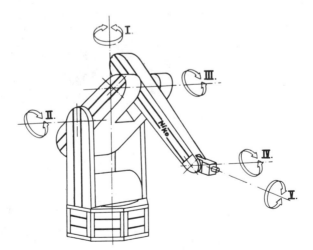

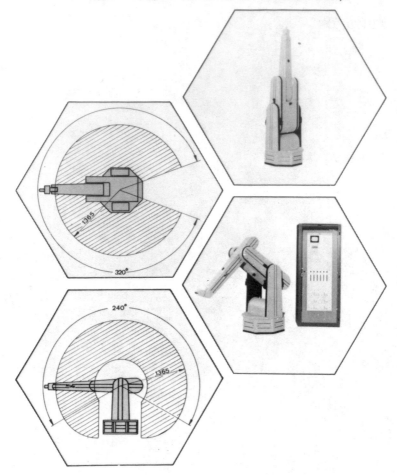

Specification Control System

- micro-processor-control
- quasi path control
- positioning
- memory capacity
- memory extension each
- max. memory capacity
- speed
- storage
- extension of input and output each

NIKO 150

5 movement-axes

(max. point to point distance 30 mm)

incremental – digital

400 points in space

200 points in space

1200 points in space

99 programmable areas

in none-volatile memories (EPROM)

16

■ programming	teach-in-method
■ power supply	380 V; 50 Hz
■ connected load	7 kw
■ ambient temperature	$0-40^0$ C
■ screen indication	program-flow service instruction indication of state diagnosis of errors checking program
■ interface V 24	programming of EPROMs print-out of program read in of program
■ service panel	control on-off selection switch for different modes of operation indication of state key-board for movement-axes and gripper
■ teach-in-operating field	type of service - path measurement - typing - step preselection - going to the programmed point - cancelling step - putting in - cancelling - functions - putting in - change
■ external inputs and outputs for	gripper; welding gun; MIG-wolding device; TIG-welding device; selection of welding programs
■ dimensions	control cabinet 800x600x2000 service panel 290x120x 400 teach-in-field 230x 80x 280

Specification Mechanical system

	NIKO 100	NIKO 500
■ MECHANICAL STRUCTURE		
degrees of freedom	1 translational axis 5 rotational axes	
drive	DC-disc-rotor-motor	
power transmission	harmonic-drive-gear	
■ POWER		
accuracy of repetition max. throat	± 0,35 mm	± 0,35 mm
manipulation weight max. throat	20 kg	60 kg
■ OPERATING RANGE		
axis 1/X	340^0	340^0
axis 2/Y	270^0	270^0
axis 3/Z	500 - 1000 mm	500 - 1250 mm
axis 4/A	340^0	340^0
axis 5/B	340^0	340^0
axis 6/C	340^0	340^0

■ MAXIMUM SPEED

axis 1/X	90°/ sec.	90°/ sec.
axis 2/Y	110°/ sec.	110°/ sec.
axis 3/Z	0,3 m/ sec.	0,5 m/ sec.
axis 4/A	120°/ sec.	120°/ sec.
axis 5/B	120°/ sec.	120°/ sec.
axis 6/C	120°/ sec.	120°/ sec.

■ MOUNTING AREA 0,3 m² 　 0,3 m²

■ WEIGHT 1050 kg 　 1200 kg

■ LOCATION OF AXES

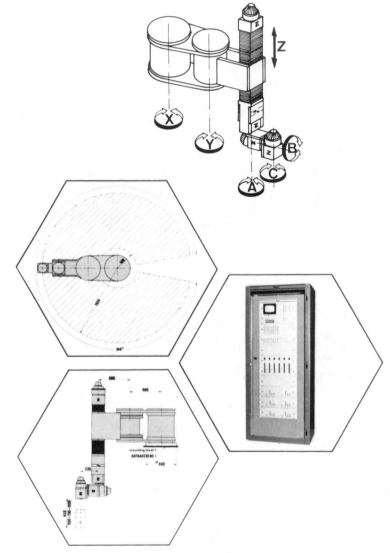

Specification Control System

	NIKO 100	NIKO 500
■ micro-processor-control	6 movement-axes	
■ quasi path control	(max. point to point distance 30 mm)	
■ positioning	incremental – digital	
■ memory capacity	400 points in space	
■ memory extension each	200 points in space	
■ max. memory capacity	1200 points in space	
■ speed	99 programmable areas	
■ storage	in none-volatile memories (EPROM)	
■ extension of input and output each	16	
■ programming	teach-in-method	
■ power supply	380 V; 50 Hz	
■ connected load	10 kw	11 kw
■ ambient temperature	$0-40^0$ C	
■ screen indication	program-flow service instruction indication of state diagnosis of errors checking program	
■ interface V 24	programming of EPROMs print-out of program read in of program	
■ service panel	control on-off selection switch for different modes of operation indication of state key-board for movement-axes and gripper	
■ teach-in-operating field	type of service - path measurement - typing - step preselection - going to the programmed point - cancelling step - putting in - cancelling - functions - putting in - change	
■ external inputs and outputs for	gripper; welding gun; MIG-welding device; TIG-welding device; selection of welding programs	
■ dimensions	control cabinet 800x600x2000 service panel 290x120x 400 teach-in-field 230x 80x 280	

Specification Mechanical system

	NIKO 200	**NIKO 600**

■ MECHANICAL STRUCTURE

degrees of freedom — 3 translational axes
3 rotational axes
drive — DC-disc-rotor-motor
power transmission — harmonic-drive-gear
ball screw
spur gear drive

■ POWER

	NIKO 200	NIKO 600
accuracy of repetition max. throat	± 0,35 mm	± 0,35 mm
manipulation weight max. throat	20 kg	60 kg

■ OPERATING RANGE

	NIKO 200	NIKO 600
axis 1/X	500 - 6000 mm	500 - 6000 mm
axis 2/Y	500 - 2000 mm	1000 - 2000 mm
axis 3/Z	500 - 1000 mm	500 - 1200 mm
axis 4/A	340^0	340^0
axis 5/B	340^0	340^0
axis 6/C	340^0	340^0

■ MAXIMUM SPEED

	NIKO 200	NIKO 600
axis 1/X	0,75 m / sec.	1 m / sec.
axis 2/Y	0,75 m / sec.	1 m / sec.
axis 3/Z	0,30 m / sec.	0,50 m / sec.
axis 4/A	120^0/ sec.	120^0/ sec.
axis 5/B	120^0/ sec.	120^0/ sec.
axis 6/C	120^0/ sec.	120^0/ sec.

■ MOUNTING AREA — according to the stroke

■ WEIGHT without gantry — 1400 kg / 1650 kg

■ LOCATION OF AXES

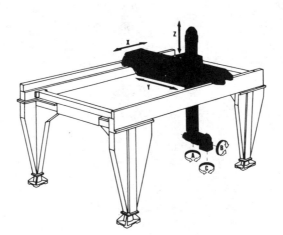

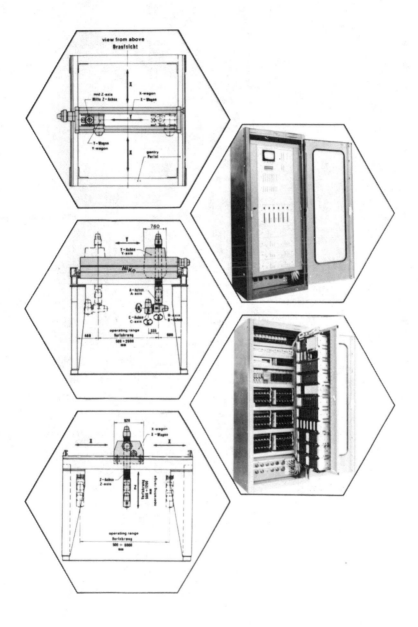

Specification

Control System	NIKO 200	NIKO 600
■ micro-processor-control	6 movement-axes	
■ quasi path control	(max. point to point distance 30 mm)	
■ positioning	incremental – digital	
■ memory capacity	400 points in space	
■ memory extension each	200 points in space	
■ max. memory capacity	1200 points in space	
■ speed	99 programmable areas	
■ storage	in none-volatile memories (EPROM)	
■ extension of input and output each	16	
■ programming	teach-in-method	
■ power supply	380 V; 50 Hz	
■ connected load	6,5 kw	10 kw
■ ambient temperature	$0-40^0$ C	
■ screen indication	program-flow service instruction indication of state diagnosis of errors checking program	
■ interface V 24	programming of EPROMs print-out of program read in of program	
■ service panel	control on-off selection switch for different modes of operation indication of state key-board for movement-axes and gripper	
■ teach-in-operating field	type of service - path measurement - typing - step preselection - going to the programmed point - cancelling step - putting in - cancelling - functions - putting in - change	
■ external inputs and outputs for	gripper; welding gun; MIG-welding device; TIG-welding device; selection of welding programs	
■ dimensions	control cabinet 800x600x2000 service panel 290x120x 400 teach-in-field 230x 80x 280	

Westinghouse Electric Corporation (Series 4000 Arc Welding Robot).

This robot is a solid-state-controlled automatic welding system designed for application versatility. It utilizes the new pulsed gas-metal-arc welding spray transfer process to join many types of metals and alloys in virtually any shape. It is ideal for many precision welding applications for both long or short quantity production runs. The Series 4000 Robot provides increased production with improved weld quality, greatly reduced welding costs, and energy efficiency for high profitability.

The Series 4000 arc welder is designed for automatic operations at a production line station or as an integral component of a completely automated assembly line. The system is composed of four major components: an arc welder robot, a control cabinet, a welding power source, and a welding-wire feeder. It is designed to approach total automatic operation, with all component operations integrated through the programmable control unit for controlled coordination of the welding parameters.

Westinghouse Series 4000 welding robot. (Specifications on p. 252.)

Westinghouse Electric Corporation (Series 5000 Industrial Robot System).

This is a high-technology automation system designed to increase productivity in manipulating, inspection, and assembly operations. It incorporates the control sensitivity and precision movement required to accomplish delicate assembly operations in areas such as the automotive, electronics, aerospace, and electrical industries.

Specifically designed for application versatility, this robotic system offers a variety of standard manipulator modules and special fixtures when needed and has the capability for a high number of inputs and outputs for auxiliary equipment. This flexibility combined with a versatile programming system results in the ability to adapt the Series 5000 robot to

Dimensions in Millimeters

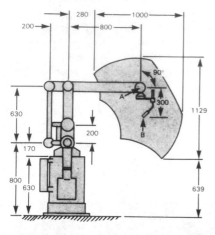

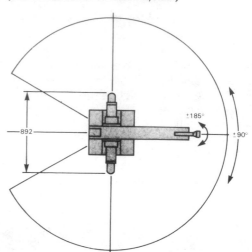

Westinghouse Series 4000.

Specifications

Mechanical

Type: 5-Axis articulated

Net Weight: 370 kg. (815.85 lbs.) without cable

Load Capacity: 10 kg. (22.05 lbs.) within 200 mm (7.87 in.) area from wrist bend axis center

Drive System: D-C Servomotor

Position Repeatability: ±0.2 mm (±.008 in.)

Ambient Temperature: 0° to 50°C

Controlled Travel:
Base: ±150° from Vertical (300° total)
Upper Arm: −45° to +50° from Vertical (95° total)
Forearm: +65° to +135° from Vertical (70° total)
Wrist Bend: +30°-+210° from Vertical (180° total)
Wrist Twist: ±185° (360° useful arc)

Maximum Speed:
Combined Base/Arm: 1000 mm/sec. (39.37 in./sec.)
Wrist Bend: 120°/sec.
Wrist Twist: 180°/sec.

Wrist Holding Position: Wrist maintains posture independent of base/arm movement

Home Position Detection: Proximity switch

Emergency Braking: One brake each for stem, upper control arm, and lower forearm motions

Control System

Controller
Cabinet Construction: Self-standing, dust-tight w/door interlock

Dimensions: 654 mm x 1615 mm x 769 mm (25.5" x 63" x 30")

Ambient Temperature: 0° to 45C

Power Requirements: 230 VAC or 460 VAC, 3 phase, 60 HZ; 380 VAC, 3 phase, 50 HZ

Program Method: Point-to-point teach/repeat

Number of Control Axes: 5 axes controlled simultaneously

Speed Control: Constant linear speed at the arc-point

Position Control: Software servo-system

Position Detection: Resolver

Memory: Integrated-circuit
Interpolation: Linear
Coordinate System: Orthogonal
Capacity: Up to 20 programs totaling 1000 points
External Synchronous Signals: 31 Inputs, 31 Outputs
Timer Function: 0.1 to 9.9 sec. each
Editing of Teach Points: Insertion, substitution and deletion
Jump Function: Included

Control Panel: Flat "touch-pad" type, dust-tight enclosure, with 9" CRT, 512 characters, with 3 times enlargement capability

Teach Pendant: Remote hand-held unit, with controls for advancing/reversing of steps

Control Pendant: Remote hand-held unit which includes control for weld parameter adjustment during welding operation.

Abnormality Detection/Display Functions: Servo or CPU malfunction, overrun, overload, operator error, wire seizure, interruption of arc, and decrease in gas pressure.

Welding Power Source
Type: Direct Current

Dimensions: 430 mm x 510 mm x 950 mm (17" x 20" x 37.5")

Weight: 125 kg. (276 lbs.)

Output: 16 to 42 V D-C, 50-500 amps

Input: 18.5 KVA, 230 or 460 VAC, 3 phase, 60 HZ; 380 VAC, 3 phase, 50 HZ

External Input Command: Analog input for current and voltage wire-inching command

Rated Current: 500 amps

Applicable Wire Size: 1.2 mm (.047 in.)

Welding Parameter Control: (direct digital setting)
Current: 0 to rated current
Voltage: 0 to maximum
Speed: 100 mm to 2000 mm/min. (4.0 in. to 78 in./min.)

Confirming/Control Functions: Start of Arc, weld wire advancement, weld parameter regulation

Protective Functions: Automatic crater-handling and arc-striking mechanisms specific production requirements and environments. It is suited for manufacturing operations where fast, repetitive manipulation is required to assemble a variety of parts into components and subassemblies. In addition, quick setup and changeover make the Series 5000 particularly adapted for quick batch runs of different product styles and configurations.

Available in one- or two-arm standard models and two- or three-arm long models, the Series 5000 system utilizes a unique operating feature. All arms act independently, yet in collaboration, to accomplish the programmed work cycle.

Whether this robot is used to automate a particular manufacturing stage or is integrated into a complete automated manufacturing process, this system can provide improved product quality with increased production.

The Series 5000 Robot is constructed with an open support structure that leaves the working area accessible from all four sides, so set-up and maintenance time are reduced. In addition it is designed with sensing capability and program simplicity that enable quick recovery from irregular handling situations, often without interrupting the work cycle.

A series of modular components make up the operating arms. Suspended from the carriage modules are the work-handling components of the Series 5000 Robot. By suspending the arms from the carriage, the system designers enhanced the open access construction of the frame, leaving the assembly area free of obstacles that could hinder production, set-up, and maintenance personnel. This design also keeps all robot operating components within the frame structure, permitting more efficient utilization of valuable floor space.

Westinghouse Series 5000.

Carriage Module

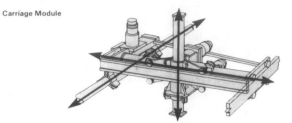

Vertical Axis Revolving Module

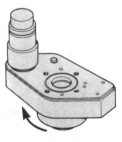

Horizontal Axis Revolving Module

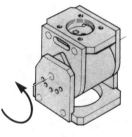

Gripper Module

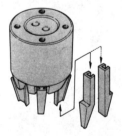

Conveyor Transport Module

Westinghouse Series 5000 two-arm assembly robot.

Specifications

Mechanical

Frame: Bridge-type construction of structural steel

Linear motion: Along 3 axes (X,Y,Z)

Rotary motion: Vertical rotation (axis C), horizontal rotation (axis A)

Drive mechanism: Rack-and pinion

Drive motors: Direct-current, closed-loop feedback

Maximum axis length:

"X" axis   1400 mm (55.1 in.) standard model
            2800 mm (110.2 in.) long model

"Y" axis   410 mm (16.1 in.) standard model
            410 mm (16.1 in.) long model

"Z" axis   410 mm (16.1 in.) standard model
            410 mm (16.1 in.) long model

Controlled travels:

"X" axis   1270 mm (50 in.) standard model
           2250 mm (88.6 in.) long model

"Y" axis   410 mm (16.1 in.)

"Z" axis   410 mm (16.1 in.)

Minimum distance between arms: 130 mm (5.1 inches)

Positioning speed: 32 m/min. (1.75 ft/sec)

Acceleration: 4m/sec^2 (13.1 ft/sec^2)

Positioning accuracy: ±0.15 mm (0.006 inches)

Repeatability: ±0.10 mm (0.004 inches)

Minimum programmable movement: 0.05 mm (0.002 inches)

Maximum weight of component to be moved: 10 kg (22 lb.)

Maximum force developed at each axis: 20 kg. (45 lb.)

Machine overall dimensions:
    Standard Model 2200 x 1090 x 2760 mm
        (86.6 x 42.9 x 108.7 in.)
    Long Model 3600 x 1090 x 2760 mm
        (141.7 x 42.9 x 108.7 in.)

Basic machine weight:
    Standard Model: 1500 kg. (3300 lbs.)
    Long Model: 2000 kg. (4400 lbs.)

Control

Number of axes controlled: up to 9 independently or simultaneously.
Number of force and/or displacement transducers, for pick-up devices or other specific tools: up to 6 controlled simultaneously.

Input/outputs
    Number of input channels: 23
    Number of output channels: 29

User Interface
    Terminal with alpha-numeric keyboard
    Printer for program listing and registration of production control data — 120 characters/sec.

Memory: 32 RAM, 16-bit words

External storage: magnetic-tape cassettes

Power: 220V, 60 Hz; 380V, 50Hz; 440V, 60Hz.

Westinghouse Electric Corporation (Series 7000 Welding Robot).

This is a "real-time" controlled robot, designed for fully automated gas-metal-arc or flux-core welding. Quick response control with accurate mechanical functions make it highly efficient and productive in any process that requires accurate, repetitive welding from light thin-wall to heavy fabrication applications. It is ideal where continuous welding of long pieces or of many small pieces is required.

The Series 7000 features an innovative adaptive control system that provides an automatic search function which locates the programmed weld joint. This control system also provides continuous automatic real-time tracking of the weld joint that enables the robot to compensate continuously during welding for production conditions such as inadvertent product movement, poor fit-up, weld distortion, or unfavorable tolerance stack-up.

Single or multipass welding in any combination of linear, circular, or curvilinear weld lines, in straight or weave patterns, is possible with the Series 7000. It can be used to join mild carbon steel, high-strength steel, stainless steel, and many other metals and alloys. It will improve product quality and increase production through consistently accurate weld deposition at increased cycle speeds.

The Series 7000 Robot Welder is a five-axis orthogonal configuration consisting of a steel superstructure that provides movement along the three primary axes (X, Y, and Z), a flexible wrist that provides $\pm$ 50° of bend and $\pm$ 270° of twist, and a welding head. The various transversing axes are driven by electric dc servomotors with a rack-and-pinion drive mechanism for the X axis and ball screw mechanisms on the Y and Z axes. Precision ball-bearing "way-systems" that can handle loads in any direction are used on all three primary axes.

There are two basic types of the Series 7000 Robot, horizontal and vertical. Both models are modularly designed with 40 different combinations of axis sizes, so the stroke lengths can be matched for a particular application.

Westinghouse Series 7000 welding robot.

Specifications

Robot
Dimensions: Dependent upon axes configurations

Axis System: 3 Orthogonal Axes, 2 Rotary Wrist Axes

Optional Axis Lengths:

"X" Axis	2000 mm (78.7 in.)
	3000 mm (118.1 in.)
	4000 mm (157.5 in.)
	5000 mm (196.9 in.)
	6000 mm (236.2 in.)

"Y" and "Z" Axes	800 mm (31.5 in.)
	1250 mm (49.2 in.)
	1600 mm (63.0 in.)
	2000 mm (78.7 in.)

Wrist:
Bend: ±50°
Twist: ± 270°

Positioning Speed 12 m (472 in.)/Min. Maximum

Welding Speed 1.2 m (47.2 in.)/Min. Maximum

Repeatability ± 0.4 mm (±0.015 in.)/Axis

Control System
Type: Computer Based Controller with real-time sensing control

Dimensions:
Controller Cabinet:
 900 mm x 1700 mm x 950 mm
 (35.4 in. x 66.9 in. x 37.4 in.)
Operator Console: 260 mm x 1300 mm x 360 mm
 (10.2 in. x 51.2 in. x 14.2 in.)

Memory Capacity: 800 Points (Dependent upon programming)

Memory Mode:
 Internal: CMOS RAM
 External: Digital Cassette

External Signal: 32 input / 32 output

Teach System: Teach-Playback

Tracking Function: Straight and Circular, Arc Sensing

Coordinate Shift Function: Relative position can be defined by 3 coordinates. Teaching data can be shifted by programming.

Welding Programming: Set as required on each weld line by programming

Monitoring Function: Emergency Stop and Temporary Stop for internal and external condition abnormalities.

Program Editing: Addition, correction, deletion and checking

Program Recording: Printer (Optional)

Built-In Function: Weaving; Sequence correction control prior to welding; multi-layer welding; self-diagnosis.

Standard Welding Power Source
Type: Direct-Current

Dimensions: 500 mm x 1020 mm x 650 mm
(20.0 in. x 40.2 in. x 25.6 in.)

Weight: 210 Kg. (463 lb.)

Output: 45 V D-C, 50-500 Amps

Input: 32 KVA; 220 or 460 VAC, 3 phase, 60 Hz;
380 VAC, 3 phase, 50 Hz

Duty Cycle: 100%

External Input Command: Analog input for current and voltage wire inching command

Rated Current: 500 A (also available in 750 A and 1000 A)

Cooling System: Air cooled

Wire Sizes: 0.035, 0.045 or 0.062 inch diameter

Welding Parameter Control:
 Current: 0 to rated current
 Voltage: 0 to rated maximum
 Speed: 1200 mm (47.2 in.)/Min. (Maximum)

Confirming/Control Functions:
Auto-check for power supply, automatic detection of gas pressure, retractable wire feed

Protective Functions: Torch anti-collision protection, automatic shut-off for extended idle periods.

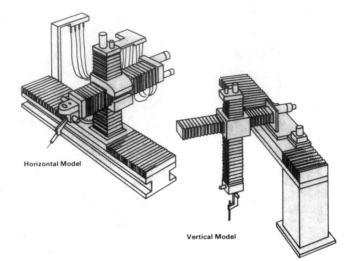

Horizontal Model

Vertical Model

Westinghouse Series 7000.